*White power and the
liberal conscience*

To Beryl and Charles

PAUL B. RICH

White power and the liberal conscience

Racial segregation and South African liberalism 1921-60

MANCHESTER UNIVERSITY PRESS

Copyright © Paul B. Rich 1984

Published by

Manchester University Press
Oxford Road, Manchester M13 9PL, UK
and
51 Washington Street, Dover, N.H. 03820, USA

British Library cataloguing in publication data

Rich, Paul
   White power and the liberal conscience.
   1. Race discrimination—South Africa—History—
   20th century. 2. Racism—South Africa—History—
   20th century
   I. Title
   305.8'00968   DT763

   ISBN 0-7190-0940-5

Library of Congress cataloging in publication data

Rich, Paul B., 1950-
   White power and the liberal conscience.
   Bibliography: p.
   Includes index.
   1. South Africa—Race relations. 2. Liberalism—
South Africa. 3. South Africa—Politics and government
—1909-1948. 4. South Africa—Politics and government
—1948-1961. 5. South African Institute of Race Relations.
   I. Title.
   DT763.R477   1983   305.8'00968   83-9853
   ISBN 0-7190-0940-5

Printed in Great Britain
by Butler & Tanner Ltd, Frome and London

CONTENTS

PREFACE

This study has grown out of my doctoral thesis at the University of Warwick, which was completed in 1979. The research for this thesis was pursued mainly in the extensive and underused South African archives between 1975 and 1977. Further work in England, though, has led me to revise a number of my original conclusions on the nature of South African liberalism.

The decision to study the time span of 1921 to 1960 was partly prompted by a desire to relate some of the wider themes which are at present emerging in South African historical research to the historiographical debate that has raged between liberals and neo-marxists in recent years. At the same time, while Janet Robertson's book *Liberalism in South Africa, 1948-1963* has provided a general survey of liberal politics in South Africa post-1948, little has been written at length for the previous period during the formative phase of South African industrialisation.

In the period since the research for this study, a number of significant developments have occurred in South African historiography. One of the most interesting has been the growing interest in social history, especially in the urban context, prompted, by the resurgence of the African Studies Institute at the University of the Witwatersrand. At the same time, though, there has yet to be any real interest developed in intellectual or socio-cultural history, which can in a variety of ways complement a successful social history. The rewriting of this thesis has thus been influenced by a recognition of the importance of intellectual history, and a hope that further and more detailed micro-studies might reveal the nature and significance of ideas in South Africa's social and economic transformation.

I have inevitably a large number of people to thank for helping to make this work possible. Innumerable librarians and archivists in both South Africa and England have patiently assisted my trying to find often difficult and obscure documents. Furthermore, stimulating discussion with a number of colleagues has helped in the clarification of a number of hypotheses. I would like to thank especially John Rex, who assisted in the supervision of the thesis, and Colin Bundy, Terence Ranger and Jack Spence for offering detailed criticisms of various parts of it. I am furthermore indebted to Brian Willan and Tim Couzens for pointing out valuable archival sources. I am also extremely grateful to Anna Cunningham of the Church of Province Archives, University of the Witwatersrand, and Mike Berning and Sandy Ford of Rhodes University Library, Grahamstown, for providing invaluable assistance in my research. Finally I would like to thank Jacqueline Kalley for assisting with the bibliography and Rose Goodwin at the Research Unit on Ethnic Relations, University of Aston, for typing evolving versions of the manuscript.

University of Aston,   Paul B. Rich
July 1982

List of Abbreviations

ABM	Files of the American Board Mission
ARTCM	Archive of the Transvaal Chamber of Mines
ArSAIRR	Archive of the South African Institute of Race Relations
HAD	House of Assembly Debates
MSS	Brit. Emp. British Empire Manuscripts held at Rhodes House, Oxford
NA	Files of the Union Native Affairs Department, Union Archives, Pretoria
UG	Union Government

INTRODUCTION

This work looks at the formative phase of South African liberalism from the period after the first world war to the establishment of the Liberal Party after the 1953 general election. This was a time of growing industrial and class conflict as South African industrialisation and urbanisation proceeded under the impact of two world wars. It was also a period of rising political nationalism, within both the Afrikaner and African populations, as the drift to the towns and cities broke up rural social relationships and enhanced the pressure towards newer ethnic forms of social solidarity in the burgeoning urban areas.

South African liberalism interacted uneasily with these new developments, though amongst small circles of missionaries, educationalists and philanthropists there was a tradition of paternal concern, or 'rescue', and welfare work to alleviate the hardships of city life. Much of the ethos of this concern was Victorian in conception, since the main impetus for the South African 'liberal tradition' prior to the establishment of Union in 1910 had come from the nineteenth-century Cape. Here a restricted, colour-blind franchise had been ensconced in the 1853 constitution, and the trend of missionary concern for the training of a small intermediary class of African educators and political leaders in such missions as Lovedale and Healdtown had been strongly influenced by the mid-Victorian ideal of social upliftment through the instilling of values of hard work and self-help. Originally, this missionary programme was directed to the rural areas and the training of a class of African master farmers and peasants, especially in the Eastern Cape.

This 'great tradition' of Cape liberalism, as Stanley Trapido has termed it, reached its apogee in the 1860s and 1870s as it underpinned an alliance between the Eastern Cape African peasantry and British mercantile capital that enjoyed a strong influence on the echelons of goverment in the Cape Colony at that time.[1] However, by the last quarter of the nineteenth century, this economic base for Cape liberalism came under strain as the opening up of, first, the Kimberley diamond mines and later, after 1883, the gold mines on the Witwatersrand introduced a powerful new dimension into Cape politics.[2]

The mining revolution in South Africa heralded a steady erosion of the Cape liberal tradition in its classic mid-Victorian form, as the requirement for an ever-expanding supply of African migrant labour started to conflict with the fostering of a prosperous Eastern Cape peasantry. Furthermore, with growing British imperial interest in the sub-continent from the 1880s onwards, a new tone emerged in the dominant political ideology in the Cape. Whilst the idea of keeping African societies separate from the colonial white society in the Cape was not a new one — indeed it can be perceived in many respects in one of the pioneering tracts of Cape liberalism, Dr. John Philip's *Researches in South Africa* (1828) — the phase of British imperial intrusion marked a growing *racialisation* in political discourse. Introducing the Glen Grey Bill in 1894 to provide for local African councils in the Glen Grey district in the Eastern Cape, the Cape Prime Minister, Cecil Rhodes, argued for the measure in terms of avoiding 'labour troubles', as in England or the recent strike by black car porters of the Pullman Car Company in Chicago.[3] It was also as a means of avoiding such proletarianisation that white supremacy could be secured:

... if the white maintain their position as the supreme race, the day may come when we shall all be thankful that we have the natives with us in their proper position. We shall be thankful that we have escaped those difficulties which are going on amongst the old nations of the world.[4]

A talk the same year by the novelist and magistrate, William Charles Scully, to the Lovedale Literary Society also argued for a measure similar to the eventual Glen Grey Act to check African tribal tenure. It was by means of 'scientific agriculture' that the white race could be maintained in South Africa, for 'up to the present the Aryan race has never secured a permanent footing on the African continent' and the Portuguese example — 'who have a strong admixture of African blood' — showed white settlement being confined to the coast.[5]

This racialisation in political dialogue within white settler society escalated in the period up to and after the Anglo-Boer War of 1899-1902 and pushed the more paternalistic mode of Victorian Cape liberalism on to the defensive.[6] Whilst the ideology of 'segregation', which eventually emerged in the first decade of the twentieth century, owed a considerable amount to similar ideas of white supremacy in the Jim Crow South of the United States in the 1890s and 1900s, the ultimate meaning of the concept in the South African context was considerably different. As George Fredrickson has recently argued, a direct parallel in South Africa to Southern segregation was far more evident in the case of the Cape Coloured population, subordinated within a single colonial society, than the practice of segregating separate African societies into tribal and precapitalist reserves.[7] South African 'segregation' in practice meant a carrying of racial separation to a far more advanced and sophisticated stage than its American equivalent, where ideas for separate areas of Negro landholding received scant attention even by the strongest supports of white supremacy.[8]

However, the growing internationalisation in white political debate on race in the 1890s and 1900s had a profound impact on liberal thinking in South Africa and started a chain of transatlantic political and ideological ties which were to have an important influence between the 1920s and 1950s. As the American historian, Jack Temple Kirby, has pointed out

The years of South African accommodation, American colonial expansion and the southern racial settlement witnessed increased communications and a heightened sense of comradeship among whites on three continents. Englishmen, Boers, English South Africans, and Americans paid close attention to developments on either side of the Atlantic, read and reviewed each other's books, and took comfort in comparing each other's racial problems and solutions.[9]

In the South African case, though, it was almost as if the political defeat liberals experienced in failing to enshrine an expansion of the nominally colour-blinded Cape franchise in the other provinces at the time of Union in 1910 led to a lurch towards American modes of thinking through despair at the Cape Victorian legacy. Here was a newer mode of discourse, accruing from the greater impact of sociology and the social sciences on missionary and welfare circles and a group of concepts linked around the idea of managing inter-ethnic and race relations. It was also linked in American intellectual circles to a growing revolt in the early decades of the twentieth century against the more conventional assimilationist ideology of Americanism, linked to the fate of self-serving and isolated individuals. In its place came a set of ideas linked to a group - and communally-based society which was the forerunner of more contemporary pluralist and multi-ethnic social models in western social science.[10]

These ideas did not start to reach any systematic formulation in South African liberalism until the 1930s where, as this study shows, the ideas of Alfred Hoernle and liberal pluralism started to have an important impact on liberal political discourse.[11] However, the emergence of the segregationist notion had an important impact almost from the time of its importation into South Africa. One of the earliest uses of the concept of 'territorial segregation' was by the Cape liberal, Richard Rose-Innes, member of a prominent Cape legal family, who linked it to the establishment of reserves for Africans as 'reservoirs of labour'.[12] The model from which this accrued was the Glen Grey Act of Rhodes, and Rose-Innes established a continuity of Cape liberal thinking with the wider debate on segregation as part of a Union 'native policy' which took place after the Treaty of Vereeniging in 1902, under the hegemony of the Milnerite 'conquest state' in the Transvaal.[13] The following year the Johannesburg accountant, Howard Pim, a Quaker and friend of Alfred Milner, began using the 'segregation' notion the same year as part of the discussions surrounding the work of the South African Native Affairs Commission, chaired by the Secretary of Native Affairs, Sir Godfrey Lagden. 'Segregation' for Pim meant keeping African communities rooted on the land and avoiding the pitfalls of permanent urbanisation and proletarianisation. However, looking at the American parallel, there was a dominant historical tendency, Pim perceived, for 'the two races' to 'steadily drift apart', so the Afri-

cans were afforded the means to live 'under natural conditions which he understands and has created for himself'.[14]

The historicism and determinism implicit within this original conceptualisation of 'segregation' in the South African
context begs certain questions about the nature of racial
ideology generated by the dominant white settler society. An
interesting feature of this is the relative absence of what may
be termed 'biological racism' and deterministic theories of
genetic and biological racial inferiority of South African
blacks. While clearly an area that needs more detailed historical research, the general conclusion can be made that South
African racial ideology did not need to employ in quite the
same manner theories of biological racial inferiority as in the
American instance, since the concept of territorial racial
separation acted as a form of cultural and ideological buffer.
As was later to be the case with the Afrikaner theorists of
'apartheid', who took over much of the ideological discourse
of 'segregation' (though linking it more strongly with concepts of ethnic and national self-determination[15]), the theorists of territorial segregation employed a more conventional
mode of social particularisation. This was based upon what
William Empson has termed the 'pastoral process', whereby
complex ideas are made simple by a ruling class seeking to
reinforce a social order by bolstering up more traditonal
stereotypes.[16] Thus Pim's conception of the 'naturalness' of
the reserves as terrains for African societies was an extrapola-
tion of more conventional colonial stereotypes of African
societies as pastoralised and rural entities that merged back
into the African landscape.[17] Only a minority of the white
social theorists in the debate on 'native policy' in South
Africa before Union resorted to a biological determinism in
order to rationalise an ideology of segregation. As in the case
of Fred Bell, who succeeded Pim as president of the Transvaal
Native Affairs Society in 1909, this biological racism was of a
second-hand variety, resting on the claims of the American
race theorist, Robert Bennett Bean, Professor of Anatomy at
the University of Virginia, that Negro brains were inferior to
Caucasian ones.[18] Though evidencing the interaction of white
race theory between South Africa and the United States, Bell's
arguments were important not so much for their assertion of

biological race differences but for their buttressing of the ideology of territorial segregation:

> ... I would make the individual black man in white areas as much of a
> 'fish out of water' as the white man would be in black territories. The
> native should have no locus standi in white territories and the incon-
> venience of this position would act, automatically, as a stimulus to
> separation... In opposton blacks and white are each antagonists,
> industrially, socially and politically. But separate and apart each may
> follow his own line of progress without detriment to the other.[19]

This version of radical territorial segregation formed the ideological basis for successive government policy after the establishment of Union in 1910 and forced the inheritors of Cape liberalism increasingly on to the defensive. In 1911, following a white mine strike, the industrial colour bar was entrenched in the Mines and Works Act. In 1913 the Natives Land Act initiated the process of territorial demarcation of land on a Union-wide basis, with African landholding initially being confined to some 9 per cent of the total area of the Union. In 1923, following the wave of strikes and passive resistance campaigns by Africans after the first world war, the government passed the Natives (Urban Areas) Act, based upon the dictum enshrined in the 1921 Transvaal Local Government Commission, chaired by Colonel Stallard, that Africans were only to be in urban areas in so far as they ministered to the needs of the white man.[20] Given the seemingly inexorable logic of this segregationism and its political rationality in buttressing white political and economic hegemony in an industrialising society, the inheritors of Cape Victorian liberalism were forced to reassess their political and ideological standpoint so as to evolve some form of political and social role for themselves in the new order that was emerging.

This new role, which is substantially the focus of this study, was developed by the survivors of the old Cape liberal tradition who came together with a new generation of academics, missionaries and social workers in the years after the first world war in an effort to establish a specifically South African tradition of political liberalism. Though not initially successful, the ultimate fruition of these efforts in the inter-war years can be said to have been reached in 1953 with the establishment of the Liberal Party, though by this time it was too late to act as an effective political catalyst to forces seeking to resist the political entrenchment of Afrikaner nationalism.[21] Overall the weak position of the liberals in such areas as politics, education and welfare work leads to a questioning of the recent thesis propounded by Martin Legassick that South African liberals were 'agents of social control' and the entrenchment of racial segregation.[22] In a number of respects, South African liberals lacked from the start a cohesive middle-class base to which they could appeal in philanthropic and welfare terms, like their equivalents in Victorian and Edwardian England. The harsh peripheral or 'booty' capitalism (to employ a term of Max Weber) in South Africa lacked the element of a concerned middle class, as in England, that had grown up within a milieu of nineteenth-century social and political optimism.[23] As the logic of segregationism advanced, the ideological and political base for such welfarism became eroded in South Africa, as the direction for social welfare and subsistence for Africans increasingly pointed to the economies in the reserves. Thus, whilst seeking to mediate the obvious contradictions thrown up by the reality of black poverty and social breakdown in the burgeoning slums in South African towns and cities, the South African liberals and welfare workers were forced to confront the dominant segregationist tenets that implied a process of enforced rustication and movement of Africans as far as possible back to the rural reserves.

Consequently the dominant political logic of segregationism ultimately defined the direction of political thinking amongst South African liberals for most of the period covered by this study. As we see in Chapter one, initial efforts to delineate a specifically urban welfare role increasingly broke down in the 1920s in the face of the rural segregation programme, and this led to moves by liberals to tackle the issue of the economies of the reserves. Chapter two thus looks at the debate on establishing co-operative societies to link up the reserves through some form of trading nexus. Anthropological study of African societies also developed in the period between the wars, and Chapter three looks at the impact anthropology had on liberal thinking as regards the cohesion of African societies and the resistance to incorporation into a single homogeneous social model implied by racial assimilationism. By the late 1930s, divisions of opinion within the liberal camp began to widen as a more radical body of left-inclined liberals led by William Ballinger began to criticise what they saw as the political accommodationism of the Institute of Race Relations under the directorship of J.D. Rheinnalt-Jones. This liberal radicalism gained a political base during the second world war as the African National Congress under the presidency of Alfred Xuma became increasingly disaffected with government segregation policy and the seeming political neutrality of the Institute of Race Relations. These developments continued to the political crisis in 1946 as the African challenge and the crucial role played by some of the white liberals in the period of 1946-48 to formulate a wider structure of 'natives representation' to meet the criticism of the A.N.C. leadership. The failure of this by the 1948 election and the defeat of the Smuts government left the liberals further isolated under the Nationalist government of D. F. Malan. The moves towards establishing a Liberal Party, after the success of the Nationalists in the second election of 1953, marked a more desperate search by liberals to achieve political influence at the centre after the established avenues of political representation, built up over the preceding two decades or more, became blocked by a new government machine mobilised behind the ideology of apartheid.

The development of liberalism in South Africa also reflected some of the ideas of an emergent intelligentsia in the period of South African industrialisation. While moving beyond the more optimistic beliefs of Victorian liberalism in the Cape and the progressive expansion of a colour-blind franchise within a parliamentary system of government, South African liberals between 1921 and 1953 never satisfactorily grasped the ideological challenge thrown up by territorial segregationism. Though this period saw the emergence of an awareness of the strength and tenacity of ethnicity, whether in the form of Afrikaner nationalism or African ethnic resistance to cultural and social assimilationism, the nascent plural model which liberal theorists developed was rooted in a pessimistic view of political trends. While this period was therefore of importance for later South African debate centred on concepts of multi-ethnic and plural societies, the narrow political parameters in which this was conducted by liberal circles and the increasing alienation of a radical black opposition indicates the limited degree to which such concepts could have had practical political application.

ONE

The Joint Councils and the Institute of Race Relations

1 Urban welfare work

'Johannesburg', wrote the American Board missionary, Frederick Bridgman, soon after arriving on the Witwatersrand in 1913, was 'the very pivot upon which the future of the native in South Africa swings'.[1] However, introducing a note of anxiety, he also recognised that it was useless to expand missionary work on the Rand unless the missionary can in some way or other find the means with which to multiply himself.[2] Stated in this way, Bridgman defined a central problem confronting while liberals and welfare workers, during the period of rising industrial conflict in South Africa's industrial heartland and the segregationist triumph of the Stallardist reaction. How were welfare organisations to be adapted to confront the issues thrown up by the South African pattern of industrial transformation and the growing political divisions centered around perceived differences of race? The strongly Victorian character of many missions in South Africa and their work in rural areas did not leave them with much expertise to adapt quickly to an urban situation, and it was by no means clear how an urban African following could be created in order to sustain a new phase of urban missionary enterprise.

The most obvious African group that could be first won over were those mission-educated Africans in the urban areas who were beginning to emerge as an identifiable élite or petty bourgeoisie. By 1921 there were an estimated 9,756 African teachers, ministers, chiefs and headmen in South Africa, in addition to some 1,634 interpreters and clerks, many of whom resided in urban areas.[3] The clerks and interpreters, as well as the teachers, frequently formed a vital intermediary element between the emergent urban African proletariat and the apparatus of native administration, especially in so far as they were in crucial linkage positions at times of stress, such as in court cases or working the pass law system. However, as a social category, this petty bourgeoisie lacked any strong sense of its own social identity and was often prone to political factionalisation and volatility. In the period after the 1918 Armistice, especially, the petty bourgeois leadership of the Transvaal Native Congress became strongly radicalised by the upsurge of African working-class consciousness on the Witwatersrand, though at the same time its experience of the oppression this class faced was different amongst different sections of the petty bourgeoisie: some teachers and ministers often saw themselves as more civilised than their working-class compatriots, while interpreters and clerks often had virtually the same wages as those in manual jobs. In addition, some groups were more attuned to the interests and struggles in the urban areas, whilst others, especially if they had plots of land, were more interested in rural issues. Thus there was by no means an automatic and cohesive class alliance between white liberals and missionaries and the African petty bourgeoisie as a whole.[4] Indeed, during the post-war radicalisation there was some loss of following amongst the white missions on the Rand: in 1917 there had been a secession by some Zulu members of the American Board Mission in Doornfontein, whilst in 1919 Bridgman reported a boycott movement among his African followers:

No church, no membership card, no marriage certificate, which has anything to do with a white missionary is to be recognised or countenanced in anyway. So far as I can see we are living in days in Johannesburg at least analogous to the days preceding the Boxer uprising in China. If matters keep on with the present trend and at the present rate, there are bound to come terrible days in South Africa.[5]

Bridgman's sense of isolation indicated how the petty bourgeoisie's radicalisation could leave the missions seemingly helpless to act on African political ideas or activity. The phase of radicalism was relatively short-lived, however, as after 1921 the onset of depression and unemployment had a neutralising effect on the Transvaal Native Congress leadership and helped to rechannel political activity out towards the rural areas.[6]

Even as the white missionary activity began to pick up again in the early 1920s, this still left the question of how an appeal was to be made to the slumland culture that had grown up in the Johannesburg 'yards' and shaped a strong communal consciousness around illicit liquor and the culture of 'marabi'.[7] This collective solidarity of the African working class strongly distanced itself from the western-educated culture of the more'civilised' sections of the petty bourgeoisie who were most attuned to the activities and appeals of the white liberals. Given these cultural fissures that underlay the political divisions, the strategy open to the white liberals was necessarily limited, though in the early 1920s Bridgman and his fellow workers of the American Board Mission led the way in seeking some form of political accord.

The tradition of the social settlement movement in the United States, founded amongst the new communities of immigrants from southern and eastern Europe in the early years of the century, left the American missionaries considerably better placed to confront a situation of multi-ethnic urbanisation than their British counterparts.[8] To this extent Bridgman and the American Board sought to impress on his fellow missionaries the scale of the challenge and lead them, if possible, in the direction of founding a similar settlement movement on the Rand. Arguing that the church as a whole clung to the'medieval fallacy' of 'saving souls while ignoring the body in which the soul lives', Bridgman urged that there was a need for recreational facilities for Africans on the Rand to divert them from political pursuits. It was'healthful, uplifting recreation' which was the key means to win over the 'raw native', who was otherwise a prey to the 'snares' of the 'gleaming allurements of city life'.[9]

This attempt at 'rescue work' by the American Board Mission in the post-Armistice era took a number of different forms to fit a variety of conditions of African social and industrial life on the Witwatersrand. By 1918, Bridgman was joined by a fellow A.B.M. missionary, Ray Phillips, who soon proved adept in the use of film shows at mine compounds and welfare societies as part of this goal of recreation. Most famously, this was used during the 1922 white mine strike to divert the attention of restive African mine workers from joining in the strike agitation.[10] In addition, Bridgman, together with his wife, was instrumental in the establishment of the Helping Hand Club For Native Girls in Hans Street, Fairview, which sought to insulate African female domestic servants from the pressures of city life. 'As a class', Bridgman complained, African servants were 'bold, impudent and of loose character',[11] and the general ethos of the club was to instil a Victorian conception of social deference into the newly arrived African female city immigrants.[12] A similar campaign was mounted by the Community of the Resurrection, and right through the inter-war period white welfare bodies sought to train a relatively docile class of African domestic servant to service white middle- and lower-class suburbia.[13]

However, the key objective was the main body of the African intelligentsia who were perceived to have such a crucial influence over the main body of African political and social thinking. Bridgman was again an early recogniser of the general 'suspicion and aloofness' of this class to missionary influences and an important early stimulus in the move towards a more co-ordinated welfare effort on the Rand in the period after the first world war. Though the Joint Council movement got off the ground in 1921 in the wake of the 1920 African mine strike, pressures for such bodies began as early as 1919 from a more secular section of the emergent white liberal intelligentsia. As the new University of the Witwatersrand became established in that year on the basis of the old Transvaal School of Mines, a former official of the Witwatersrand Council of Education, J. D. Rheinnalt-Jones, appeared on the scene. At the time Jones was the editor of the journal *The South African Quarterly*, which was generally pleading for a more enlightened approach to native policy, and he was drawn into inter-racial activities through the founding of the Eclectic Club, which replaced the defunct Johannesburg Native Welfare Society that had lapsed with the post-war militancy. This stimulated Ray Phillips, who was already influenced by the Native Affairs Reform Association in Durban, to found a literary and debating society, with a title The Gamma Sigma Club (after the Greek dictum 'know thyself') that suggested a parallel with a similarly-named organisation in the United States.[14] Contact in a body such as this, with 'keen-witted native leaders at their wits' end in Johannesburg, ready to try anything',[15] convinced many white liberals of the value of such groups where Africans like R. V. Selope Thema, Selby Msimang and Horatio Mbelle could involve themselves in dialogue with white missionaries, educationalists, welfare workers and advocates. Though the discussions were described as 'often heated',[16] the groundswell for interracial co-operation was laid through the dissemination of liberal ideas that emphasised the role of individual rights and liberties at the expense of nationalist and group identities. The advocate O. D. Schreiner, for instance, acted as a powerful influence on Selby Msimang's thinking:

Mr Justice O. D. Schreiner gave us a lecture (at the Eclectic Club) I have never been able to forget. This was the time when we were all developing real hatred for a white person. In other words, Black Nationalism. We were already accusing ministers of religion of hypocrisy of holding the bible in one hand while on the other hand they helped to confiscate the land. Mr. Schreiner disillusioned me completely. I learnt of one that might not visit the wrongs of one person to the whole race of natives to which he belongs.[17]

This pattern was not followed completely throughout the African political class at this time, for a radical group of nationalists continued to campaign on Garveyist lines via the A.N.C. paper *Abantu Batho*, and R. V. Selope Thema, until at least February 1920, was a member of this group. During his stay in Britain before his return to South Africa in 1919, Selope Thema reported that he had 'come in contact with men and women of all nationalities and colours who are pledged to free the world from the clutches of the economic vultures of capitalism'.[18] Presaging, therefore, a very different model of 'interracial contact' to what the white liberals in South Africa had in mind, Selope Thema pointed out, on the basis of post-war railway strike in Britain, that the popular cry of the working classes is 'direct action' and that 'the waters of international revolution are rising and the flood of proletarism [sic] is threatening to sweep away capitalism and militarism and establish the real permanent peace of the world'.[19]

However, in the wake of the 1920 mine strike by African workers, a series of developments ensued, designed to neutralise the faction centred around *Abantu Batho* and strengthen structures of co-optation. The African press as a whole had tended to be treated with a certain amount of disdain by the white liberals, [20] and the precedent of the strike made the establishment of a white-controlled paper directed at the African intelligentsia even more pressing. Thus, in the same year, the Native Recruiting Corporation established *Umteteli wa Bantu* in order 'to voice sound native opinion in the country'.[21] The people instrumental in this were H. M. Taberer of the N.R.C. and Ray Phillips, who earned the long-lasting dislike of the African radicals for his attempts to control African thought. *Umteteli's* establishment hastened the demise of the shaky *Abantu Batho*, which continued to be printed on the outmoded and worn printing presses that had been used when the paper was established in 1912 with assistance from the Swazi Queen Regent. The printing workers on the paper, however, were enticed away by higher wages on *Umteteli* and, though the paper struggled on through the 1920s finally to die during the depression, it lost the original influence it had enjoyed in shaping African political thinking on the Rand and elsewhere in South Africa.[22]

The establishment of *Umteteli* was further complemented by moves to create the Bantu Men's Social Centre as a means of fulfilling Bridgman's ideal of establishing recreational facilities for the growing African population on the Rand. The scope of the centre was for the most part confined to the African petty bourgeoisie, with the overall control over policy retained by a sub-committee that included a number of prominent white liberals. Howard Pim was secretary, and Ray Phillips was Organising Secretary; other committee members included Walter Webber of the Chamber of Mines and Frederick Bridgman. The African role on the committee was confined to electing seven of the total of fifteen members and, of the seven, three had to be white. This relatively peripheral influence produced an initial wave of African hostility, and Bridgman described the attitudes of some African leaders as 'supicious, jealous and offish'.[23] Furthermore, the centre was clearly dictated by the interest of the chief donors: the Chamber of Mines gave £3,000 for the establishment of the centre which was estimated to have cost some £15,000 in all, while the Chamber of Commerce in Johannesburg also gave a donation.[24] However,

Bridgman's aim of making the centre a place where African men could find 'wholesome companionship, entertaining amusements and healthful recreation' began to achieve some fruit, despite attempts at obstruction in 1920 by the 'reactionary element' who attempted, according to Bridgman, to 'discredit' the whole idea. With the 'more reasonable element' in African political leadership coming out in support of the scheme,[25] the centre began to establish itself from the end of 1920 and to play a significant role in the evolution of a western-educated urban black élite during the 1920s. Indeed the centre acted as one of the more crucial institutional underpinnings behind the move towards educational, cultural and political co-optation of the African petty bourgeoisie in the aftermath of the industrial struggles of 1918-20. By 1927, the centre was reported as having a total membership of 365, though the actual numbers of Africans coming in contact with it was far larger because of the high rate of resignations and new memberships. In addition to such sporting facilities as volley-ball, tennis, cricket and boxing, the centre provided a series of educational classes for junior clerical work such as book-keeping, typewriting, English, arithmetic and elementary science.[26] The Gamma Sigma Club was also continued in the centre, and this may well have been an important educational - forming experience for a future president of the A.N.C., Dr. A. B. Xuma, who came into contact through the club with such prominent white liberals as C. T. Loram, J. D. Rheinnalt-Jones and the A.B.M. missionary James Dexter Taylor.

The exact role of the Bantu Men's Social Centre in white liberal activities in the 1920s can be seen to change, however, as the aim of 'healthful recreation', in the urban context by Frederick Bridgman, began to be transformed into a wider objective of accommodating liberalism to territorial segregation as the decade advanced. Charles T. Loram from Natal was crucial in shifting the emphasis away from reform *per se* in the urban context, towards defining welfare activities in the context of a policy of confining as far as possible the educational, social and political aspirations of the African petty bourgeoisie to the reserves. The report of the Native Churches Commission in 1925 was a landmark in this respect for, with Loram as one of its members, the spectre of Ethiopianism was finally exorcised from official thinking, at least in South Africa. African Church separatism was now seen as a process that was likely to continue and should, the commission argued, be given government recognition. Furthermore, the fissiparous tendencies within this separatism no longer represented the potential for a united Ethiopian ideology of 'Africa for the Africans', but rather the continuation of tribal ties into the industrial setting. 'A feature in the separatist movement which is disconcerting to the parent churches', Loram wrote on the commission's findings, '… is the friendly and even cordial relationship which exists between the seceeding Natives and those who remain loyal to the parent Church. It shows clearly how racial or at least tribal considerations rank higher in the Native mind than church divisions, and how likely it is that the separatist movement will spread.'[27]

Loram took over, in many respects, the role of chief ideologist of white liberalism in the 1920s from such figures as Frederick Bridgman and Howard Pim. In the aftermath of the 1920-22 strike wave and the decline in the political significance of independent church movements, the focus of attention for the South African state had clearly shifted to the educated South African intelligentsia in the towns, and Loram, as a member of both the Native Affairs Commission and the Native Churches Commission, was in a good position to shape governmental thinking on this. Furthermore, his previous work for the Phelps-Stokes Commission on education in Africa gave him a good insight into contemporary colonial ideas on updating education in the African setting to fulfill the objectives of rural development. Loram's ideas reflected a shift in emphasis in the 1920s in government and informed white opinion away from seeing African political consciousness in monolithic 'black peril' terms, goaded by 'Ethiopianism', towards a more sophisticated conception rooted in evolving African class differences. The 1920 mine strike illustrated the degree of African proletarianisation and the continued possiblity of their being influenced by radical political groups like the International Socialist League or, after 1921, the South African Communist Party. The key point was to recognise the crucial mediating role played by the African intelligentsia and to instil in them some form of political accommodationism linked to

alternative political outlets through the rural reserves. Thus
Loram, together with other fellow liberals like Rheinnalt-Jones, was in may ways a crucial figure in accommodating
inter-war liberalism with government segregation policy. This
was to occur in the 1920s, mainly through the Joint Council
movement and then, after 1929, via the Institute of Race Relations.[28]

2.   The Phelps-Stokes Commission and the formation of the Joint Councils

The internal trend in South Africa towards co-optation of African political leadership remained fragmentary at the start of
1921. The establishment of *Umteteli*, the founding of the Eclectic and Gamma Sigma clubs and the development of the
Bantu Men's Social Centre all remained partial solutions, each
hindered by a good deal of African suspicion and political
hostility. It was probably true that no white liberal in South
Africa had sufficient personal charisma to rally African political leadership behind the idea of 'inter-racial co-operation', and
the possibility of demonstrating concrete examples of its success remained tenuous. There was the precedent of similar
attempts in the American South, but apart from the small
number of Africans who had been to America for education,
this remained a very distant ideal to most Africans in South
Africa at this time. Furthermore, despite the continuing general popularity of the Tuskegee ideal of Booker T. Washington
and his successor after 1915, Robert R. Moton, it was no
longer the case by 1920 that all African opinion formers in
South Africa accepted Washington's ideas without question.
Breaking to some extent with the previous adulation of Tuskegee by leaders like John Dube and Pixley Seme, S. M.
Molema wrote in his book *The Bantu Past and Present* in 1920
of the ideas of W. E. B. Dubois. Taking up the ideal in Smuts
1917 Savoy Speech of 'independent self-governing institutions', Molema reflected the thinking of a section of the African intelligentsia in South Africa after the first world war in
demanding that the process be taken to its logical conclusion
and that' seperation must be equal'.[29] Morevoer, Molema articulated the more widely felt despair in Europe in the values of

Victorian liberalism after spending a period at the University
of Edinburgh (together with the future A.N.C. president James
Moroka) studying medicine. 'British liberalism is offering nothing to the Bantu of South Africa', Molema wrote, 'except
such morbid creations and fancies as "the Native problem".'[30]

In this context, it was essential for some new external influence to show itself in South Africa for any wider movements
towards 'inter-racial co-operation' to be a success. This was
duly provided by the Phelps-Stokes Commission in the course
of 1921 as the Director of the Phelps-Stokes Fund, the Welshman Thomas Jesse Jones, and the commission's African member, Dr. J. E. K. Aggrey from the British colony of the Gold
Coast (Ghana), toured South Africa collecting information on
African education. The tour was significant for the marrying of
ideas on educational segregation, like those of C. T. Loram
(who helped to arrange the tour) with those of Jesse Jones who
was director of the Research Department at the Hampton Institute in Virginia and lecturer in sociology there. As Loram
argued in 1917 in his book *The Education of the South African
Native*, education for Africans should be directed towards the
objective of resisting cultural assimilation with whites and, on
the basis of his experience in such areas as reforming the
curriculum at Amanzimtoti,[31] should be geared towards industrial training in the reserves. For Jesse Jones, too, education
for American negroes should be based on the principles of
industrial training similar to those of Tuskegee which, in the
Southern case, could be demonstrated to be economically successful by the use of comparative statistical analysis. Both
therefore defended an educational ideology based upon assumptions of racial differentiation, and both essentially saw
the value of education for blacks in the context of rural social
control, despite the considerable growth in the United States
during the first world war of extensive negro urbanisation.[32]

The special significance of the Phelps-Stokes Commission,
however, was its linking of the ideas on industrial training,
developed in such centres as Tuskegee and Hampton in America and Lovedale in South Africa, with missionary and administrative concern in African colonies and the problems of
rural education.[33] This linkage was reflected by the inclusion of
Aggrey on the commission, for here was a shining propaganda

example of the relevance, as far as the Phelps-Stokes Commission was concerned, of the Tuskegee ideology to colonial conditions. Aggrey had graduated from Livingstone College in North Carolina in 1904 and had long been acquainted with Jesse Jones. Afer becoming vice-principal in 1919 of the college at Achimota in the Gold Coast, established by the progressive British administration of Sir Gordan Guggisberg, Aggrey was a key political figure to use in demonstrating the possibilities of the Tuskegee ideal. Furthermore, Aggrey's Anglophilia served as an important means to dispel any doubts, as reflected for instance by writers like S. M. Molema, in the values of British liberalism, which could now be shown to be the essential basis behind the objectives of African self-help and self-reliance. In the course of the South African tour, Aggrey went out of his way to influence the thinking of the African intelligentsia and participated in no fewer than 120 meetings with African students and religious and political leaders. Appealing to 'British Justice' which was 'being felt now more than ever before because of the war and because of the restlessness', Aggrey was able to exploit politically the divisions that had emerged by 1921 in Garvey's Universal Negro Improvement Association through corruption and the disaster of the Black Star Shipping Line.[34] This proved especially effective in student centres such as Lovedale, and Aggrey appealed to his African origins in his objective of weakening Garveyite sympathies, in a manner that white missionaries, such as Father Bernard Huss of Mariannhill, engaged in a similar task, were unable to do.[35] 'What we need is some great messiah of the Anglo-Saxon race to rise up and give fair play and reciprocity', Aggrey declared at one meeting. 'I have dedicated my life to see that we work for cooperation. I pray that before long South Africa will be the best place on earth for white and black; so that Great Britain will lead the whole world.'[36] At the same time, reflecting the gradualist basis of this approach, Aggrey argued that 'we Africans must, like infants, learn to stand before we can walk and walk before we can run'.[37]

Aggrey's appeal clearly lay in his ability to demonstrate to sections of the African intelligentsia the political advantages of working through institutions that afforded direct contact with white liberals and governmental, academic and commission

representatives. The air of glamour about his own career and
the possibilities of being able to influence government and
'white' thinking probably appealed to even radical African political leaders. R. V. Selope Thema, for instance, was especially
impressed by Aggrey's description of the inter-racial bodies in
the American South which demonstrated the possibility, so
Aggrey argued, of altering ingrained political attitudes.[38] Furthermore, Aggrey stressed that Africans had the *right* to join
the proposed Joint Councils, as opposed to the previous system
of selective invitation to the old Native Welfare Associations,
and this gave the Joint Council idea a wider political potential
for many African leaders. By 1921 the political possibilities had
already become somewhat narrowed as the decline in popular
upsurges left the scope of 'agitator' politics considerably diminished. The success of political agitation, as Michael Twaddle has pointed out, depends upon a continual threshold of
political credibility[39] — this had been the case in the wake of
rising prices, the decline of the reserve economies and the
dissemination of radical ideaologies in the course of the first
world war. On the other hand, short of the creation of a full
fledge political movement, 'agitation' *per se* does not offer the
basis for a political career for the more aspiring politicians who
engage in it, and there is the consequential risk of becoming a
specialist in a narrowly defined political field. Thus political
co-operation occurs when institutions open up the opportunity
for upward career mobility, introducing what Morris-Jones describes as 'nodal points or moments of crucial choice in the
course of a career' when the less adaptable politicians tend to
be eliminated.[40] In this respect, the establishment of the Johannesburg Joint Council did offer some such avenues of mobility,
and Professor D. D. T. Jabavu, for instance, championed African membership on the Native Affairs Commission in 1920.
There had been hopes, too, for the local councils, established
under the Native Affairs Act, considerably revamping the powers of the Glen Grey councils and extending them to the rest of
the Union. In the initial stages of optimism in 1921, the Joint
Councils were probably seen by many African leaders to complement this process of 'representation', though in later years
they became the last bastions in a general process of declining
political influence by the time of the legislation of 1936. In

terms of information and factual discussion, the Joint Councils clearly provided invaluable assistance to many African leaders whose education had often ill-equipped them to scrutinise complex government legislation. It was precisely in this sense of growing political adaptability that Selby Msimang later recorded that the Johannesburg Joint Council provided much needed help on such measures as the 1923 Natives (Urban Areas) Bill. 'For the first few months', Msimang recalled, 'the whole thing was in the form of a test. Africans felt that they could not put all their confidence in the whites, they had got to show in some way their sincerity.' With the introduction of the Urban Areas bill, the white members of the Joint Council were provided with an opportunity of demonstrating their interest in lending concrete assistance and 'they took the trouble to explain the provisions of the Bill and went through it clause by clause'.[41] As a consequence, when the Native Affairs Commission visited Bloemfontein to discuss the bill, Msimang said 'the notes we had made through our discussions in the Joint Council assisted us greatly. I was able to put across the various ideas that came across in our discussions in the Joint Council.'[42] But the other side of this process was a strong decline in political radicalism for, even though Msimang wanted to organise a large demonstration 'of all the people from Randfontein to Springs' to protest against the Urban Areas bill and march to Pretoria, he was unable to carry his fellow African members of the Joint Council on the issue.[43] By this time, the Joint Council had been able to institutionalise itself sufficiently to ensure that its African members eschewed for the most part popularly based politics.

The political co-optation centred in the Joint Council in Johannesburg, however, was not all-embracing. After an initial attendance by the Native Mine Clerks Association and the Native National Congress, which were both able to elect representatives on to the committee of thirty members, external pressures soon enforced their withdrawal. In the case of the Mine Clerks, the Chamber of Mines sought its separation from Joint Council activities through fear of its possible radicalisation. As in the case of Kimberley, where De Beers established its own structures of internal co-optation with the local African petty bourgeoisie through its support for the Brotherhood

Movement and the Lyndhurst Road Native Institute,[44] the chamber on the Witwatersrand feared outside participation in its own system of rewards and favours that buttressed social control. In the aftermath of the 1920 African mine strike, this attitude was probably well reflected in one memorandum of the Native Recruiting Corporation which argued that:

The native has an inbred respect for his superiors and will quickly recognise and appreciate the justice granted to the more skilled of his class and will look at these men to guide him rather than the highly educated native who is fast becoming more and more under the influence of undesirable Whites who will only use the natives as a means to attain their own mischievous ends.

This distinction between the 'more skilled' Africans on the mines and the 'highly educated native' probably guided the Chamber's policy. In the case of the latter group, the issue was seen as essentially a non-mining one, coming under the province of such institutions as the Bantu Men's Social Centre, the Joint Councils and literary and debating societies. The proneness of this group to radical political ideologies, as represented by the *Abantu Batho* faction in the Native National Congress, made it an object of continued chamber mistrust, and it was partly for this reason that the Native Recruiting Corporation had been instrumental in establishing *Umteteli* in 1920. Thus it was not surprising that, when the Native Mine Clerks under their leader, A. W. G. Champion, sought to introduce a discussion on African wages at the second meeting of the Joint Council in June 1921, the Chamber sought to bring the association to an end. The following year the Chamber withdrew recognition from the association in the light of the 1922 Rand Strike by white mine workers, and consequently the Association had to withdraw from the council in October 1922.[46]

This withdrawal by the most prominent association of clerical and white collar workers on the Witwatersrand, whom Charles van Onselen has designated 'collaborators' in the mining industry,[47] left the Joint Council's African component very much dominated by the more conservative sections of the African petty bourgeoisie who had to some extent no real alternative avenues of political advancement once they had been deprived of a mass following. It was not surprising, there-

fore, that the Mine Clerks' withdrawal was followed by the
formal disassociation by the radical A.N.C. leadership centred
around *Abantu Batho*. Always distrustful of the council, the
radical group, led by D. S. Letanka, C. S. Mabaso, L. J. Mvabaza
and T. D. Mweli Skota, attacked what they alleged was Joint
Council interference in A.N.C. politics and forced R. V. Selope
Thema to give up his post as Provincial Secretary of the A.N.C.
in the Transvaal.[48] Aided by the development of Kadalie's
I.C.U. on the Witwatersrand, the A.N.C. refused to collaborate
with the Joint Council throughout the early 1920s. The isolation that this produced for the African followers of the Joint
Council was evidenced in 1924 when Selby Msimang got the
council to establish a special sub-committee to organise pub-
licity for the council which he said was only vaguely known
about by Africans living on the Rand.[49] As a Chamber of Mines-
backed paper, *Umteteli* continued to give the Joint Council
unstinting support throughout the 1920s, claiming that 'the
chief hope of the Native people lies in such inter-racial co-
operation as that which has been begun by the Johannesburg
Joint Council'. Its protestation, however, that it was 'certain
that the movement will spread' and 'the government will
sooner or later be *compelled* to give it recognition'[50] began to
look increasingly implausible as the 1920s progressed, (emphasis added).

The Joint Council, however, did act as an important channel
by which some African organisations on the Rand were able to
obtain white liberal support on specific issues. A good example
of this was the 'night passes' issue when the Council was
pressured by Mrs Charlotte Maxeke and the Bantu Women's
League. As a prominent African member of the Joint Council,
Mrs Maxeke opposed Champion's attempt to have the wages
issue discussed in June 1921 and was clearly anxious to maintain the support of such prominent white liberals on the council as Ray Phillips and Howard Pim. These connections proved
useful in 1925 when the Pact government proposed to introduce night passes for African women. Ray Phillips took the
lead in the lobbying of the governmnent on the matter, carefully pointing out in a letter to General Hertzog on 18 January
that 'we could deplore any action on the part of the Natives
which would lead to any increase of anti-white feeling on their

part'.[51] The response from Hertzog indicated the government's willingness to accede to the Joint Council's request for holding the issue in abeyance, provided that the Joint Council itself agreed to act as an informal policeman for the government by placing before it 'any effective and acceptable alternative scheme of solution of the problem'.[52] Ray Phillips then sought to mobilise a campaign to change the government's policy and reported on 9 February that 'energetic efforts' had been made to secure the co-operation of the African National Congress in the calling of a joint conference on the issue.[53] In the event, the A.N.C. refused any such collaboration and, though individual member attended the conference which was held on the separate days of 14 February and 7 March, no formal support from the A.N.C. was obtained by the Joint Council. Instead, the Joint Council had to be content with the support of the essentially conservative Africans' organisations on the Rand, such as the Native Ministers Association, the Native Mine Clerks Association, the Native Teachers Association and the Bantu Women's League. Even so, the meetings failed to reach agreement on the issue of whether African women should be made to secure parental or magisterial assent before travelling to an urban area, with both Selby Msimang and A. W. G. Champion opposed to the whole idea.[54] Though the Joint Council won the admiration of some leaders of African opinion such as Sol Plaatje for 'its definite stand and active protest' over women's night passes,[55] the ambiguity of the Joint Council's strategy and its failure to obtain A.N.C. approval indicated its only partial political support from the African petty bourgeoisie.

By the middle 1920s, the Joint Council's somewhat unreliable support from the African political and educational élite reflected in many ways the contradictions engendered by the government's segregation policy. As the 1923 Natives (Urban Areas) Act had indicated, the main place of abode for Africans was in the rural areas, and the restrictions on African property holding in urban areas indicated the problem an urban petty bourgeois class faced in getting itself established.[56] Even the two most prominent African members of the Joint Council in Johannesburg, Selby Msimang and R. V. Selope Thema, were unable to overcome these hindrances for both had only flimsy economic roots in the city in the 1920s.[57] Though they both wrote regular articles for *Umteteli*, attempts at forming businesses were haphazard, and when Msimang eventually gave up the secretaryship of the Joint Council and formed a general agency business with Selope Thema to collect rents for the property owners in Alexandra Township and Sophiatown, the effort proved unsuccessful. After working as a clerk to pay off debts of some £80, Msimang found a much more promising offer in the management of three farms owned by a land syndicate at Driefontein, near Ladysmith, in his native Natal.[58] The problems confronting Msimang and Selope Thema in establishing urban businesses almost personify the positon of the African petty bourgeoisie at this time, and indicate why so many members of the African political élite were willing, in the final analysis, to accommodate themselves to governmental policy and take advantage of territorial segregation to acquire rural landholdings. 'It seems to me', Msimang wrote, 'that if we allow things to drift as they do we shall not only delay the final settlement of the Native areas for another ten or twenty years but we may afford an opportunity to those whose ambition it is to oust us out of the land altogether and to convert the existing recommended areas into white settlements or cotton growing farms for poor whites under state or company patronage'.[59] There was a tendency, therefore, for African members to fall in with the general trend of segregationist thinking in the Joint Councils in the 1920s, belying the idea that they acted as significant forces on liberal opinion in the direction of assimilation.[60]

With this general weakness in the urban African petty bourgeoisie, the Joint Council looked increasingly to rural areas for African political support. This policy was shaped to a considerable degree by the more segregationist turn of liberal thinking in the wake of the 1923 Urban Areas Act, the victory of the Pact in 1924 and the publication of the four bills in 1926. This was aided after 1926 by the growing impact of C. T. Loram on Joint Council policy as the Native Affairs Commission declined in its ability to influence government thinking. As chairman of a Commission of Enquiry into the Training of Natives in Medicine and Public Health, Loram championed the idea of welfare work and the training of African doctors being primarily focused in rural areas. Thus, it was not surprising that, when A. B. Xuma returned in 1927 from America as a qualified medical practitioner, Loram, together with H. M. Taberer, advised the wife of the late F. B. Bridgman not to appoint Xuma as a superintendent of the newly opened Bridgman Memorial Hospital for Africans on the grounds that he would be better employed among 'his own people' in the reserves.[61] The general direction of liberal ideology in South Africa increasingly moved to an 'apolitical' stance, with welfare work by the Joint Councils and other welfare bodies serving as the social and economic underpinning of co-optation of the African petty bourgeoisie. This became much clearer in the years after the publication by the Pact government of the four native bills in 1926.

3 The Cape franchise and the establishment of the Institute of Race Relations

The publication of Hertzog's four native bills in 1926, with the implicit threat behind them of the eventual destruction of the common franchise in the Cape, led to a debate in liberal circles on the exact 'political' role the Joint Councils should take. Loram argued that with funds from the Carnegie Corporation in the United States, the councils needed to keep a 'respectable' image if they were to continue to be supported by their American benefactors, whilst at the same time avoid rousing political hostility inside South Africa due to their overseas connections.[62] From at least 1923 onwards, Loram became increasingly influenced by what he saw as the significant political potential of the Dutch Reformed Churches, which he considered could do the job of political lobbying far more effectively than the English-speaking liberal bodies. In that year a conference was held under the auspices of the Federal Council of the Dutch Reformed Churches in Johannesburg, where a number of papers, including one by Edgar Brookes, was given on the need to develop welfare politics within an overall policy of territorial segregation. The conference impressed Loram as 'the largest and most important unofficial conference on Native Affairs ever held in South Africa',[63] and after the victory of the Pact in the 1924 election, he advocated a low-profile strategy for the Joint Councils, leaving the Dutch Reformed Churches in the vanguard of actual political pressuring on a government that now had a distinctly Afrikaner complexion. This meant, furthermore, a tightening up of the national organisation of the Joint Councils and the creation of a federal controlling body, since this would be likely to lead to pressures for more direct political involvment. As Loram wrote to Rheinnalt-Jones:

American experience would keep the Joint Councils aloof from national issues. If the JC is bound to a votes for Blacks policy for example it will find it harder to get the Blacks in Pretoria a swimming bath. Without achieving practical local reform the JCs will fade away. Keep your big political organization separate tho the personnel may be the same in both cases... You will see that I have departed from my view of a National Joint Council. I see that the JCs need to be local and non political. Let the Dutch Reformed call the political meetings... [64]

Following these informal pressures in the early 1920s to depoliticise the Joint Councils, Loram went on to the offensive in 1928. Having ceased to exert much influence via the Native Affairs Commission, Loram turned his attention to establishing a body that could co-ordinate Joint Council work and bring it more closely under the aegis of the research work of American-style 'race relations'. As a representative of the Phelps-Stokes Fund in South Africa, as well as acting as an unofficial adviser to the Carnegie Corporation, Loram was in a strong position to lobby these bodies for funds at a time when the Joint Councils were starved of money. The Phelps-Stokes Fund agreed initially to pay Rheinnalt-Jones a salary of £200 a year as the 'executive secretary' of the Joint Councils, and the Carnegie Corporation also authorised a grant of £750. [65]

This American backing for Loram's aims was not met with an unqualified welcome from the liberals involved in the Joint Councils. To an older generation represented by Howard Pim, it represented a dangerous new turn of events where the area of political involvement became more narrowly defined. Furthermore, for those in the Cape the re-organisation of the Joint Councils could mark a playing down of liberal opposition to government proposals to end the common franchise. In 1928 a tie had been forged between the Johannesburg and Cape liberals around the franchise issue, which many on the Rand recognised as a key means in upgrading the 'status', as Rheinnalt-Jones defined it, of the Africans. 'Without status', he

wrote, 'all efforts at upliftment will take many more genera-
tions to be effective.'[66] The Rand-Cape connection began with
a Franchise Defence Organisation organised by Howard Pim as
the chairman and Rheinnalt-Jones as secretary. This body cir-
cumvented the rather cautious Joint Council in Cape Town[67]
and began to lobby for potential support amongst members of
Smuts' South African Party opposition in the House of Assembly. Despite the caution of a number of potential M.P. sympathisers like Henry Burton and C. P. Crewe, for an election
was looming on the horizon,[68] the body expanded its activities
after a National European Bantu Conference in Cape Town in
February. Here Pim spelt out the new thinking, which is ex-
amined in more detail in the next chapter, on the need to
expand African agriculture in the reserves and establish trading
outlets with the urban areas.[69] Furthermore, the advance of
industrialisation also necessitated a modification in the pass
laws to allow ease of access to the urban areas, and the removal
of the Colour Bar Act. All this necessitated maintaining the
Cape franchise, and a resolution defending it was passed at the
conference. Loram's equivocation on this angered Pim, who
declared his lack of trust in him for 'he is a Government
servant every time with the merits and defects of his class'.[70]

Greater involvement with the franchise issue led to the
establishment in April 1929 of the Non Racial Franchise Association, before the election of that year. With the support of
such prominent Cape liberals as Sir James Rose-Innes, who
was president, Morris Alexander, Henry Burton and J. W. Jagger, the organisation sought to influence both the S.A.P. and
the white electorate on the need to retain the common Cape
franchise. As its manifesto declared, to remove it, as the current Franchise Bill of the Pact government intended, would
'drive all the Bantu, civilised or uncivilised, into one group by
giving them a common allegiance'.[71] Despite Smuts' careful
dissociation of the S.A.P. from the association, the victory in
the election for Hertzog's Pact government was attributed by
many S.A.P. members to the Association's activities.[72] Thus
the election had the effect of distancing many South African
liberals from the mainstream of white party politics, for in the
early 1920s they still enjoyed channels of influence with members of both political parties. At the same time, it also streng-

thened Loram's hand in his move to establish an Institute of
Race Relations, the initial committee of which was already set
up on 9 May, before the election.

After gaining the consent of the Carnegie and Phelps-Stokes
funds for the creation of such a body, Loram secured his own
election as chairman of the organising committee, while
Rheinnalt-Jones was secretary and Howard Pim the treasurer.
The objectives of the body were clear from the initial meeting,
for extracts from the Carnegie Corporation report of 1924 were
distributed to the members, defining the policy on non-political involvement. 'The deliberate and conscious propagation of
opinion is a perfectly legitimate function for the individual,'
the report stated, 'but it is becoming greatly recognised that it
is not the widest use to which trust funds can be put.'[73] This
was the policy that Rheinnalt-Jones, appointed as 'Adviser' to
the Institute from 1930 onwards, sought to implement, and for
the most part the Institute avoided direct political involvement in favour of informal pressure on government ministers
on an individual basis, or else the factual presentation of issues
devoid of any strongly political comment.[74]

4 The challenge of the International and Commercial
Workers Union

The establishment of the Institute also terminated, for a period
at least, a debate which had been going on in Johannesburg on
the kind of response liberals should make to African urbanisation and the creation of radical black political leadership. In
the immediate post-war years, as we have seen, the main
response had been in the direction of Joint Councils and the
social settlement ideas of Frederick Bridgman, which had led
to the establishment of the Bantu Men's Social Centre and
women's hostels. However, by the mid-1920s, the growth of
the International and Commercial Workers Union marked a
new phase in African politics which many in the Joint Councils seemed unsure how to meet. To the novelist Ethelreda
Lewis, who first suggested the idea to the Witwatersrand liberals of bringing in orthodox trade-union assistance as part of a
plan to reorganise the I.C.U. to prevent Communist infiltra-

tion, this tardiness of both the Joint Councils and the Churches to take greater action indicated weaknesses in their whole approach.

Ethelreda Lewis's criticism stemmed from a philanthropic concern, typical of many white liberals in the 1920s, to protect African societies from what she perceived as their over-hasty penetration by western economic pressures. Restating a forceful pastoral vision of the essentially rural nature of African society, she pleaded for a strategy of 'evolution' rather than 'revolution' in African social change, which necessitated as much attention as possible being placed on the possible disruption by Communist agitators.[75] However, it was indicative of the state of the new liberalism that she was unable to win over any of the business community in Johannesburg to support her scheme for recreational facilities for Africans; nor could she win C. T. Loram's support for devoting the limited Joint Council resources of £750 a year for five years from the Carnegie Corporation to providing diversionary educational and recreational facilities to stem any possible Communist undercover activity (which at this time mainly consisted of night schools).[76] Forced, therefore, to look overseas for assistance in her 'mission', as she termed it, to influence the ideas of the African political leadership, Ethelreda Lewis represented more the last phases of the older post-war urban settlement liberalism on the Rand, than anything substantially new.

By the time that William Ballinger arrived in South Africa in 1928, the I.C.U. was already severely split and wracked by corruption, and in his attempts to restructure the organisation he received little support from the Joint Council liberals beyond the payment of his salary from Britain, which was organised under the auspices of the accountant, Howard Pim. The actual decision to go ahead with William Ballinger's visit was substantially out of Ethelreda Lewis's hands, as it became subject to the emerging African lobby in London centred around Winifred Holtby and Norman Leys and the T.U.C. lobby represented by Arthur Creech Jones and Walter Citrine.[77] In effect, Loram and the Institute indicated a growing concern to stem the old external, metropolitan influences which were seen to have far less weight politically as South Africa moved towards attaining Dominion status in the 1931 Statute of

Westminster. The exercise of bringing in Ballinger was not repeated and, in attempting to obtain continued outside recognition of the 'urgency' of the situation, Ethelreda Lewis met a realisation of this fact in Britain also. Neither Exeter Hall nor *The Times* could be expected to influence South Africa in the way they used to, wrote Sir Willoughby Dickinson of The World Alliance for Primary International Friendship Through The Churches,[78] and though the liberal circle organised around The Friends of Africa in London sought the partial continuation of this, it was only a shadow of its former self. Nevertheless, the continuing existence throughout the 1930s of an organisation with metropolitan links did check the complete introversion of the South African Institute, which could keep up only limited ties with external bodies such as the conservative John Harris of the Anti Slavery Society. As the next chapter shows, this alternative to the otherwise monolithic conservatism of the Witwatersrand liberalism also provided the political context in which an intellectual critique of the new liberalism was mounted.

TWO

Widening horizons

1 *African societies and market economics*

As the economic status of the African reserves in South Africa continued to decline throughout the 1920s, it became clear to a number of liberals that a simple faith in Victorian ideas of improvement and self-help would no longer do. The seemingly insatiable appetite of the mines, farms and burgeoning industry in South Africa for black labour had ensured an increasingly restrictive application of segregationist doctrines by the latter part of the 1920s. Even the small number of liberally inclined segregationist writers like Edgar Brookes, who published an important work, *The History of Native Policy in South Africa from 1830 to the Present Day*, and supported Hertzog in the 1924 election, became disillusioned.[1] As Hertzog's Pact government came under mounting pressure from agricultural interests, earlier promises to revive the idea of establishing 'neutral' areas, on lines of the draft Land Bill of 1912, were abandoned.[2] So, too, was any idea of extending parliamentary representation on the Cape model to the rest of the Union, though Brookes had pressed in the mid-1920s for some form of elective representation for 'detribalised' Africans living in the urban locations via either chiefs and headmen or the councils established under the 1920 Native Affairs Act.[3] By 1927, things began to change as Brookes, like so many liberals of his generation, became impressed by the example of American blacks. Visiting the United States that year, the former apologist for racial separation began to move in a different political direction after seeing a relatively prosperous negro middle class, and resigned from the Nationalist Party. He eventually became an active member of the Institute of Race Relations after its foundation in 1929,[4] and began championing the idea of incorporating an acculturated class of Africans into 'western civilisation'.[5] This still left, though, the question of what was to happen to the large number of peasants and labour migrants left in the reserves and rural locations, and their relationship to the South African economy.

In this respect, a number of other liberals began to learn of some of these economic developments, analysed by William Macmillan from first-hand experience in the late 1920s and vividly portrayed in his book *Complex South Africa* in 1930. Furthermore, Margaret Ballinger (née Hodgson), travelling around South Africa in 1929, noted in the Ciskei that the introduction of the cash nexus via labour migrancy hindered rather than aided agricultural innovation. Economic stress did not necessarily mean that people were automatically encouraged to go out and work, for 'all prefer to starve together', while squatters were reluctant to migrate 'partly because people themselves won't expel them — naturally they are relations — partly because there is nowhere for them to go'.[6] The net result, therefore, was further overcrowding of the type that Macmillan observed in Herschel and elsewhere.

By 1930 a growing band of liberals centred around the Johannesburg Joint Council began to turn their attention to the idea of fostering rural co-operatives amongst the African peasantry and also, as research widened, to link them if possible to the Protectorates in order to establish a separate and autonomous African market outside the direct control of the 'white' industrial economy. 'I am wondering,' Howard Pim wrote in January of that year to Sir James Rose-Innes, 'if we have begun to understand living alongside a people to whom competition is unknown and markets [sic]. Who hold all necessities of life in common... How can the rules of our economics be applied?'[7]

This question of how to 'apply' western market economics in a different cultural and economic situation became an important subject of liberal discussion in the early 1930s. By this time a number of new paths of analysis were being pursued at the academic level which were to have a significant impact, given the close connection between the universities in South Africa and bodies like the Joint Councils and the Institute of Race Relations. Foremost was the unfreezing of anthropology from the rather static positivism of the 1920s into the more historically oriented conception of 'culture contact' that sur- *culture-contact* rounded the work of the journal *Africa*. These developments will be discussed more fully in the next chapter. In addition, there was the development of historical study generally and the formulation, especially by Eric Walker, of the conception of South African society as the product of a frontier situation that had been the cultural and political source for the generation of racial attitudes carried over into the industrial period. The implication was that many of the unilinear assumptions of Victorian liberalism could not be seen to hold directly in the South African situation, since they were derived from a British historical trajectory where racial ideology was not so embedded. Eventually, it was hoped, the logic of South African industrialisation would remove what was seen as the atavistic racial ideologies derived from the past, but in the meantime South African liberalism would have to live with these anachronisms and accommodate itself to them in the best way possible.[8]

This was the mood of a more pessimistic liberal intelligentsia that became increasingly resigned by the 1930s to the idea of the eventual removal of the Cape franchise. It reflected, too, the declining faith of a number of liberals in the course of African politics. The fissures in the I.C.U. in the late 1920s left William Ballinger disillusioned with the prospects of African trade unionism by 1930, as it seemed that there was little or no chance of re-establishing a large black trade union organisation in a period of economic depression. Ballinger had come out to South Africa in 1928 originally hoping to pledge his life's work to this enterprise,[9] but it appeared that some other form of organisation was needed in order to generate economic wealth amongst Africans. 'The I.C.U. is more adapted in policy and structure', he wrote to Arthur Creech Jones, 'for mass production — the next phase of industrial development in Africa — than are the other unions.'[10] This idea of 'mass production' helped shape William and Margaret Ballinger's research into the economies of the Protectorates and the question of establishing African co-operatives.

2   The issue of the Protectorates

William Ballinger's growth of interest in the Protectorates
emerged from a number of sources. By the time he came to
work for the I.C.U. in 1928, the union had moved from its
original base amongst industrial workers and had started to
gain extensive support amongst rural farm workers. Ballinger,
on his tours looking at the rural organisation of the union,
immediately came up against the whole land issue, which he
saw as being one of the crucial reasons for the union's weakness: '... the failure to procure land for people was the principal
factor that led to the downfall of the organisation', he declared
in 1929.[11] With the proclaimed establishment by Kadalies's
rival faction of an African Native Land Settlement Corporation
Ltd, with a nominal capital of £100,000, Ballinger, too, sought
to move into the land purchase racket.[12] The I.C.U. of Africa
reported the same year the establishment of a Native Development and Trust Company Ltd, registered at the Volksrust farm
of Pixley Seme, in the hope that 'with the assistance of the
African Congress combined with the I.C.U. this will prove a
success and restore the confidence of the masses'.[13] The company had a nominal capital of £25,000 and appears to have
strengthened Seme's political position to the extent that he
could take over the presidency of the A.N.C. in 1930, in alliance with a conservative faction of chiefs.[14] The experience of
this was important in impressing upon Ballinger the varying
methods that needed to be developed to link up African landholding in different parts of the Union.[15]

The Protectorates research, however, also emerged out of
William Ballinger's frustration with what he perceived as the
short-sightedness of the liberal bodies in Johannesburg as they
came increasingly under the 'race relations' syndrome after
1929. Whilst indebted to a number of liberals such as Howard
Pim, who organised the payment of his salary during the time
he worked with the I.C.U., Ballinger felt that the Johannesburg
liberals had little understanding of the mechanics of trade
unionism and, with key figures like C. T. Loram suspicious of
his intentions, he felt increasingly excluded from the development of the new race relations infrastucture.[16] As a consequ-

ence, the old support from Winifred Holtby, Arthur Creech Jones and I.L.P. circle support in England continued to be viewed as useful, even though he had moved from the original objective of reorganising the I.C.U. In London, a group of liberals led by Winifred Holtby, Mrs Pethwick-Lawrence and F. S. Livy-Noble (a former warden of the Bantu Men's Social Centre in Johannesburg) formed a committee to look into the position of Africans resident in London and the accompanying problems of social alienation and racism,[17] and this body maintained contact with Ballinger as he began the Protectorates research. Eventually it was to emerge in 1934 as The London Group on African Affairs. Many of the assumptions of English liberals, who were critical of British colonial policy in Africa, began to filter through into the Ballinger's work and to shape the interest in 'development' after years of neglect by the British Colonial Office.

Unlike the South African liberal 'establishment' after 1929, the British liberal circle was far less influenced by American ideas on 'race relations'. In Britain itself, the term did not come into any sort of popular usage until well after the second world war, and issues of race were still seen largely in terms of 'the colour problem' and 'the colour bar'.[18] Unlike South Africa, where the anti-slavery tradition in the Cape had been implanted by John Philip at second hand, London was still the home for a strong moral concern on issues of race. Winifred Holtby reflected this in one of her lesser-known novels, *Mandoa Mandoa*, an exotic 'irrelevant comedy' which touched upon the strong moral objections by such campaigners as Norman Leys and McGregor Ross to British pro-settler policy in Kenya in the 1920s.[19]

In the 1920s British colonial policy became influenced by ideas on colonial 'development', though substantially in terms of aiding unemployment in Britain rather than to foster colonial development for its own sake. Furthermore, until the 1929 Colonial Development Act, this was still pursued very much in a piecemeal fashion.[20] Most of the actual assistance that did go to Africa went to the East African colonies,[21] and virtually no assistance went to the southern African Protectorates. There was thus a growing fear among some liberal critics that these were going to pass under some form of white settler control. This did not necessarily mean simply handing them over directly to South Africa, despite the provision for their ultimate incorporation under the Act of Union of 1910. After the 1922 referendum in Southern Rhodesia, rejecting unification with South Africa, British policy-makers had another white settler block to turn to, as the course taken by the Pact government after 1924 increasingly influenced British politicians against handing over the Protectorates to the Union. British policy on the Protectorates in effect represented less a simple promotion of 'trusteeship' and a general moral aversion to South African segregation policy, than a desire to maintain the British 'imperial factor' through connecting the Protectorates with the white settler states in East and Central Africa. Any concern to protect African interests in the Protectorates tended, therefore, to be qualified by a wider set of strategic interests in fomenting a British sphere of influence across the Zambesi, where white settlers were to be 'co-trustees' in a bloc that could check Afrikaner nationalist power to the south.[22] This became especially clear in the 1929 election in South Africa, in which Smuts's S.A.P. was defeated in a welter of charges by Hertzog that his 'Black Manifesto' would lead to 'a black Kaffir state... extending from the Cape to Egypt in which white South Africa would vanish'. Pact policy under Hertzog appeared to be increasingly opposed to any collaboration with British imperial policy to the north, and this became compounded by the renewal of South African claims in the early 1930s for the incorporation of the Protectorates into the Union.[23]

It was, therefore, the lurch towards increasing support in British colonial policy for British settler interests in East and Central Africa which worried the liberal circle in London. While still anxious that the Protectorates might be handed over at some date to South Africa, the British liberals were especially angered by what they saw as a consistent policy by Leo Amery, the successor to Lord Milner at the Colonial Office in the 1920s, of watering down the trusteeship provisions of the Devonshire Declaration of 1923, in which African interests in the East African colonies were declared to be paramount.[24] Amery, as a former member of the Milner Kindergarten, was ardently in favour of entrenching the white settler interest in

Kenya, while in southern Africa he saw this as linked to a growing collaboration with South African mining capital and the rising interest of Sir Ernest Oppenheimer in the Anglo-American Corporation. As he observed in 1927 on visiting southern Africa, the 'future policy of the Empire in South Africa is going to depend largely on the Protectorates and Rhodesia, both as regards native development, and on a smaller scale as regards British white developments'.[25]

Ideas for 'native development' in the southern African Protectorates therefore became bound up with a rising climate of moral concern in British liberal circles by the late 1920s and early 1930s on the direction of South African segregationist policy. The specifically Afrikaner nature of the South African Government after the emergence of the Pact in 1924, and the triumph of 'Afrikaner provincialism' over the older Cape liberalism, began to be recognised in a lot of British political discussion as a result of a new series of critical books by radical liberal critics of colonialism. Lord Olivier, for example, wrote *The Anatomy of South African Misery* in 1927 (after discussions with William Macmillan in England the previous year), while Leonard Barnes, who had worked with the Ballingers for a period in their Protectorates research in the late 1920s, brought out *Caliban in Africa* in 1930 and *The New Boer War* in 1932.[26] These works indicated that it would probably be unwise for British political decision-makers to involve themselves too closely with South Africa, at least on the formal political level, and that it would be far more important to turn to the Protectorates as a means of exerting British presence in the region.

This shift of liberal ideas outside South Africa also had some effect on the thinking of those liberals inside South Africa who were more sensitive to external changes of opinion. Liberals in both Britain and South Africa began to turn at the same time towards the Protectorates, which began to appear as useful areas for the testing of new ideas on social and economic 'development'. Perhaps feeling that the chance of shifting the direction of the South African experiment in segregation was minimal, liberals in Britain and South Africa turned to the Proctectorates as possible social laboratories, as the period itself was one of experimentation and toying around with pos-

sible model social systems. Concomitant, therefore, with the
reports on the Protectorates commissioned by the British
government from Sir Alan Pim which were published between 1933 and 1935,[27] so South African liberals began to
turn their attention to similar areas. Howard Pim's report on
the Transkei was published in 1934, recommending a step-
ping up in land-reclamation schemes, cattle culling and economic co-operation,[28] while William Ballinger and Margaret
Hodgson (later Ballinger) also began work on the Protectorates in the early 1930s, publishing *Indirect Rule in Southern Africa* in 1931, *Basutoland* the same year and *Britain in
Southern Africa (No.2): The Bechuanaland Protectorates* in
1932.[29]

3   The work of William and Margaret Ballinger

The significance of the Ballingers' work was that in a number of respects it challenged a new orthodoxy which was
beginning to emerge in South African 'native policy' in the
early 1930s surrounding the Report of the Native Economic
Commission of 1932. This report favoured a strategy of
'adaptation' of African institutions towards European ones,
as opposed to either full-scale cultural 'assimilation' on the
one hand or complete racial 'separation' on the other.[30] It
marked a growing awareness within the echelons of Union
native administration of the growing importance of anthropological research in the implementation of policies of social
and cultural transformation, and an indication of the growing links between academic work in universities and administration by government. However, the commission failed
to discuss what the relationships were going to be between
the class of tribal chiefs, whose powers had been significantly boosted by the Native Administration Act of 1927,
and the African intelligentsia in the rural areas. For the most
part, the commission welcomed the general direction of segregation policy and dashed any hopes held by some liberals
for a policy that focused on the African intelligentsia as a
nucleus for a strategy of Tuskegee-type agricultural modernisation in the South African reserves, gradually nullifying the
powers and authority of the chiefs.

In the case of the Protectorates, avenues for political reform did not seem so blocked, and the Ballingers launched an attack on British colonial policy for bolstering the powers of chiefs, whom they saw as a 'doomed institution':

While the chiefs are desperately clinging to the old forms and justifying themselves on the grounds of defending tribal claims to the land, they are entirely ignorant of the economic and political forces which are crushing out the nation's life... They see their young men go out to work in the Union without a glimpse or appreciation of the factors involved both for themselves and for others.[31]

In the wake of the 1929 Colonial Development Act, it appeared politically feasible, especially while a Labour government was still in power and Lord Passfield (Sidney Webb) Colonial Secretary, to criticise the Colonial Service for allowing the apparatus of native administration to become 'enmeshed [with] private enterprise to exploit the resources of the country to its own benefit'.[32] What was really needed was a programme to ensure that cultivation and development were initiated by the new Agriculture Department of the Colonial Office so that the 'tribal methods' and the 'conservatism of the chief' could be eliminated. By such means the Ballingers argued, 'an effective native society' could be created

... with the joint advantage of tribal ownership of land and effective use of such land. This would make ejection or confiscation impossible, or at least very difficult, and would thus remove one of the greatest dangers of transfer to the Union. It would mean also that the Native population of the Territories would not be entirely at the mercy of the Union's Native policy but would have some bargaining power.[33]

For Britain to go ahead with transfer of the Protectorates to the Union 'would destroy the last vestige of that belief in her protection and benignant [sic] power'.[34]

The Ballingers, therefore, continued to make a strong moral appeal to the policy-makers behind British colonial policy, at a time when a similar course had declined either through a growing political pessimism amongst South African liberals, or because of direct involvement via the developing apparatus of native administration. They were aided in this task in the early 1930s by a series of political events that brought the Protectorates into the limelight.

In 1932 Hertzog renewed his bid for the incorporation of the Protectorates, backing it up this time with economic threats that included the exclusion of Africans in the Protectorates from the Union's labour market.[35] In addition, in 1933 the Protectorates issue came forcibly into public view following the forceful removal of the Regent of Bechuanaland, Tshekedi Khama, by the acting High Commissioner, Vice-Admiral Edward Evans with a force backed up by Union troops. Though Khama was soon reinstated, the affair served to highlight the position of the Protectorates, especially as Tshekedi had attempted unsuccessfully to renegotiate the concessions granted to the British South Africa Company in 1929. Through the mediation of the Governor-General in South Africa, the Earl of Athlone, the British government successfully accomplished a series of new concessions to Sir Ernest Oppenheimer's Anglo-American and De Beers companies for mineral exploitation in the territory.[36] Though Tshekedi's objections ('we know that when mining takes place in a country it won't be a nation. We know we can uplift ourselves by means of cattle not be means of mining') had not been able to reverse the British policy, it was still the hope of liberal critics in Britain that the whole affair could serve to show the dangers of actual incorporation of the Protectorates into the Union. For Leonard Barnes, the issue was a valuable card to play in at least delaying the transfer, for while 'the Prots are bound to go to the Union sooner or later and the South Africa Act contemplates as much', nevertheless liberal critics could continue 'to insist that this is not the time, and to go on doing so as often as the questions of transfer is raised, until at last we are defeated'.[37] More forceful opposition came from Margery Perham through a series of articles in *The Times* in September 1933, as a result of which a debate was instigated between her and Lionel Curtis, formerly of the Milner Kindergarten and anxious to see the Milnerite vision at least partially accomplished through incorporation.[38]

The controversy served also to enhance the role of the Ballingers' research, especially as the more conservative liberals in the Institute of Race Relations equivocated on incorporation. In 1933 Rheinnalt-Jones considered the incorporation of Basutoland as 'inevitable', while not being sure about the other two.[39] Two years later the issue again reached the level of serious political discussion as the British government began to modify itself towards Hertzog and the Afrikaner Nationalists in the wake of Fusion. Rheinnalt-Jones sought to use the debate as a means to enhance the prestige of both himself and the Institute. Writing to Livy Noble of the Friends of Africa, he argued for a commission of enquiry to be set up on the whole incorporation issue, containing representatives from the British and South African governments together with African representatives and 'missionaries'. Recommending D. D. T. Jabavu, John Dube and Z. K. Matthews as the African representatives from the Union of South Africa, Rheinnalt-Jones suggested a number of additional white liberal possibilities including Professor Hoernlé, Professor Walker, Edgar Brookes and himself. 'At present', he continued, 'I am the only link in South Africa between *all* the missions... The Institute has been useful in acting as a consultative agency without being either a government department or a missionary institution. But possibly even the Institute and myself might be suspect, being in the Union!'[40] The proposal got as far as being sent to Lord Lugard for serious consideration.[41] By this time William Ballinger had come out in marked opposition to this kind of accommodationist political stance. Those in charge of the Joint Councils, he wrote to Livy-Noble in 1933, 'either cannot, or do not want to see, that they are not supported, so far as the non-Europeans are concerned, by the rising Native middle class'.[42] He accused the Institute of being manipulated by the Chamber of Mines, especially in the case of the appointment of Edgar Brookes to the Institute in 1933,[43] and argued for a much more active policy of political involvement to defend African and coloured interests. Following his attendance at the Non-European Conference in the Cape in 1930, he claimed that Abdurahman and D. D. T. Jabavu backed his candidature for a parliamentary seat, though in the event he was ineligible as a non-South African citizen.[44] In 1933, he became the supervisory editor of the radical A.N.C. paper *The African Defender*, which was established by a group inside the African National Congress to fight the conservative policies of the president, Pixley Seme. Despite its decline, the I.C.U. of Africa was not completely defunct either, and Ballinger claimed that the

I.C.U. of Africa was still the 'parent I.C.U.' of eight existing separate sections and argued that he was only unable to rejuvenate the organisations through lack of funds for travelling around South Africa.[45]

Furthermore, William Ballinger claimed the successful development of some African co-operative enterprises, which he saw as the partial answer to the problem of development in the Protectorates. In the first year of operation, the Western Native Township Co-operative, based in Orlando, made a small profit, and Ballinger jubilantly reflected that 'the tree of Native co-operation is well rooted and is going to throw out many strong and varied branches'. Contact was established with the resident magistrate in Swaziland, T. Ainsworth Dickson, in the hope of being able to develop marketing links between Swazi producers of butter, tobacco and other commodities and the African market on the Rand. Ballinger wrote to Livy-Noble:

If you could get those in charge of the Colonial Development Fund to spend a few thousands on co-operative activities, it would do much to assist the Natives to adapt themselves to the better aspect of our economic system and money economy. As it is today, the most intelligent Natives are suffering from the shocks of a money economy, which is so far removed from their subsistence economy, and the breakdown of our commercial-industrial system which leaves them so bewildered. When they invest, or rather put on fixed deposit £25 of their surplus from co-operative retail sales, I have to warn them about high rates of interest and the meaning of fluid as against frozen capital.[46]

The apparent success of the first year's operation of the Western Native Township Co-op led to efforts by Ballinger's friends in England to seek support from the British government for co-operative enterprises in the Protectorates. Winifred Holtby succeeded in gaining contact, via the Rev. A. G. Fraser, Principal of Achimota College in Ghana (where Aggrey had been vice-principal), with Lord Lothian[47] As secretary of the Rhodes Trust, former member of the Milner Kindergarten and a minister in the National government until his resignation in 1932, Lothian represented one of the most valuable contacts between liberal opinion on colonial development and official government policy. Ballinger sent to Lothian a summary of what the scheme had achieved so far, arguing that 'for various reasons, African natives grasp far more quickly the principles of co-operative than of individualist economics, and that if a beginning could be made which would in some way link native production within the Protectorates to a market outside, a partial solution at least would have been reached for the present problems of the Territories'. Pointing out that the Western Native Township Co-operative had made a profit of £340 in the year following its opening in April 1932, allowing for a dividend of 5 per cent to be paid, Ballinger argued that 'such stores are both needed, and can, under European supervision, be developed'.[48] The Resident Commissioner in Swaziland's enthusiasm for the idea also gave credence to Ballinger's scheme, and it was hoped that the Swaziland Protectorate Authorities would assist the marketing of cattle, butter, 'Native hand-made cigarettes' and 'kaffir corn and mealies', thus possibly supplying the basis for 'the transition stage between industrial and tribal economics'.[49]

Despite finding the Rhodes Trustees cautious, Lord Lothian himself was enthusiastic towards the scheme. 'Obviously,' he wrote to Howard Pim in December 1933, 'it would be of immense advantage if agriculture could be made more productive in the native territories with a steady market within the Union, thus keeping the money in the country and giving the natives an economic interest which might save them from rushing prematurely into politics.'[50] Similarly, approaches were made to the co-operative guilds in England for funds to develop the scheme, though in the event only a small sum of money was forthcoming. The overall objectives, however, behind the fund-raising were not achieved, and by 1934 it became clear that Ballinger, together with his small number of liberal supporters in Britian, would have to go it alone. Even before the scheme was started, it was clear that the British government was not going to be over-enthusiastic for its success. In 1932 J. H. Thomas, the Colonial Secretary, refused to support a proposal from Lord Olivier and a group of supporters behind the co-operative idea, that Ballinger should be put on the staff of the High Commissioner for South Africa, Sir Herbert Stan-

ley.[51] Furthermore, until at least 1933, it was the general view
of the Dominions Office, according to Alan Pim, 'that absorp-
tion is ultimately unavoidable on general economic grounds
though they dislike the idea and this ultimately defeatist view
must affect the attitude of the Treasury to financing essential
developments',[52] Even while the resistance to incorporation
was sufficiently strong, after Fusion in 1934, the development
of South African mining after the Union came off the gold
standard represented another key factor in British policy — not
wishing to antagonise the basic labour requirements of the
mining industry. In this respect, British colonial policy in the
early 1930s, so far as southern Africa was concerned, had not
yet moved towards a developmentalist view that sought to
initiate any independent economic projects in the Protectorates that might run counter to the requirements of migrant
labour. British policy at this time was guided by the view that,
even with the Union becoming 'unBritish', the pro-British settlers of East and Central Africa were still too small to form an
effective counter bloc and that both economic and political ties
with the Union were likely to persist for some time to come.[53]
Though there were critics of South African policies in the
British government in the 1930s, such as the High Commissioner, Sir William Clark, in 1938,[54] for the most part British
opposition to South African segregation in the 1930s failed to
link itself to the 'forward thinking' which had been initiated by
Amery in the 1920s and institutionalised through the creation
of the Colonial Development Fund in 1929.

Accordingly, though some liberals such as William Macmillan were anxious, on leaving in 1932, 'to hold up South Africa
as *the* awful warning',[55] liberal opinion on segregation outside
the Union remained unclear throughout most of the 1930s. It
was only after the Italian invasion of Abyssinia in 1936, and
the growth of Pan-African consciousness through a body like
the International African Service Bureau, that radical opinion
began to focus upon South African policy in the late 1930s.[56]
Calling for public demonstrations against South Africa and
hostile to the seemingly complacent moderation of the London
Group on African Affairs (directed by F. S. Livy-Noble after
Winifred Holtby's death in 1935), the I.A.S.B. nevertheless
failed to generate widespread public feeling on the issue before

the outbreak of war in 1939, and this compounded the general isolation of William Ballinger and The Friends of Africa throughout the 1930s.[57] After 1934, as South Africa came off the gold standard, the main focus of South African liberal interest shifted back towards the Union as it became clear that a coherent South African native policy was likely to emerge with Fusion. External liberal opinion was too weak to exert much of a break on this process.

4 Co-operatives inside South Africa

William Ballinger's political isolation was exacerbated by the fact that for a number of South African liberals it was clear that there was little chance of a scheme of co-operatives in the Protectorates linking up with similar movements inside South Africa. While the liberal-controlled paper, *The Bantu World*, extolled the virtues of economic co-operation, claiming that 'there is not a town in South Africa where Europeans of standing cannot be found — businessmen, accountants or auditors — to advise and keep Natives engaged in such work',[58] the political leadership inside Congress was unlikely to direct their main energies in that direction. Though the A.N.C. President, Pixley Seme, evinced some enthusiasm in that regard, it was recognised by no less a person than the Secretary of Native Affairs, Major Herbst, that this was unlikely to gain much support. As far as black settlement in the Protectorates was concerned, he admitted to Howard Pim that 'Union natives would not go to Bechuanaland' and were unlikely to support any settlement scheme.[59]

In addition to this African resistance to links with the Protectorates, there was the growing recognition, even by William Ballinger, that co-operatives were not proving especially successful even inside the Union. It was generally accepted by the Johannesburg Joint Council in the early 1930s that any co-operative ventures needed to be well organised and that 'expert guidance' was needed to get them off the ground. The previous efforts of Father Huss in the Transkei looked less and less impressive, and Howard Pim confessed to Alexander Kerr that a talk given by Huss at the Bantu Men's Social Centre in 1933 was 'unintelligible' and that there was 'very wide distrust of the co-operative movement in the Transkei'.[60] Accordingly there was a growth of interest in bringing in an outside special-ist, such as the former Indian administrator C. F. Strickland, who had written a book *Introduction to Co-operation in India* in 1928 and was widely acknowledged to be an 'expert' on matters of 'applying' western ideas to communally based tribal communities. Pim believed that it would need 'considerable propaganda' to make the co-operative idea a success; there was support for the idea of sending out Strickland to South Africa to help co-ordinate Ballinger's efforts and, as Winifred Holtby put it in a letter to William Macmillan, 'as part of an experi-ment towards the solution of the economic problem of the Prots'.[61]

The year 1934, however, proved a turning point as Strick-land's visit failed to materialise since there were insufficient funds for the trip. Pim died the same year and William Mac-millan, who had earlier been won over to the co-operatives idea, had already left South Africa to do research on the copper belt before moving on to the West Indies. The London Group failed to be able to persuade the British Co-operative Societies to finance the activities of the Ballingers,[62] and even though there was some support in the Institute of Race Relations for spending some of the £2,500 offered by the Carnegie Corpora-tion in the 1930s, William Ballinger by this point had shifted his interest; this followed the offer by the Institute of a grant in 1934 to accompany the round of the Wage Board and help to present the African case for improved wages based upon stu-dies into their cost of living.[63] Thus, it was not altogether surprising that the one co-operative that William Ballinger did have a hand in helping to establish, in Orlando, with assistance from Howard Pim's firm of accountants, Howard Pim and Hardy, soon got into difficulties. The management of the con-cern had little experience and there was widespread pilfering of the goods, so that by 1935-36 it was reported that the profit margin had fallen to between 10 and 15 per cent on a turnover of £3,000.[64] Though three African co-operatives were registered at the office of the Registrar of Co-operatives in that year, it appeared that the most successful base for co-operative trading was a kinship one, with ethnic ties and control by chiefs reducing the incidence of corruption. One of the more successful efforts was that of the Bakgatla Co-operative Society Limited under Chief Makapan at Makapanstad, near Pretoria, whose objectives extended beyond trading to 'tribal co-ordination' and the integration of the four separate groupings of Mosetlha, Mocha, Makau and Pilane.[65] Another relatively successful example of a co-operative society fostered as a result of Ballinger's efforts was a second one at Orlando under the Rev. S. S. Tema of the Dutch Reformed Church, while at Boksburg the Rev. N. Tansi of the A.M.E. Church also had a co-operative society.[66]

5 The move towards unions

Given these fragmented attempts at economic co-operation, it was not surprising that there was a growing interest in establishing black trade unions amongst the burgeoning black working class in South Africa's towns and cities. Though the Institute of Race Relations kept up a small interest in co-operatives in the latter part of the 1930s, especially via the Bantu Welfare Trust which approached the administrator of the Transkeian Territories for information on their working,[67] the main shift occurred in the direction of unions. In 1934, attempts were being made to revive African Unions after the collapse of the Communist dominated South African Federation of Native Trade Unions and the lean years of depression. On the Witwatersrand, the only two African unions that appear to have survived the early 1930s were the clothing and laundry workers, and the Laundry Workers Union became the nucleus of the Joint Committee that was formed in 1934 to extend union formation to African workers in South Africa's burgeoning industry.[68] As the number of African industrial workers grew in the 1930s, from 66,751 to 134,233 between 1932-36, so in turn did the number of unionised workers, who were estimated to toal some 20,000 by 1940. For William Ballinger, it seemed a ripe opportunity to return to his union-organising activities of the late 1920s and learn by past mistakes. Hopeful that African unions could be modelled on lines similar to the British Transport and General Workers Union, Ballinger claimed a limited success in 1934, announcing to Livy-Noble that he had been instrumental in the establishment of a Native Building Workers Union.[69] But his previous attachment to the I.C.U. of Africa and continued links with the Joint Council probably led a number of black trade-union organisers to treat Ballinger with a good deal of suspicion. This weakness in Ballinger's organising ability was compounded by the arrival of a serious rival on the Witwatersrand in 1935 in the form of Max Gordan, a former industrial chemist and Trotskyite from Cape Town, who soon proved adept at submerging himself in the work of trade-union formation. Aided by links with his former friend from the University of Cape Town, Lynn Saffery, who was now secretary of the Institute of Race Relations, Gordan became secretary of the Laundry Workers Union and proceeded to develop tactics of working inside the existing legislation governing trade unions, while at the same time appealing to African workers' current needs by developing schemes for legal aid, literacy and book-keeping classes.[70]

The comparative success of Gordan and Saffrey in the late 1930s, before Gordan's internment by the Smuts government in 1940, has led to the view that Ballinger was left a marginal figure, 'confined', in Baruch Hirson's words, 'to the periphery of events'.[71] Certainly, Ballinger failed to develop trade-union organisation amongst African workers in the same degree as his political rivals, and his exact political role remained unclear. Though his wife, Margaret, claimed at a conference on the question of recognition of African trade unions in 1939 that Ballinger was a 'representative of Native Trade Unions',[72] the basis of his political support was problematical. Only a limited degree of backing had been secured from the All African Convention in 1936 at the time of the election for Natives' Representatives in the Senate, and in the event Ballinger was beaten in the campaign for the senatorship of the Transvaal and Orange Free State, not only by Rheinnalt-Jones of the Institute of Race Relations, but by the former Communist Hymie Basner as well.[73]

On the other hand, it is important to recognise that Ballinger's ties with the Friends of Africa acted as an important check on a monolithic white liberalism that was getting more and more under the control of Rheinnalt-Jones and the Institute. In the years after 1936 and the Native Franchise and Native Trust and Land Acts, the bulk of white liberal opinion

inside the Union shifted away from any former interest in the
Protectorates and the incorporation issue towards seeking to
make the segregationist provisions of the Native Trust and
Land Act workable, having been prepared, from as early as
September 1935, to sacrifice the Cape franchise as part of this
objective.[74] Rheinnalt-Jones, in particular, saw the Land Act
as opening up opportunities for development in the reserves.
On the question of agricultural innovation, Jones wrote on
similar lines to the Native Economic Commission arguing
that 'more has been achieved in this direction than is generally realised — enough to justify confidence that the Bantu
can be developed into a reasonably progressive agricultural
people working in harmony with the restricted conditions of
close agricultural settlement'.[75] Given such possibilities, and
with a 'splendid lot of men' in the Native Affairs Department,
it no longer made sense, Jones wrote to Livy-Noble, to consider the additional incorporation of the Protectorates, for '...
the Union Native Administration has enough... for the next
ten years to carry out the promises made to the Native in
regard to the land and Native development to prevent it
giving adequate attention to the Territories and the spending
of money which should be spent on them'.[76] The result of this
strategy, however, as later chapters seek to show, was the co-
option of the Institute into the working of the government's
trusteeship policy and the growing isolation of white liberals
from the emergent African nationalism in the 1940s.

For William Ballinger and a minority of more radically
inclined liberals, this path of co-optation appeared as a disaster, even before the end of the 1930s. 'There can be little
doubt', he wrote vitriolically to Xuma in May 1939, 'that
Jones imagines that he has a right to corner Natives and all
they do or intend to do. If he ever wakes up to the fact that
many of the Natives in Southern Africa are very conscious
that they are Africans he will die of shock.'[77] Though increasingly isolated politically, William Ballinger's opposition to
the idea of 'segregated co-operatives for Natives under the
control of the Institute and Department of Native Affairs',[78]
acted as a basis for the development of a critique of the
strategy adopted by Rheinnalt-Jones and the Institute by the
start of the second world war.

This critique, however, rested initially upon a different political trajectory to that of mainstream South African liberalism. In so far as the political vision of the Ballingers and the Friends of Africa in the early 1930s rested upon a rejuventation of the Protectorate territories in southern Africa, they appealed back in many ways to the former British imperial presence expressed through the High Commission. As John Benyon has argued in a recent analysis, the High Commission represented up to 1910 an important intermediary mechanism, co-ordinating metropolitan imperial impulses with local initiatives within southern Africa. Furthermore, in the years after Union, the legacy of the High Commission was still strongly felt for

... the new political unit of 1910 bore a deep impress from the activity of the High Commission, which had been the pre-union co-ordinator of the sub-continent's affairs. The impress left behind as much diversity as uniformity. In many of its boundaries, some of its inter-government relationships, several aspects of its 'native policies' and problems — not least those of the land and labour — in part of its economic development and communications network, a number of its institutions, and in the persistence of certain political attitudes among white, black and brown peoples modern Southern Africa bears the stamp of High Commission action.[79]

This 'diversity' was still sufficiently clear in the 1930s for the Friends of Africa strategy to bear some degree of political credibility within South African liberal politics. As Union 'native policy' was only in the process of acquiring an ideological rigidity, based upon the conception of both racial segregation and the subordination of the African reserves to the status of labour reservoirs for the white-controlled economy, it did not appear obvious that liberal political action was necessarily confined only to the sphere of territory formally controlled by the Pretoria government. The experience, though, of appealing unsuccessfully to the British Colonial Office, and receiving only marginal support from within British establishment circles after the establishment of the National government in 1931, acted as an important political watershed for a number of left-leaning liberals in South Africa. The tie with the metropolitan liberal tradition looked increasingly what it really was, namely a Victorian anachronism that bore little political meaning as South Africa obtained Dominion status and her own sovereign national flag. Though it was still conceivable

for some Cape African leaders such as D. D. T. Jabavu to appeal
to the Privy Council in London in 1929 at the time of the Rex
v. Ndobi case on African landholding in the Eastern Cape,[80] in
formal terms these were recognised as a thing of the past. By
the time of the 1936 Bills, even Jabavu recognised that it would
probably be necessary to go down fighting,[81] since there was no
possible external political escape route as Britain became an
increasingly distant country, locked with its own issues of
industrial depression, high unemployment and continental
fascism.

But what was to be the future strategy, then, for liberals
indelibly printed with a South African political label? The
Institute did not enjoy total political sway, despite the efforts
to control the activities of more radical activists via the Joint
Councils. In 1933 the Cape Town Joint Council was reported
as being 'strongly antagonistic'[82] to the Institute, while in 1935
the Rev. R. G. Milburn proposed in a memorandum that the
Joint Councils should be constructed as a 'liberal association'
so that 'all political progressives should act together' outside
the Institute's control.[83] Even key Cape liberal elder statesmen
such as James Rose-Innes doubted the wisdom of an 'apolitical'
approach, considering that there was a danger of the Institute
becoming 'all thing 'all things to all men'.[84]

Despite these reservations, however, the Institute became
more fully organised in the mid-1930s, as the Loram definition
of 'race relations' in a neutral, positivist mould took hold of the
Institute's activities. The new anthropology that had been
taught to a body of students in South Africa from the early
1920s undoubtedly contributed to this and, in turn, spilled
over to define the growing political self-consciousness of South
African liberal ideology. It was in reaction to this emergent
liberal orthodox that the more radical political liberalism, that
had been partly set in motion by the Friends of Africa, emerged
during the second world war.

THREE

Anthropology and cultural idealism

1 The impact of anthropology

Alongside the emergent political divisions amongst South African liberals in the early 1930s, there was a growing ideological and intellectual influence from research in anthropology. Unlike other disciplines, anthropology bound liberal opinion-formers and intellectuals closely to the apparatus of government, as a reassessment took place of 'native policy' under the banner of 'trusteeship'. In 1925 an ethnological section was formed inside the Native Affairs Department, and a tie was forged with the universities through courses in anthropology and native administration at the University of Cape Town and the University of the Witwatersrand. Anthropology rapidly established for itself a strong professional status in South Africa as a social science that was pliable to the needs of administrators, and it was significant that General Smuts personally invited A. R. Radcliffe-Brown to establish the social anthropology course at the University of Cape Town in 1921, leading to the foundation of the first distinctly South African anthropological journal, *Bantu Studies*. With close recognition paid to developments in the discipline in Britain, the South African courses became in part academic outposts of their British equivalents, such as the anthropology taught at the London School of Economics by Professor Malinowski. The collection of ethnological data on African societies became professionalised into something considerably more than the mere collection of exotica by gentlemen scholars and missionaries, as had been the case before the first world war. This fact-gathering now became systematised into a more coherent theory of 'culture contact' that emphasised the continuity and functional stability of African social institutions, and not their simple collapse in the face of missionary proselytisation. Indeed, with the rise of various forms of segregationist ideology, this anthropology increasingly emphasised the cultural differences between 'western civilisation' and African society in South Africa, and the continuing links, even in the urban context, of first-generation African city dwellers with their pastoral and rural background.[1] As in the case of American social science, therefore, South African anthropology provided an important basis for the conception of a situation of 'race relations' derived from the growing interaction between an urban, market-oriented society with a rural, folk-oriented one.

At the same time, a number of liberal opinion-formers perceived from an early stage the importance of this anthropology in the fostering of welfare and social work in South Africa's burgeoning towns and cities. In 1921 C. T. Loram pointed out that the strikes at Lovedale and Port Elizabeth and the bloodshed at Bulhoek in the Eastern Cape 'demonstrated to the people of South Africa that in the adjustment to each other of the two races... we have a situation as difficult as that in Ireland, and as vital to South Africa as was the Great War to the people of Europe'.[3] The need was, he argued, for a 'scientific' approach in a manner akin to the natural sciences, but one moreover that reflected the present state of 'contact' between the 'European' and 'native races':

It is not that we have studied some Native matters in a scientific manner. The philologist has found, and is still finding, much in the languages of our Native peoples of interest and importance; the ethnologist has studied the varieties of the human race found in our country, but the majority of these studies have been made of the Native in his primitive or isolated state, when he has been little or not at all influenced by contact with white civilisation, and when he has not, therefore, become a problem to the European in the same sense in which the less romantic but much more troublesome educated or semi-educated Native is a problem. It is from the Native in contact with the European that the Native problem arises, and there is a great dearth of studies of the Native in this relationship.[4]

Loram' plea did not fall on unreceptive ears, for despite the general image of British anthropologists between the wars as being only concerned with studying African societies in a completely isolated or 'tribal' state,[5] those involved in establishing the subject in South Africa were concerned to relate it to immediate political issues. A. R. Radcliffe-Brown, for example, indicated precisely this type of concern during his short stay as Professor of the School of African Studies at Cape Town. 'The one great problem on which the future welfare of South Africa depends', he wrote in the first number of *Bantu Studies*

is that of finding some social and political system in which the natives and whites may live together without conflict; and the successful solution of that problem would cetainly seem to require a thorough knowledge of the native civilisation between which and our own we need to establish some sort of harmonious relation.[6]

This conception of a 'harmonious' political system, derived from the 'functionalism' concept in British anthropology, helped to define the new political strategy of inter-racial accord in the 1920s. Scientism and positivism were already endemic to liberal ideology before the first world war, as was seen in the case of Howard Pim in his farewell address to the Transvaal Native Affairs Society in 1909, but this now became boosted by a growing belief in the power of 'scientific' investigation to act as a key for inter-racial 'harmony'. The emphasis upon contemporary 'contact' indicated a lessening of the concern for the historical past which was seen as the repository of South Africa's racial ills — an assumption that was to spill over into the 'frontier thesis' after 1930.[7] The point was to generate the correct political mechanisms on which to build a new harmony that could eventually erode these atavistic legacies from another era. This almost Fabian-like belief in the power of the state to shape and modify social beliefs and values was perhaps best expressed by the Welshman, J. D. Rheinnalt-Jones, in 1926. Arguing against an historical approach to native policy, Rheinnalt-Jones emphasised the values of a positivist standpoint on which to base research on race relations:

Political experience and historical knowledge have not given us the panacea for our racial difficulties, but have led us instead into a wilderness where the road is lost in the thick undergrowth of racial pride, passion and prejudice. We may well turn aside to look for other paths, even though they may prove less direct.[8]

Jones then turned to the arguments advanced by the advocates of complete racial separation, who had taken comfort from the theory of a 'primitive mentality', propounded by the

French anthropologist Levy-Bruhl. The evidence for this he dismissed as thin, for 'the emergence of the Bantu from the power of animism and the tribal organisation that is based upon it' was 'inevitable'.⁹ The implication, therefore, was that the success or failure of government 'native policy' was to be judged by the yardstick of the degree to which it promoted the 'assimilation' of western 'rationalised civilisation' by African societies. In a sense, this reformulated many of the ideas of the nineteenth-century 'civilising mission' fostered by the missions in newer, more secular terms whilst avoiding a more detailed economic analysis of the role and function of African societies in the workings of the South African political economy. On the positive side, this anthropological discussion led to a decline, in official discourse at least, of the more overtly racist thinking, derived from the phase of social Darwinism and eugenics from the turn of the century. The refutation of an inherently 'primitive mentality' indicated that there was a certain similarity in all human groups. However, this biological racism became replaced by a cultural or Eurocentric chauvinism which judged African societies in terms of their capacity to adapt to western norms. In many respects these 'cultural' differences meant the 'racial' differences of the more traditional parlance under a new label, and anthropology did nothing substantial to open up the framework of analysis to newer avenues of political economy. Indeed, as in the case of W. M. Macmillan in the early 1930s, it substantially added to the closing of these in academic and intellectual investigation.

Furthermore, the response from the government itself over the following five years or so indicated the oblique nature of this anthropological critique. In a sense the 'scientific' nature of Rheinnalt-Jones's attack on the primitive mentality school was as blunted as the scientific pretensions of the racism he was attacking: science, in this context, could be seen to be used to support a case both for and against racial separation.¹⁰ There was still the problem of translating the more general anthropological attack on cultural separation into a concrete programme that would lead to completely different social and political order to that presumed by the protagonists of segregation. This, as previous chapters have indicated, was lacking in liberal thinking in the 1920s as the issues became defined by

the thrust of government segregation policy. The ultimate
ends of South African liberalism thus grew increasingly unclear.

2   *The State's response:'Adaptation' and 'Trusteeship'*

The reason for this uncertainty lay, in part, in the links forged
between government policy-makers and administration officials in the Native Affairs Department, and the white liberals,
together with an important reformulation of government segregation policy behind the notion of 'trusteeship'. Despite
Rheinnalt-Jones's opposition to the Native Administration Bill
in 1926, by that year there had already been established an
important Bantu Studies course for Native Affairs administrators at the University of the Witwatersrand. As a part-time
lecturer in Bantu Studies there from 1927 to 1937, when he
became a senator, Rheinnalt-Jones looked upon his academic
lecturing as in many ways more important than his work on
the Joint Councils.[11] This priority given to Bantu Studies was
reinforced in the early 1930s when, through Loram's assistance
and funds from the United States, the Bantu Studies course
under the professorship of the language scholar C. M. Doke
was expanded into a department in its own right, without any
ties to History.[12] In addition, Rheinnalt-Jones's control of the
Institiute of Race Relations and the growing restrictions on the
more radical activities of the Joint Councils were factors contributing to compromise with government policy.

By the early 1930s, therefore, a new ideological consensus
began to be formed between the more conservative sections of
the liberal intelligentsia centred around the Institute and the
government policy of trusteeship. Previous informal liberal
attempts at development in the reserves were given up in
favour of state control as the Native Economic Commission in
1932 spoke through a report in favour of a 'wise, courageous,
forward policy of development in the Reserves'.[13] This rap-
prochement with state policy implied a moving away from the
previous emphasis upon assimilating Africans into western
civilisation towards one of adaptation which was the principal
ideological emphasis of the report:

The inevitable effect of the under-development of the Reserves is that the orientation of the most advanced Natives has been towards the European. Instead of finding in their own area a fruitful field for using their energies, and their knowledge to uplift their people, they have been forced out from among them and have become 'exiles' elsewhere. To develop the Natives and the Reserves: to make the dead hand of tribalism relax its grip; to convert tribalism into a progressive force; to set the Native mass in motion on the upward path of civilisation, and to enable them to shoulder the burden of their own advancement — such must be... the main approach to the solution of the Native problem in its economic aspect.[14]

NEC 1932

'adaptationist' ideal

This 'adaptationist' ideal was reinforced by the commission's support for government attempts to develop the reserve economies. The Native Administration Act of 1927 was seen as beneficial in this respect, since it allowed the Native Affairs Department control over all the native administrators in the reserves. By the time of the report's publication, the Director of Native Agriculture, R. W. Thornton, had 155 African demonstrators working in the field (though it was estimated that at least 400 would be needed over the next decade).[15] In addition, the commission considered that the key basis for 'development' in the reserves lay less in the provision of more land, but in the effective utilisation of existing areas. Its central reading of history in South Africa since the 1913 Natives Land Act was that if there had been an 'intensive campaign of Native agricultural education', the African demand for further land would be 'less insistent and less urgent'.[16] Agricultural demonstrators were thus essential means towards breaking down peasant conservatism, ensuring the introduction of better livestock strains, stock limitation, fencing, paddocking and irrigation and a careful programme of land reclamation. Praising the efforts of Father Huss in his efforts to introduce co-operative societies in the Transkei, the commission recommended State action in this sphere, with the emphasis upon a Native Agricultural Bank, since European private capital was virtually excluded from the reserves. At the same time, echoing the emphasis made by liberals upon instilling sound business ethics into the aspirant African trader class in the reserves, the commission urged that 'very close watch should be kept on the use made of the borrowed money', for 'it must be remembered that to the Abantu money economy is a new thing'. It was necessary for there to be 'education on the use of credit', which the commission considered could be achieved by 'imposing very strict limits on the purposes for which money can be borrowed' and by 'employing existing Native agencies, such as Councils and Chiefs to supervise this'.[17]

The Native Economic Commission, therefore, sought both to nationalise many of the more informal efforts at capital mobilisation in the reserves and to create a class of traders and small businessmen, whilst at the same time, through the ideology of adaptation, manipulating tribal and traditional social mechanisms as the main basis of social control.[18] The strategy in effect resembled quite closely later State efforts at manipulating tribal institutions through the creation of Bantu Authorities by Drs. Verwoerd and Eiselen in the 1950s. It also acted as a forerunner for the policy proposed by the Tomlinson Commission in 1955, of economic development of the reserves and the enhancement of the rural petty bourgeois factions centred around such chiefs as Chief Matanzima in the Transkei, Lennox Sebe in the Ciskei and Chief Mphephu in Venda.[19]

The report thus came to represent an important new ideological reference point for liberal thinking in the 1930s, and the final eclipse of the older Victorian notion of a civilising mission which was represented by the minority reservations to the report's conclusions by Dr Alex Roberts, a former teacher at Lovedale and member of the Native Affairs Commission. By the 1930s, this Victorian concept came to be formulated in terms of 'assimilation' in opposition to the commission's concept of 'adaptation'. 'The way of progress for the Native people', Roberts wrote in his reservation, 'lies along the path of the Native assimilating as rapidly as possible the European civilization and culture.'[20] Roberts did not appear to mean by this the complete destruction of the reserve economies and the mass migration of the African peasantry to the towns; in 1922 he had spoken rather of the need to build villages around the urban areas for African migrants which would be made 'so attractive that no longer even the best natives will desire to live in European towns'.[21] But undoubtedly Roberts had been disappointed by the trajectory of urban segregationism since the 1923 Natives (Urban Areas) Act,[22] and he sought the incorporation into the urban areas of at least a section of the African working class. His minority report, accordingly, written with two other members of the commission, Anderson and Lucas, recommended the raising of African wages in the urban areas in order to increase the efficiency of African labour power and to raise the level of living standards in order to help alleviate the slum problem that confronted many urban municipalities.[23] In many respects these arguments, therefore, presaged the later debate after the onset of the second world war when liberal economists looked to the increase of African purchasing power as a means of increasing the South African home market and enhancing the growth of secondary industry.[24]

In comparison to Roberts's clear view opposing the notion that a complete system of urban segregation could be attained in the Union,[25] much liberal thinking in the wake of the report buttressed the concept of adaptation by reference to anthropological concepts of African cultural cohesion. The notion of culture contact, especially, which had been developed inside the International African Institute and its journal *Africa* by such anthropologists as Lucy Mair, Monica Hunter and Ellen Hellman, emphasised the separateness of African culture from western civilisation, though the relativity of these two notions in the context of the fascist permeation of Europe in the 1930s came increasingly to be stressed. The editor of *Africa* was a former professor of ethnology in Berlin, Diedrich Westermann, who, in a book entitled *The African Today* in 1934, pointed out the efforts within European societies to revive group associations of the kind that still existed in African societies.[26] Reflecting a loss of faith in western individualism which frequently led to social atomisation, anthropologists in South Africa were, by the 1930s, seeking to explain social change in a far more overt manner than the rather static positivism of the 1920s, but this recognition of change through the culture contact approach still necessitated the recognition of the tenacity of African social institutions. Thus, thinking in this regard was strongly in tune with the British philosophy of 'indirect rule' that was popularised by Lord Lugard in the 1920s, but which still sought the 'hearty co-operation of the educated Natives'[27] in order to make it work. In a South African context, however, this led to a close accord with the segregationist implications *alliance with rural black elites*

of the adaptationist approach and the search for political alliances with the rural African political leadership in the reserves, as opposed to the newer élite in the towns.

The philosopher Alfred Hoernle, who succeeded Howard Pim as president of the Institute of Race Relations on the latter's death in 1934, also reflected this changing intellectual mood. In some unpublished notes he wrote of his agreement with the chairman of the Native Economic Commission, John Holloway, that the cultural basis for the assimilation of the American negro was substantially different from that of South Africa 'where Bantu culture still exhibits a considerable de-

Hoernle

grees of cohesion and vitality... not unreasonably we begin to regret the indisciminate breaking down of Bantu culture and to talk of giving the Bantu a chance to build up on the basis of their own cultural heritage'.[28] Aware, too, of the equally strong group-based challenge to liberalism from the rising Afrikaner nationalism of the 1930s, Hoernle noted, after attending a conference of the newly formed Rasseverhoudingsbond van Afrikaners of M.D.C. de Wet Nel in 1936 that 'we simply cannot Christianise without to a greater or less degree de-Afrikanderising... We cannot administer to Native tribes as we do in the Union without Europeanising the people through contact with our methods of government.'[29]

Hoernle's thought contributed towards shifting liberalism away from its original missionary base and towards qualifying it with a more cautious political pragmatism that recognised the power of rival group and ethnic allegiances. Even the mainstream of Christian liberalism, such as Edgar Brookes and Jan Hofmeyr, recognised the strength of this anthropological investigation, and in 1935 Hofmeyr called for a 'new liberalism' based upon a 'sympathetic first hand acquaintance with the Native peoples — or, to put it differently, eager study and thoroughgoing investigation, with a view to giving form and substance to the otherwise possibly dry bones of idealism'.[30] This 'constructive segregation' Hofmeyr saw as leading to a 'class of detribalized urban native as a permanent factor, of accepting the members of that class as co-workers in the building up of South Africa's economic life'.[31] However, this remained a longer-term objective, and in terms of immediate political strategy the Institute liberals found themselves driven to co-operating with government segregation policy. Hofmeyr, for instance, could point out no new avenue beyond 'accepting the position thus created at least as a foundation on which to build a more adequate structure of race co-operation in the future' — and this was in reply to a warning from Alfred Xuma of 'very serious conflicts and antagonisms between the White and Black races in South Africa, unless better councils... prevail'.[32]

3   The challenge of Heaton Nicholls

This incorporation of the Institute and liberal activities into the working of government segregation policy was quickly perceived by the more ideologically aware of the government's own supporters. The segregationist George Heaton Nicholls from Natal, for example, sought to draw the Institute into a series of political alliances that he had already helped to forge in Natal between sugar planters, the Native Affairs Department and the African political leadership led by John Dube.[33] The role of John Dube in the scheme was important, for Nicholls had approached him as early as 1931 to sound out African leadership's opinion on land allocations to the reserves, offered in exchange for the removal of the Cape franchise. As a result of a tour of the Union, Dube succeeded in gaining considerable support for a memorandum on 'Land Settlement' that sought to create compact African reserves in each province of the Union on lines similar to the Transkei, in addition to establishing a Union Native Council for members elected from provincial councils.[34]

This employment of Dube was also significant, since he had fallen out in the 1920s with the white liberals led by Howard Pim and John Harris over their support for increased white control over his financially insolvent Ohlange Institute. As a consequence of Dube's failure to secure financial support from philanthropic circles in Britain, especially, via John Harris and the Aborigines Protection Society, by 1929 the Ohlange Institute had fallen under increasing control from Natal sugar-planting interests. Marshall Campbell, a prominent sugar magnate who later became a senator, was asked by Dube to become one of the trustees of the Institute, so that by 1931 it was not surprising to find Dube so beholden to Heaton Nicholls.[35] The longer-term consequence, however, was the gradual weaning away of sections of the African petty bourgeoisie and tribal chiefs in Natal from liberal influence centred around the Joint Councils, which had generally been rather weak there anyway. Though this model of political co-option was unlikely to appease the Cape members, whom Heaton Nicholls despaired of completely winning over,[36] it appeared likely by 1935 that some sections of African political leadership, led by Dube, would stand outside D. D. T. Jabavu's Cape-based and Joint Council-influenced All African Convention in their opposition to the Native Bills of that year.[37]

This appeared increasingly likely with the general political ineffectiveness of the Institute in the course of the opposition mounted against the Bills in 1935–36. Despite hopes by D. D. T. Jabavu for a last-ditch struggle against the Native Representation Bill in 1935, so as 'to give the government a full run for their money by dying hard so that we may go down still fighting',[38] it became clear in the course of 1935 that the liberals in the institute had too much at stake to risk a complete confrontation with the government. On the 16 May, Edgar Brookes advised Rheinnalt-Jones against any policy of non-co-operation towards the Bills,[39] and on 26 May Jones himself went to consult Smuts on a scheme for a series of conferences with African leaders on the Bills. Though Smuts was in favour of one general native conference, the liberals in the Institute favoured a series of Union-wide conferences which could increase their general political influence, and this proposal was agreed upon through the influence of D. L. Smit, the Secretary of Native Affairs.[40] With the isolation of Jabavu's All African Convention in the coming months, some liberals became involved at the local level with establishing political alliances of their own with sections of the African petty bourgeoisie in supporting the removal of the Cape African franchise. In Natal Edgar Brookes, who sought the senatorship there under the proposed legislation, championed an alliance with John Dube. Following the opposition of the conference in Natal to the bills and its championing of the Cape African franchise, Brookes warned Dube of 'the grave danger' involved in his 'selling the pass' and allowing the more radical sections

of African political leadership to prevail.[41] In the hope of out-
manoeuvring the radicals, who were widely believed to be
influenced by the activities of Carl Faye, a Zulu linguist in the
Natal Native Affairs Department involved in the establishment of the Zulu Society, Brookes suggested that Dube press at
the A.N.C. Congress in Natal on 15 December for the immediate establishment of the Natives Representative Council,
which could then act as a platform for working out the other
legislation on land, native representation and the Cape franchise with the government. This *de facto* acceptance of the government's policy clearly depended upon Dube being able to
maintain congress support, though Brookes, working in con-
junction with Douglas Shepstone and the Chief Native Commissioner in Natal, H.C. Lugg, kept open the option of supporting Z. K. Matthews should Dube fail.[42] In the event Matthews was not needed and Dube maintained Congress support
for the effective acceptance of the government's proposals,
providing the Cape franchise was not abolished.[43] Thus
Brookes led the way in effectively integrating liberal political
activity in Natal into the alliance already forged by Heaton
Nicholls between the Natal sugar planters, the Native Affairs
Department and the African petty bourgeoisie. This process
was further extended in 1937 when Brookes became senator for
Natal on the basis of support from the Zulu Paramount
Mshiyeni ka Dinuzulu and the tribally based Zulu Society that
was centred in the offices of the Native Affairs Department.[44]

Given this political trend, and the eventual support for the
Bills by John Dube after he went to Pretoria with the Zulu
Regent Mshiyeni,[45] it was not surprising that Heaton Nicholls
began to recognise the potential importance of the Institute in
the co-optation process. Writing to Rheinnalt-Jones in November 1935, he urged the Institute to abandon its ivory tower
outlook and to 'set to work to study what can be done along the
material lines of the Bills'. Indeed, he believed the Institute
'could do much to assist in the coming development, and
incidentally bring a better relationship, if you go with the
national current; but on no other terms'.[46] This tended to be
the trend of policy in the Institute as both Brookes and Rheinnalt-Jones became elected as Natives Representatives in 1937
in the wake of the bills passing into law. Rheinnalt-Jones, for

example, began to integrate some of his Institute work with that of the Native Affairs Commission, then under the control of Heaton Nicholls, seeing his role as a communicating link between African chiefs, farmers and headmen on the one hand and the commission on the other. Writing to John Dube in 1937 shortly after his election as Senator, Rheinnalt-Jones boasted of his being successful in getting African chiefs and headmen to speak to the Native Affairs Commission, which 'welcomed my presence and told the chiefs etc. that I was there to help'.[47] This close collaboration led to playing down opposition to the commission's policy on land allocations under the Native Trust and Land Act. Despite repeated claims by Rheinnalt-Jones that the white liberals had done their best to persuade the South African Parliament not to pass the Act,[48] it became increasingly clear that he saw his role as one of explaining and justifying previously worked out government policy. The tribal basis of the policy prohibited him from campaigning for land claims by groups outside recognised tribal structures, such as the Hlubi clans of Chief Msiti in the Orange Free State. Despite the fact that these people had been a recognised chiefdom until the end of the Anglo-Boer War, there were no land provisions for them under the 1936 Act, and Jones doubted, in a letter to one of the group's leaders in Matatiele, whether it was worth applying for land to the Chief Native Commissioner, Northern Areas, who was 'finding it quite impossible to do anything for scattered tribal people in the O.F.S., or even for some not so scattered'.[49] Such a response tended to indicate Rheinnalt-Jones desire to shield the apparatus of native administration from attack and to smooth over the administrative process of the trusteeship policy.

4   *Alfred Hoernle and cultural idealism*

It was, therefore, in the general political context of growing liberal collaboration with the evolution of the government's trusteeship policy that the reformulation of liberal ideology by Alfred Hoernle on to a cultural idealist basis in the late 1930s occurred. 'I have always recognised that the argument for *complete* segregation is very strong,' Hoernle wrote to Nicholls's in April 1937, 'what I have criticised is the incomplete segrega-

tion which is, to me, a mere sham.' Heaton Nicholls idea of
'keeping the Bantu race in its own reserves' had an attraction
to Hoernle who was prepared to support it in its full 'literal-
ness', especially if by total segregation there would be ensured
the ending of 'the disruption of Native social and economic life
by the prolonged absences of the men for the purposes of
earning wages in white employment', which could not be
really described as 'segregation'.[50] Such considerations were
probably reinforced in Hoernle's mind by the fact that by the
late 1930s, it was becoming increasingly obvious that African
political leadership was reluctant to accept automatically the
guidance and paternal authority that had been hitherto the
prerogative of the Institute and Joint Councils. As Xuma had
warned Hofmeyr in 1936, African political opinion mobilised
through both the A.N.C. and All African Convention was
becoming radicalised, forcing the hitherto 'moderate' leaders
into severing their former uncritical class alliance with the
white liberals. This process became clear by 1938 in Johannesburg, where the African membership of the Joint Council became strained after the success of the radical faction in the
Transvaal African Teachers Association and the Transvaal African Congress. This group had supported Hymie Basner in the
1937 election against Rheinnalt-Jones and, though they had
been beaten through the weighting of the voting in favour of
the chiefs, had nevertheless made a considerable impact on the
urban intelligentsia.[51] Thus, on an issue such as the Protectorates, when it was discussed by the Joint Council, a number of
African members present wholly opposed the idea of their
transfer to the Union. 'Our Natives manages to disappoint us
all, more or less', Hoernle wrote to John Harris of the Aborigines Protection Society; 'I have known them in much better
form... '. The 'general effect' of the discussion was to set
Hoernle thinking on the value of tribal structures:

The general effect on me at least — and much against my wife — was
to set me wondering (not for the first time) how these detribalised
Natives can really speak for the Native peoples as a whole; or how
much helpful advice they can really give to the Natives in the
Protectorates. Compared with a chief who has a real following among
his tribe, these advanced Natives have no following at all; and would
be in oppositon, if they had to live and work under a chief. This
fundamental division between the (more or less) detribalised, when

added to solid surviving tribal jealousies and enmities, makes any strong and wise leadership of Natives by Natives impossible.[52]

With growing doubts in the ability of liberal organisations like the Institute of Race Relations and the Joint Councils to maintain their ideological and political influence over the African political élite, Hoernle undertook his rethinking of liberal ideology in his Phelps-Stokes lectures of 1939, *'South African Native Policy and the Liberal Spirit'*. Here the cultural idealist arguments on the value of social communities as the essential basis of social control became linked, in Hoernle's analysis, with an interpretation of liberalism heavily influenced by the liberal Hegelian school of idealists of late nineteenth-century England. The static notion of a 'liberal spirit' thus became bound up with the preservation of 'culture' in the group-oriented sense of the cultural idealists:

... individuals live their lives as members of social groups, and the excellence of their lives is relative, therefore, to the culture (in the widest sense) of their group; the culture to the pattern of which individual lives are moulded, the culture from which they draw the materials, as it were, for a life worth living. The liberal spirit, in this aspect, shows itself as a respect for social groups other than one's own, for cultures other than one's own, for sentiments and traditons other than one's own, though always coupled with a willingness to share one's own.[53]

Out of this cultural relativism, Hoernle formulated a liberalism that was strongly influenced by the English traditon of political pluralism represented by his teacher at Oxford between 1898 and 1905, Bernard Bosanquet, and his friend Harold Laski.[54] This held that intermediary social groups between the inidvidual and the state had personalities of their own, though in the South African context these took on a 'cultural' mantle that would be later defined as ethnicity. Recognising, therefore, that within this cultural pluralism, Afrikaner nationalism was a growing political force, Hoernle gloomily reflected on the 'heartbreak house' of contemporary South African race relations. Perceiving that the choices were threefold, in a manner similar to the Native Economic Commission, Hoernle argued for a policy of separation as opposed to parallelism or assimilation. Such separation meant though 'the sundering or dissociation so complete as to destroy the very possibility of effective domination' if the 'liberal spirit' was to be achieved.[55]

However, this did not, Hoernle recognised, represent a very practical political programme, and he was forced to concede that there was 'no ultimate hope for the liberal spirit'.[56]

5   The political implications

Hoernle's liberal idealism marked a mood that dominated much of the liberal thinking in South Africa during the late 1930s. In one sense, the Phelps-Stokes lectures reflected a growth in liberal intellectual pessimism in the possiblilities of South African political progress and a decline in a faith in the inherent beneficence of a white 'civilising mission' derived from the nineteenth-century belief in continued social progress. Hoernle was in an especially good position to interpret this for he came from a background that had not been so closely associated with this Victorian spirit. Entering a Land-esschule at Pforte, near Naumburg, in Germany in 1896 at the age of sixteen, Hoernle had been brought up in the same educational milieu as the German professional middle class that Fritz Stern has seen as forming the basis of German liberal resignation and *Vulgaridealismus*. The general pervasiveness of idealism has been offered as an important explanation for the failure of the German liberal intelligentsia to take a stronger political stand against the rise of National Socialism. It was the idealisation of *Kultur* and the reverence for the past achievements in the arts and sciences which led to an intellectual degeneration of German liberalism into 'little more than the ritualistic repetition of phrases and pieties'.[57] Hoernle's liberalism bore marked resemblances to this, except that his conception of culture became strongly shaped by the developments in anthropological work in South Africa during the 1930s, especially as they were imbibed through the influence of his wife, Winifred, who taught anthropology at the University of the Witwatersrand.[58]

Not all liberals necessarily accepted this form of political resignation, and those from the Christian tradition especially saw it as challenging an essential tenet of standing and fighting for one's political beliefs. The Bishop of Johannesburg, Geoffrey Clayton, accused Hoernle of 'abandoning hope', which he saw as the basis of the Christian message,[59] and it was clear that, as South Africa went into war, a more optimistic mood began to prevail. The domination of anthropology in so much of the social science research work in the 1930s at the University of the Witwatersrand began to be eclipsed by the start of the war. Audrey Richards, lecturing in social anthropology at the University in 1940, reported a mood of restlessness amongst the students who were keen to go off to fight in the war.[60] Certain key classics had been published during the decade of the 1930s, such as Monica Hunter's *Reaction to Conquest* (1934), Audrey Richard's *Land, Labour and Diet in Northern Rhodesia* (1939) and Eileen and J. D. Krige's *The Realm of a Rain Queen* (1943 but completed in 1939).[61] More were to follow in the 1940s, but the subject began to be increasingly eclipsed by the growing interest in economic forces as the South African economy began to industrialise through the enforced protection afforded by the war. Much of this economic liberalism that grew up in the 1940s, however, was of a neo-classical kind, and it can be concluded that South African liberalism remained much the poorer for the loss of W. M. Macmillan in 1932 after the failure to get the course in Bantu Studies at Wits tied to history and not anthropology.[62] While thinking on the nature of colonial development widened during the 1930s as comparative surveys were done of peasant societies in areas like the Caribbean and West Africa, liberalism in South Africa became increasingly isolated as it moved from a conservative, neo-Durkheimian concern to protect the cultural homogeneity of African societies and insulate them in some respects from missionary influences, to a simplistic belief in the inherent beneficence of free market forces. Beginning with the work of an economist like E. H. Hutt at the University of Cape Town in the 1930s,[63] this grew into a popular belief disseminated by journals like *The Forum* and *Trek* in the 1940s that the South African social system would become liberalised through the development of secondary industry and the growing requirement for urban black labour force.

For the Institute of Race Relations, these developments represented an important area for future research, especially in new modes of social control in the urban context. While there had been some research on African slum conditions in the

1930s by anthropologists such as Ellen Hellman and Eileen Krige, much of the general ethos of this was still one of the degree and influences of the rural hinterland on first generation city migrants. Throughout the 1930s little attention was paid to the general social and cultural processes that underlay the conditions in South Africa towns and cities and the formation of a black working class.[64] Liberal thought substantially reflected the general trajectory of urban legislation itself, which for the most part, via the Amendment Acts of 1930 and 1937, entrenched still further the Stallardist presuppositions of the original 1923 Natives (Urban Areas) Act. Liberals thus mainly hoped to exploit whatever loopholes lay in the legislation in order to help foster a small class of African petty bourgeois property owners and small businessmen who were led by such figures as A. B. Xuma in the Sophiatown township in Johannesburg, R. G. Baloyi in Alexandra and R. H. Godlo in East London. This African property-owning interest was expressed especially through the Native Advisory Boards which had been established under the 1920 Native Affairs Act, and some important political ties were forged with the white liberals during the 1920s and 1930s.[65]

The onset of war in 1939, however, led to a growing governmental recognition of the whole urban issue as large numbers of black workers moved into industrial jobs vacated by whites who went off to fight in the war. In 1941 Smuts appointed a committee under the chairmanship of the Secretary of Native Affairs, D. L. Smit, to investigate social and economic conditions of Africans in the urban areas, and in a memorandum to the committee, which was published as a pamphlet *The Union's Burden of Poverty*, Rheinnalt-Jones and Hoernle articulated the thinking among liberals as a result of the war-time burst in industrialisation. It was becoming plain that the old pastoral conception of locating African societies in the rural reserves was breaking down, as a number of Africans were becoming permanently urbanised; the point was, though, what was the nature of their status to be in the urban context? For Hoernle, there was still no reason why the perceived evils of proletarianisation, as he saw them, in European societies could not be avoided in South Africa:

... there is no good reason why an efficient industrial worker should be a 'proletarian' ... or live under slum conditions. All through modern industrial countries, the pressure is, and has been for years, to give the workers a 'human' or 'civilised' standard of life. With the control of Nature with which modern science has endowed us, any economic system must be accounted a failure, root and branch, if with proper planning it cannot do that. The African industrial workers are as much entitled, in return for efficient work, to live on this plane as workers of any other race.[66]

This was an argument for planning and what would now be seen as a 'modernisationist' plea for the application of a politically neutral technology to raise living standards. This was much in keeping with the general ethos produced by the experience of total war and of state-led social engineering in the societies of the West. In July 1942 the executive committee of the Institute of Race Relations appointed a sub-committee to work out ways of implementing the aims of the 1941 Atlantic Charter, signed by Roosevelt and Churchill, to African conditions.[67] The Rooseveltian conception of 'Four Freedoms' marked a new era in western liberalism, born as it was out of the experience of the New Deal in America in the 1930s, whereby the state pump-primed a mixed economy and used Keynesian methods of economic tuning to prevent the capitalist system falling into deep recession, as had happened in 1929. At the same time, with the growth of war-time collectivism that saw the rise, especially in Britain, of the social democratic left and a Labour government in 1945, there was a growing trend towards welfare state ideas of the Beveridge type. These were important considerations if it was to be accepted that there was going to be a permanent African urban population, with a low standard of living and high claims on limited social wefare provision.

While South African liberals from the Institute and Joint Councils had little chance directly to shape the exact course of government policy (though, as we shall see in chapter five, they were able to launch after 1946 some strong pleas for some governmental reform), the occasional opportunity they had at the local level indicated how far any strongly political liberalism had been emasculated in the 1930s. In the case of Alexandra Township in Johannesburg, for example, there was a Health Committee which was chaired in the early 1940s by Alfred Hoernle. This committee sought to defend the location from the encroachments by white property speculators who were anxious to buy up the area in order to extend the profitable northern suburbs. These interests were organised through the North East District Protection League, and the challenge they presented in the form of 'racial friction' indicated a need for some form of philanthropic segregation in order to ward off 'European encroachment'. Supporting the right of African standholders in the location, the committee argued for isolating the area as far as possible from the surrounding white residential areas and so remove the economic basis behind the white speculators' campaign. This would, the committee argued, 'put an end, at one stoke, to the danger of mounting friction between Alexandra Township and its European neighbours, whilst giving the Township the security and confidence in its future which it needs in order to pursue a constructive policy for improving itself'.[68] The application of Hoernle's group analysis to South African liberalism had dangerous political consequences for, in their actual effect, they could be seen to produce arguments that closely resembled those the Nationalist government itself was to put forward at the time of the 1950 Group Areas Act, instituting group patterns of residential segregation throughout the town and cities of the Union.

6   The debate in the Institute of Race Relations

The stand taken by the Alexandra Health Committee can be seen in part as an attempt to win over some sections of the African petty bourgeois traders and property owners who, in Alexandra, were led by the prominent figure of R. G. Baloyi, treasurer of the African National Congress. However, by 1942–43 it was becoming clear that the democratic challenge to the liberals in the Institute of Race Relations was rising significantly. Between July 1942 and January 1943, the Institute members debated a letter sent by Alfred Xuma, president of the A.N.C., asking for clarification of the Institute's position on the pass laws, the registration and recognition of trade unions and the Union's 'native policy' generally. The request was significant for a number of reasons: Xuma's gaining of the A.N.C. presidency marked a new phase of regeneration in African nationalism during the war years after a long period of weakness and division in the 1930s and, as the next chapter discusses, this was linked with a growing democratic spirit engendered by the war itself. Furthermore, Xuma was under growing pressure from within Congress to resist what was perceived as white liberal control of African politics and pursue a more militant and independent political line.[69] This Africanist radicalism was still ill-organised and did not gain a firm political definition until the growth of the Congress Youth League under the influence of Anton Lembede in the post-war period,[70] though it was already proving a significant force in some parts of the congress organisation like the Cape, and this was compounded by influences from within the left-liberal camp centred around the Ballingers' Friends of Africa movement. By the outbreak of war, some white liberals such as Donald Molteno, one of the Cape African representatives in the Union House of Assembly, sided with William Ballinger's championing of African trade unions, while another supporter, Douglas Buchanan (who had acted as advocate for Tshekedi Khama in Bechuanaland in the early 1930s), sought to try to isolate the control of the Institute from the liberals on the Witwatersrand.[71]

The Xuma letter, therefore, acted as an important catalyst in defining these different liberal positions, which had hitherto been rather diffuse and frequently characterised as much by personal animostiy (for example between William Ballinger and the Institute liberals) as anything else. The central issue boiled down to whether the Institute was to become a more political body, willing to take up certain key issues as the Union 'native policy' itself began to fall into question. With Smuts stating at an Institute meeting in Cape Town in the previous year (1942) that 'segregation has fallen on evil days', there was a feeling of optimism in the air, and some of the more radical liberals became increasingly dissatisfied by the nominally 'apolitical' line the Institute took, which Hoernle had defined as a dispassionate and 'synoptic' view of race relations.[72] In such circumstances, the campaign for politicisation represented a challenge to the version of conservative liberalism that had been carefully fostered since 1929 by Loram, Rheinnalt-Jones and Hoernle, and marked a new strategy which Buchanan hoped would be centred around growing collaboration between the Institute and the Friends of Africa, leading to 'one strong body representing a united front behind a clear and unambiguous policy'.[73]

The Institute hierarchy, however, decided to fight back in the months after the July 1942 letter from Xuma, and mobilised allies amongst both the more conservative sections of the African petty bourgeoisie like D. D. T. Jabavu in the Cape-based All African Convention (who was under growing political attack from Trotskyite opponents), supporters from the municipalities, led by Graham Ballenden of the Johannesburg Council, and the universities like the University of South Africa which had an especial importance since this body could threaten to leave, like the universities of the Orange Free State, Pretoria and Stellenbosch had in the mid-1930s. For leaders like Hoernle, this counter-attack was stimulated by a personal dislike for William Ballinger's political standpoint: 'I feel degraded by being linked with WGB', he confessed in a private memorandum. 'After years of effort on my part I am now convinced that WGB does not understand team work and hasn't the moral basis for it. Nothing will induce me to try again.'[74] This hostility was strengthened, too, by the fact that the Friends of Africa was seen as a very small organisation with little funds, since its English links had effectively dried up at the start of the second world war when the London Group on African Affairs, run by F. S. Livy-Noble, went into liquidation. Thus it was not especially surprising that, at an important meeting of the council of the Institute in January 1943 to determine the response to Xuma and the A.N.C., the official line of dispassionate research was maintained, though it was recognised that 'scientific study and research must be allied with the fullest recognition of the human reactions to changing racial situations' while 'respectful regard must be paid to the traditions and usages of the various national, racial and tribal groups which comprise the population'.[75] The influence of Hoernle's thought here seems especially clear.

The victory marked an important phase in South African liberalism as the war drew to a close. While other societies in the West moved in accord with the democratic spirit of the times, South African liberalism would have to accommodate itself to the very reverse of this. In 1941 Alfred Hoernle wrote an unpublished memorandum, 'Reflections on the Racial Caste Society of the Union', which articulated the liberal ideological dilemma. He took up the caste study of society at precisely the time when scholars in America were beginning to argue that it was on the decline there,[76] and pointed out that in South Africa 'caste unity overrides class unity'. While the government policy of trusteeship might secure for the dominated castes a certain level of 'progress', especially the 'slow, but steady disintregration of tribal bonds and tradition', the important point was that 'no balance of improvement over retrogression does *in fact* touch, or weaken, the caste structure', for if anything it strengthens it.[77] In effect, this was a formulation that presaged in some respects Herbert Adam's thesis on the South African government's capacity to modernise continuously the structures of racial control.[78] In this context, the work of liberals was only to strengthen this overall control, for it was mere 'ambulance work' to 'make the caste society more tolerable for the underlying castes within it'.[79] The point was that there was no generally prevalent and hegemonic liberal ethos to which South African liberals could appeal in their championing of the increasing liberalisation of race relations. Despite the superficial political optimism the war engendered, it was clear to the more perspicacious observers like Hoernle that South African political change represented a parting of the ways with the societies of the West, rather than a process of growing closer towards them. This political hiatus did not become generally obvious until the 1948 election and the defeat of Smuts United Party government. For those liberals most closely aware of the narrow parameters of political change, however, it was beginning to emerge that what was left of the western liberal tradition was starting to be squeezed by a populist white ethnic nationalism on the one hand, and a democratic African nationalism on the other. Things were beginning to fall apart as the 'Heartbreak House' of South African liberalism was being rocked to its foundations.

FOUR

The growing democratic challenge

1 The radicalisation of the A.N.C.

The internal *malaise* of South African liberalism which, by the early 1940s, had surfaced in the form of growing ideological divisions within the Institute and the deep despondency of Hoernle, was compounded over the following years by a renewal of democratic optimism ushered in by the second world war. Hitherto, as we have seen, periodic upsurges of African political consciousness had been followed by periods of stabilisation when liberal political influence could be reasserted. The post-war strike wave of 1918–20, for instance, had helped to shape liberal politcal initiatives via the Joint Councils, *Umteteli wa Bantu* and the Bantu Men's Social Centre. In the early 1930s, too, *The Bantu World* had been partly established to neutralise the Africanist *Abantu Batho*, while the creation of Natives Representatives under the 1936 Representation of Natives Act strengthened local anti-I.C.U. alliance in areas like Natal through the election there of Edgar Brookes as African senator. So, at least until the late 1930s, the liberal position was never directly challenged by a democratic movement with any significantly popular following. Continued financial weakness and factional disputes in African politics ensured that there was no serious threat to the essentially paternalistic role the liberals continued to play with respect to black political movements.

By the onset of war in 1939, however, things began to change. As the extension of African trade unionism under the Federation of Non European Trade Unions indicated a potentially radical base for African political organisation, a new generation of African political leaders began to come to the fore by the 1940s who were also far less likely to accept as automatic the clientelism on which the white liberals had continued to rest their political appeal to Africans. Even before the emergence in 1943 of the Africanist-inclined Congress Youth League inside the A.N.C., under the leadership of Anton Lembede, Nelson Mandela, Oliver Tambo and others, this resistance to white liberal control became increasingly apparent. At the time of another 'African deputation' to the Minister of Native Affairs, H. A. Fagan, in 1939, which was led by Rheinnalt-Jones,[1] Alfred Xuma complained of the seeming inability of Africans to generate their own distinct political ideas:

Many of us have no views of our own; but are making expressions and acting according to instructions from our patrons. There seems to be more co-operation with and more faith in certain people on the part of the African leaders, than with their own compatriots. Because of this situation many policies which are against the interest of our people have been implemented with co-operation and blessings of some of us.[2]

Xuma's opposition was prompted in part by his growing doubts about the attempts by the Institute of Race Relations to act as a mediator in such things as African student visits overseas. As Rheinnalt-Jones sought to tie in Institute activities in the late 1930s to government trusteeship policy under the 1936 Native Trust and Land Act, so there had been moves to extend controls over the activities of African students who went to study in London. As a self-taught student in the United States, Xuma was in a strong position to attack the suggestion of Rheinnalt-Jones in an Institute memorandum that Africans from South Africa would not be 'at ease' in the company of West Africans at Aggrey House in London and would be better off in hostel accommodation at the Student Movement Club where there were fewer African students. Xuma opposed the idea of establishing a specific committee to deal with 'the welfare of non-Europeans from Southern Africa' on the grounds that it 'may tend to run the segregated South African hostel like a reformatory or detention home from which men come out educationally and culturally no better than they were when they left South Africa'. Xuma also saw it as helping to extend the South African government's own ideas on racial segregation in African higher education into an overseas context.[3]

Xuma's complaints led to the Institute, under Hoernle's moderating influence, toning down many of Rheinnalt-Jones' proposals.[4] The issue, though, pinpointed many of the African objections to perceived white liberal political and cultural control over their political movements and thinking. One of the main reasons why many African students went abroad for further education was precisely to escape the tight segregation in higher education in South Africa and the failure of attempts to broaden the basis of courses at Fort Hare. As a member of the All African Convention in the 1930s, Xuma maintained contact with one of his black American acquaintances, Max Yergan, who had acted as 'Secretary for External Relations' for the A.A.C. in New York. Yergan at this time was strongly in favour of establishing independent black educational and research efforts, and was a guiding influence behind A.A.C. efforts to establish at Fort Hare an institute for the training of African social workers in order to escape the white monopolisation of the profession through such liberal-controlled institutions as the Jan Hofmeyr School of Social Work in the Johannesburg Bantu Men's Social Centre. The attempt was not successful due to the government's opposition to the proposals, and after 1937 Yergan's interests in New York became diverted into the International Committee on African Affairs, of which he became director in that year.[5] However, the legacy of Yergan's influence in favour of independent African efforts in the educational sphere helped to shape Xuma's thinking.[6] When he became president of the bankrupt A.N.C. in 1940, he began to emphasise as far as possible the need for independent black political action that was free from white liberal control. This increasingly led him to challenge the political role carried out by both the Institute of Race Relations and Natives Representatives like Rheinnalt-Jones.[7]

One of the basic problems Xuma faced, however, together with the tiny educated leadership at the head of the A.N.C., was the inadequacy of research sources and organisational funds to finance a campaign that could resist the permeating empiricist and neutralising influences stemming from the Institute. For a brief period under the secretaryship of Lynn Saffery the Institute began to move from its role of presentor of factual information, due to the alliance forged with Max Gordon and the Federation of Non European Trade Unions.[8] By 1942 this phase had ended with Gordon's internment, and Saffery and the radicals in the Institute became progressively isolated. Institute policy, furthermore, was reaffirmed in a direction that accommodated itself to government trusteeship policy. Thus a tension began to set in as African unions continued to develop in the early 1940s under the organising influence of leaders like J. B. Marks and Gaur Radebe, the 'Secretary for Mines' in the Transvaal African Congress. The founding of the African Mine Workers Union in 1941 acted as a fillip to hopes for the extension of African unionism, for it was seen as a key means to 'create', in Gaur Radebe's words, 'an organised body capable of taking its proper place in the advance of the African people out of their present state of national oppression'.[9] The establishment in November of the same year of the Council for Non European Trade Unions (C.N.E.T.U.) acted as a further organisational base on which to build African political and industrial movements free from white liberal control. Inside the Institute, this development was only understood by a small number of white liberals, such as Julius Lewin and the renegade Communist Solly Sachs, who argued for a new approach that could avoid direct white control over African unions and, instead, entrench a semi-skilled African labour aristocracy.[10] By the end of 1941, it was clear the relations between the A.N.C. leadership and the Institute were further deteriorating as Xuma came under pressure to make the advancement of trade unions and increases in African wages one of the central planks of the A.N.C. platform; '... the Africans are getting more and more apprehensive of what they consider to be compromising their rights piece meal', he wrote to Alfred Hoernle in August 1941. While still acknowledging that 'we [Africans and white liberals] are all working for one common goal', he nevertheless considered that the Africans' personal views and attitude must be more and more essential in any scheme towards that goal'.[11]

In 1942 even this relatively conciliatory approach by Xuma to the Institute liberals became strained as the development of the A.N.C. antipass campaign led Xuma to seek clarification of the Institute's attitude toward the government's segregation policy.[12] Before the resolution of this at the Institute's council

meeting of January 1943, the additional dimension of the senatorial election in the Transvaal injected a further element of
radicalism into the policy of the A.N.C.'s leadership. By the
time Hoernle asked Xuma and the A.N.C. treasurer, R. G.
Baloyi (a prominent Alexandra businessman), to nominate
Rheinnalt-Jones in opposition to the ex-Communist Hymie
Basner, it was clear that Basner was increasingly likely to win
the election. The most that could now be looked for from
white liberals, wrote Xuma, was the less organised voluntary
support of radical white sympathisers of Congress:

... no individual European elected to the Senate is going to save the
African people from disaster. They may help but one need not go to
Parliament to serve the cause of better race relations. There are many
Europeans — unsung heroes — who are doing their bit quietly. The
salvation of the African people from disaster is the African himself
through his organisations which finally imply his proper representation.[13]

Basner's victory in the election, following the swing of several prominent chiefs in the Transvaal away from Jones,[14] acted
as a critical turning point politically. From now on, the ideological homogeneity of white liberal representation in Parliament was broken, combined with the fact there there was an
alternative radical political spokesman to whom the congress
leadership could appeal to for support. Indeed, it was precisely
this 'breakup of the present team of representatives of the
African in Parliament' which Hoernle had feared when he
sought Xuma's nomination for Rheinnalt-Jones.[15] Ever since
the first election of the Native Representatives in 1937, the
group, consisting of Senators Brookes, Rheinnalt-Jones, Malcommess and Welsh, and M.P.s Mrs. Ballinger, and Messrs.
Hemming and Burman, had agreed to act as a distinct caucus
free of links to any of the party groupings in the South African
Parliament.[16] The election of Basner for the Transvaal in 1942
directly challenged this view of Natives Representation, gover-
ned as it was by the distinctly conservative liberalism of such
leading liberals as Rheinnalt-Jones and Brookes. The basis of
Basner's election campaign had been a strong attack on both
the ostensible political neutrality of the Institute of Race Relations and the *toenadering* (coming together) of Rheinnalt-Jones
with government segregation policy. The reason, Basner's elec-

tion manifesto argued, for the 'low level of political and econo-mic thought in South Africa' was due to 'European racialist politicians' and this could only be rectified by 'energetic prop-aganda and political courage'. Of the Native Representatives, only Margaret Ballinger and Donald Molteno in the Cape had 'brought the economic facts home to Parliament and to the people of South Africa', while Rheinnalt-Jones as a 'social worker' from the Institute had essentially masked over the differing interests of 'firms and municipalities and the Native people'. Thus, appealing to the growing African trade union movement, Basner rested his election campaign on a basically anti-fascist and democratic platform:

The defeat of fascism is even more important to you than to the European section, because fascism aims at a greater and crueller exploitation of the workers and peasants of other races. Fascism's main characteristic is race oppression. If the government is in earnest about this war it must arm the African soldiers. If the Government is in earnest about this war it must give the Africans some democratic rights to fight for.[17]

   This challenge to the traditional Institute hegemony in the co-optive structures created in 1936 had a significant impact on the movement of African political consciousness in the coming years. It contributed to a growing democratic liberal-ism amongst both younger Africans and white liberals influ-enced by the wartime alliance against the Axis. By the end of 1942 Xuma was driven to admitting that on the role of the Institute there was 'no halfway house' between political invol-vement or a 'research and information bureau'; if it was not prepared to come out in favour of the former, then it would be better 'to give up the attempt to deal with everyday problems and to leave the responsibility for dealing with daily issues of race contacts and conflicts to such united bodies as the Friends of Africa and the Cape Central Committee on Race Contacts which have defined their objectives'.[18] The Institute, he charged, had been taken in a considerably different direction by Rheinnalt-Jones than what had been originally intended by such liberals as his former friend, Howard Pim, and he turned down the offer of being elected onto the Institute's council.[19]
   However, it was also clear that the rising nationalism inside Congress prevented too firm an alliance with the smaller and

less well-organised democratic liberals centred around Ballinger's Friends of Africa and Basner. Xuma himself confessed to knowing less personally about these groups than the Institute,[20] and though some selective assistance was made use of by the Congress, such as a memorandum on African wages prepared by William Ballinger (which was used to buttress the congress's evidence to the Native Mines Commission in July of 1943),[21] the emergence of the Congress Youth League in the course of that year began a movement towards avoiding close contact with any white liberals or democrats of whatever political hue. The C.Y.L. began as a movement amongst the African intelligentsia, many of whom had been educated at Fort Hare of Adams College in Natal, and had direct acquaintance with the control over higher education for Africans by such liberals as Alexander Kerr and Edgar Brookes. Unlike the groping nationalism of Xuma, Calata and the congress leadership, the league began by injecting a strongly racial conception of African nationalism that initially was hostile to the class analysis of the Communist Party and the democratic left. By appealing back to a distinctly African cultural tradition that stood antiposed to the 'white western civilisation' that was seen to be oppressing the African nation in South Africa, the C.Y.L. was able to invoke a sense of African ideological identity. This was lacking in much of Xuma's American-influenced pluralism that assumed that the A.N.C. could mobilise South African blacks in a manner similar to the political machinery of the National Association for the Advancement of Coloured People. It was thus not surprising that, in the years after 1943-44, the C.Y.L. began to spread slowly outwards from Johannesburg to small areas in Natal, the Orange Free State and the Eastern Cape where there were small groups of African teachers, medical students and professional men.[22] Foremost amongst the league's early ideologists before his premature death in 1947 was the U.N.I.S.A. philosophy graduate Anton Lembede, and it was he who injected the strong Africanist strain into a league programme that directly challenged the entire conception of Trusteeship and liberal political activities as they had been conducted since the early 1930s.[23] Trusteeship, the C.Y.L. Manifesto of 1944 proclaimed:

... has meant, as it still seems, the consolidation by the Whiteman of his position at the expense of the African people, so that by the time of the national awakening opens the eyes of the African people to the bluff they live under, While domination should be secure and unassailable.[24]

Rejecting, therefore, the entire apparatus of trusteeship established under the 1936 legislation, the league emphasised the necessity of directly challenging the psychological underpinnings of an ideology that it saw as contributing to the apparatus of state control over the African population:

While Trustees have been very vocal in their solicitations for the Afr ican their deeds have shown clearly that talk of Trusteeship is an eyewash for the Civilised world and an empty platitude to soothe Africans into believing that after all oppression is a pleasant experience under Christian democratic rule. Trusteeship mentality is doing one thing and that very successfully, to drive the African steadily to extermination. Low wages, bad housing, inadequate health facilities, "Native education", mass exploitation, unfixed security on land and halfhearted measures to improve the African's living conditions are all instruments and tools with which the path to African extermination is being paved.[25]

There was nevertheless some ambiguity in the Youth League's position, despite their fervent rejection of any collaboration with white liberals in the development of African nationalism. Many of the discussions that led to the original 1944 Manifesto, for example, still took place in the Johannesburg Bantu Men's Social Centre,[26] and it was clear that, despite Lembede's appeal back to the values of 'traditional' African society with its alleged 'democratic' and 'socialistic' features, the Youth League was very much dependent upon the existing organisation of the African National Congress.[27] In terms of actual numbers, the C.Y.L. failed to extend beyond a narrow circle of the educated African intelligentsia, and by the end of 1947 only had 278 members based in some four branches.[28] On the other hand, the addition of a strain of Africanist philosophy in congress added to a sense of intellectual reassertion amongst the African political élite which had hitherto been lacking. Congress meetings in the early 1940s were poorly organised and ill-attended,[29] while the cultural domination from white liberalism had a marked effect on African self-confidence. As late as 1943, *llanga lase Natal* wrote that African intellectuals still gave the impression of being 'intimidated' for:

They speak as though afraid of the echo of their own words. Indeed, in many instances when our men of ability and intellect were exchanging views with Europeans of liberal minds, it was left to the European to express themselves with moving sincerity of some of the problems confronting our people. If utter condemnation of conditions that perpetuate the suffering of the non European was called for the European did the talking while the intellectuals glossed over these things and kept on thinking of half loaves of bread all the time.[30]

It was this psychological and cultural dependence upon white liberals — a phenomenon once termed the 'Prospero complex' by the French anthropologist Mannoni in a study of French colonialism in Madagascar[31] — that was to a degree broken by the Youth League in the years after 1944 as an increasing radicalisation began to occur within the congress leadership. The initial period of political optimism in the early years of the war that was summed up by General Smuts' statement to the Institute of Race Relations in Cape Town in 1942 that 'segregation has fallen on evil days', began to fade by the end of 1943. It began to become clear by then that the pass laws were not going to be completely removed by the wartime government, African trade unions were not going to receive immediate recognition, while African strikes were made illegal in 1942 under War Measure 145. The Atlantic Charter, signed in 1941 by President Roosevelt of the United States and Winston Churchill, prime minister of Great Britain, formed the basis for the A.N.C. document *African Claims* that was adopted in December 1943. Rejecting completely the policy of segregation on the grounds that it was 'designed to keep the African in a state of perpetual tutelage and militates against his normal development',[32] *African Claims* indicated the growing democratisation of African political consciousness in the 1940s under the impact of ideas such as Roosevelt's 'Four Freedoms'. While restating traditional political objectives such as the extenson of the franchise, equal justice before the law, freedom of the press and the right to own and sell property, *African Claims* also sought a welfare state programme that would lead to the state provision of education for African children, free public health and medical services, industrial welfare legislation, and unemployment, sickness and old age benefits.[33]

These social democratic objectives continued to characterise the A.N.C.'s political strategy as well, at least until the 1946 African mine strike and the collapse of the Natives Representative Council. Having moved as far as possible outside the paternalistic sphere of the white liberals in the early 1940s, Xuma hoped to model the A.N.C. on lines close to that of the British Labour Party, with a new power base lying in areas like African trade unions. The initial involvement, for example, by African trade unions in the anti-pass campaign had given grounds for optimism for, at an anti-pass conference called by the Communist Party in November 1943, the largest delegation was some 43 delegates representing 26 unions, totalling in all 40,160 members.[34] Xuma, however, as president of the A.N.C., sought to guide the African unions into specifically non-political channels, so that they could focus upon industrial and economic issues while the congress itself, like the Labour Party, could deal with political questions. 'Trade unions are not political organisations', he said at a conference of non-white trade unions in August 1945, 'and to act as such is to prejudice their own functions as instruments for collective bargaining of their members.'[35]

This implied political role for the A.N.C. as the mobiliser of Africans in unions as part of a single national movement, came seriously unstuck when it came to the question of organisation and propaganda. Once again it raised the issue of how Congress was to reach its own members without a newspaper under its own control. The Youth League had an advantage here since after 1945 it had its own organ *Inkundla ya Bantu* in Natal, and its editor, Jordan Ngubane, sought to persuade Xuma to launch a campaign of propaganda through the white press in South Africa and also through overseas newspapers.[36] But though Xuma had been favourable to the idea of an independent African paper in the 1930s, when African papers had been taken over by white-controlled syndicates,[37] he was unwilling to press ahead with a scheme for an independent paper run by Congress itself. 'My fear is', he wrote, evincing his élitist political inclinations, 'that if such a paper is owned by Congress, it will suffer from mass control. It will be everybody's business and nobody's business. Incompetent people by mass vote will be placed in offices and positions that will do the cause no credit. The last Abantu Batho suffered and died from that.'[38] It was political caution like this which stultified congress's organisational efforts and progressively aliented Xuma from the Youth League and the congress radicals.

The relative failure of congress to stimulate mass involvement in a political campaign shaped by overseas social democratic models, led to a counter-movement by the Youth League, together with a small number Communist allies, to seek an early and precipitate mobilisation by boycotting all the existing institutions of segregated political representation. If congress was unable to raise the level of political awareness, then a campaign of boycott might itself lead to the crystallisation of attitudes around the institutions which kept Africans in a state of subjection. This reasoning began to prevail as the movement entered the critical year of 1946. Overseas, in India there was the final phase of decolonisation (it became independent the following year), while in New York attacks began on the South African policy of segregation, together with the administration of South West Africa, in the newly founded United Nations.[39] With the strike by African miners and the adjournment of the N.R.C. shortly afterwards, the issues became crystallised. Even the leading moderates like Z. K. Matthews and Paul Mosaka were now resigned to the fact that the 'toy telephone' of Natives Representation had completely failed to meet their hopes of a political platform through which they could influence and modify government policy: '... the Council has developed into a meeting with senior officials of the Native Affairs Department', Matthews declared, 'who not unnaturally are beginning to regard the Council as part of the set-up of their Department and the members as Government servants like themselves.'[40] In such a situation, the initiative passed to the radicals inside congress, and the Youth League organ *Inkundla* urged a 'ruthless struggle on a national scale' as a means to transform government policy.[41] In October 1946 the A.N.C. met in conference at Bloemfontein and resolved on a policy of boycott.[42]

2   The boycott issue

As these moves towards boycotting Natives Representation began in the last quarter of 1946, many of the previous pressures both at the local level and within the national leadership against alleged liberal control of African politics came to a head. In an important sense, the use of the boycott weapon came as a direct response to the defeat, through extensive state power, of the African mine strike,[43] and indicated that the strategy had passed to institutions and movements other than those of trade unions. Political struggle could now no longer be centred around the withdrawal of African labour power, which had failed to involve Africans on a wider scale outside the mines beyond simple condemnation of government methods in suppressing the strike. The alternative was to focus upon the boycott of such bodies as the Natives Representatives Council and the Advisory Boards established under the 1923 Urban Areas Act as a means (so the congress radicals hoped) of raising the wider national consciousness that was essential for a nation-wide political campaign. The Youth League therefore pressed hard for the boycott in the period after September 1946, since many of the C.Y.L. members, such as Oliver Tambo and Godfrey Pitje, had first been involved in political activity as students at Fort Hare in the early 1940s when the boycott weapon had first been used to improve the quality of food provided in the canteen.[44] As the Youth League leader A. P. Mda argued in July 1947:

If the militants within Congress join hands with the present N.R.C. members... the urban location boards, the rural election committees and progressive organisations throughout the length and breadth of the country, it should be possible to paralyze the whole segregationist machinery in South Africa, and to usher in a new period of struggle for direct representation in Parliament.[45]

In this sense, the boycott was a nationalist weapon that was being used to try to strengthen African sympathies behind its traditional vehicle of expression, the A.N.C. As such, it was still a meliorist and reformist means of effecting political change, for it was based, as *Imvo* came to argue, on the idea that '... Africans will have to educate the ruling class about their wants and activities and needs before they can be allowed much latitude of improvement'.[46] But, as with independent church separatism in the 1890s, and later with Garveyism and independent trade union activity centred around the I.C.U., the whole strategy behind the boycott campaign was to wage an independent African initiative free from white liberal control. Boycotts directly attacked the very legitimacy of the white Natives Representatives to speak on behalf of Africans, whilst it even bypassed the question of inter-racial class solidarity through the expansion of trade unions. It put into question not only the more conservative liberalism of the Institute of Race Relations and the Natives Representatives and showed it up as an outmoded form of paternalism, but also the more radical liberalism that had been espoused by the Friends of Africa, Hymie Basner and Solly Sachs.

The Boycott weapon, therefore, challenged not only the patron-client structures which had been traditionally dominated by the mainstream liberals, but even the white radicals, who had hoped for a fostering of trade union organisation as the basis behind a broad-based democratic movement that would entrench an African urban working class, as well as mobilise savings in order to generate an African business and trading petty bourgeoisie. The problem was that this group of left-inclined liberal progressives was both tiny and ill-organised, despite the growth in democratic sympathies amongst some sections of the white population during the war as a result of such organisations as the Springbok Legion. Before the emergence of the boycott issue in 1946, the only really significant achievement of this group of democrats had been the election of Basner in 1942, which had, if anything, split the white liberal camp. For the most part the ideas of the progressive liberals remained very much paper ones, though their importance was to point out the limitations of the existing strategy of the mainstream liberals and to indicate the way towards a realignment of forces into a social democratic alliance. Leo Marquard's book *The Black Man's Burden* (written under the pseudonym of John Burger) was a landmark in this respect, coming as it did from a former founder of the liberal student union, N.U.S.A.S., and a member of the Institute of Race Relations who had conducted a survey of farm labour in the Orange Free State.[47] As a member of the Army Education Corps, Marquard was affected by the rising democratic tide during the war, and the second edition of his book in 1943 applied a critical Marxist methodology to South African political economy in a penetrating insight into the limits of liberalism. The advent of the United Party in 1934, through the merger of Hertzog and Smuts, had weakened liberalism's influence, argued Marquard, and the further advent of Afrikaner nationalism left liberalism 'fighting a gallant rear-guard action... all it can do is to try to prevent the forces of reaction from having it all their own way. It is, indeed, apparent that the limits of reformism have been reached, and that any further improvement in the living conditions of the non-European proletariat will have to be achieved along the lines of industrial action rather than by liberal influence in politics.'[48]

This argument for militant industrial struggle contrasted with much of the optimism engendered in many liberal circles through wartime industrialisation and the belief that marginal changes in government policy, to allow for a larger urban African work-force, would in time lead to more substantial political change in a liberal direction.[49] However, Marquard's words were only shared by a small number of fellow liberals who pressed for moves on the industrial and trade union front in order to establish a democratic power base amongst organised African labour power. As Solly Sachs wrote angrily in June 1947:

It is high time that the liberals in South Africa descended from their lofty pedestal of abstract theory and illusions and came down to earth and faced the problem in a realistic and concrete manner. Liberalism in America and in other countries, even in England a hundred years ago, made progress only by a correct examination of the workers' needs and aspirations and by the closest co-operation with the workers' mass organisation. Liberalism in South Africa is doomed unless and until it learns to understand the workers' problems and finds a concrete base of co-operation with the masses of workers, Europeans and Non-European.[50]

But how would such a reformulation of liberalism be made and who was to make it? Undoubtedly, the wartime experience and radicalisation inside the A.N.C. influenced some of the African liberals into rethinking some of the tenets of liberalism, though it was unclear how far they were prepared to move in a leftwards direction. Jordan Ngubane, pointed out in the left-wing journal *The Democrat* that the 'fascist attack' from the Afrikaner nationalists might not immediately threaten the position of the liberals in the same way as it did the 'leftist progessive', but any 'collapse' of the latter 'would immediately

expose the Liberals to serious fascist onslaughts'. This necessitated a democratic realignment, despite the problem that the
liberals 'are not organised into a systematic political grouping
standing for clearly defined principles'.[51] This raised, however,
the question of how far the white liberals would be prepared to
move outside the constrictions of white party politics in order
both to extend their power base and to advance their cause
amongst the large mass of non-voting Africans. In this respect,
the 1946 African mine strike and the adjournment of the
N.R.C. acted as a hiatus in many liberals' hopes as it did to the
alignment of forces inside the A.N.C. The growing movement
of African nationalism and the pressure for a boycott forced
many left-wing white liberals back into the white party political camp as they became increasingly isolated from the African
nationalists. Writing to Hofmeyr on 25 September 1946, for
example, Leo Marquard indicated the growing mood of many
white liberals to look to Hofmeyr as a possible leader inside the
United Party for the attainment of liberal ideals. Reacting to a
series of police raids on the offices of the Communist Party,
trade unions, the Springbok Legion and private homes, Marquard wrote that 'African-European relations have deteriorated
and that we are rapidly forfeiting what African goodwill we
still possessed'. As one 'in contact with a considerable left-
liberal opinion', he stated that there were considerable feelings
of bewilderment at the government's 'shift away from liberalism and an appeasing of reaction'. The only hope was for a
party led by Hofmeyr which, though it could not necessarily
control the government, could still have sufficient votes 'to
enable it to hold the balance of power in such a way that no
government would be able to pass reactionary legislation'.
Such a party, based on the abolition of the industrial colour bar
and 'some form of universal franchise', would be able to attract
'to the fight for liberalism a very large number of Left Liberals,
it would have your own personal following, and it would attract a proportion of industrialists and men of the Van Eck and
Van Biljoen type. The effect on local and national politics
would, I am convinced, be far greater than most people would
anticipate. But it must be done soon if we are to avoid
disaster.'[52]

3   *The eclipse of the left liberals*

This political strategy outlined by Marquard in 1946 came increasingly to characterise liberal thinking in the run-up to the 1948 election, as it was more and more obvious that the African nationalist mobilisation around the boycott issue was going to exclude the white liberals. While Marquard, as a teacher and publisher, was not in the front line of white liberal dealings with the A.N.C.,it began to become clear that even those radicals who had been actively involved in African politics were finding their political power base ever narrowing. Hymie Basner, for instance, had been the focus for democratic hopes after his election defeat of Rheinnalt-Jones in 1942; but by 1947 he, too, was forced increasingly on to the defensive as he sought to rally African support around the idea of a national convention to rewrite the South African constitution.[53] In part, this weakness had been brought on as Basner sought to organise his own political bandwagon in opposition to that of the A.N.C. via the African Democratic Party. The campaign for constitutional reform led to the establishment by the A.D.P. of a campaign organised by Basner and his African supporter on the N.R.C., Paul Mosaka, for a £60,000 fighting fund to send propaganda overseas to Britain and America. Such activities directly offset the organisational work of the A.N.C., and Xuma accused Basner of seeking to 'fight' the A.N.C. if his plans were not accomplished.[54] But undoubtedly, for Basner, this was the only avenue left in an increasingly polarised situation where Natives Representation was under growing challenge from the boycott. As he argued at a meeting of the Cape Town Joint Council, the task of the Natives Representatives was to 'correlate the activities of all those who are exploited and unenfranchised in their efforts to achieve the general franchise and to abolish general exploitation'. Such a task involved appealing on a class basis to poor whites as well as Africans for Natives Representatives:

... [We] must educate European public opinion to the realisation that the exploitation of the poor-whites and the underpaid white workers is closely related to the absence of democratic rights, the landlessness and the economic exploitation of the Native people. They must also educate the Native people to realise the necessity of industrial organisation, peasant leagues and political parties to become pressure groups on the Government for change of the present laws and policies...

Otherwise Natives Representation is completely useless, and by confining itself purely to parliamentary advocacy can by very harmful. It can be harmful by lulling the Africans into a false sense of security that their interests are being protected and furthered in Parliament and that there is no need to bestir themselves for their own freedom and well being.

This activist view of the function of Natives Representation certainly marked a significant departure from the more limited Whig view of political representation that continued to dominate the thinking of the other Natives Representatives, such as Edgar Brookes, Margaret Ballinger and Donald Molteno, who sought as far as possible to dissociate themselves from Basner's activities.[56] On the other hand, in organising the rival A.D.P., Basner alienated certain key elements in the African intelligentsia and cut himself off from both the A.N.C. and its rival in the Cape, the All African Convention. Basner probably felt that it was essential to establish his own power base, especially as until the emergence of the boycott issue the Congress leadership had made almost no attempts to organise any mass following by appealing to the broad base of peasants and migrants. In the early 1940s, following his resignation from the Communist Party, Basner had picked up a selective following in some rural areas as he offered his legal advice to groups hard pressed by the implementation of the government's reserve reclamation programme. In the Northern Transvaal, contacts had been founded with the Zoutpansberg Cultural Association, organised by the indefatigable Alpheus Maliba,[57] while as squatter camps grew up around Johannesburg during the war years the A.D.P. established a following amongst the Sofasonke Party of James Mpanza and the Moroka Vigilance Association. Pressure from such groups was placed on the A.N.C. leadership to co-operate with Basner and the A.D.P. for, as a representative of the Moroka Vigilance Association wrote to Xuma, Basner was 'indispensable as far as the African people are concerned and he cannot be replaced'.[58]

The activities of such a body as the A.D.P. were seen, however, to rival that of Congress (despite the latter's organisational lethargy) and, moreover, to challenge the sanctity of African nationalism. One of the main objectives behind the original Youth League Manifesto of 1944 had been, according to A. P. Mda, to establish an ideological alternative to the

A.D.P.,[59] and as C.Y.L. pressure grew on the Congress leadership around Xuma, the chances for co-operation became increasingly slender. The A.N.C. working committee rejected a
proposal from Basner early in 1947 for a New Party based on
the supporters of the A.N.C. and A.D.P. on the grounds that it
would confound the 'present confusion' over the boycott issue
and, in effect, strengthen the hand of the liberals inside the
A.N.C., led by figures like Selby Msimang and A. W. G. Champion, who had modified the original congress boycott resolution of September 1946 with a proposal to launch a boycott
only when a £10,000 fighting fund had first been raised.[60] This
tendency became strengthened by the realisation in the Congress leadership that the hoped-for reform of Natives Representation, which we shall discuss in detail in the next chapter,
was not going to move much beyond the segregationist foundations of the 1936 legislation, while the proposed Industrial
Tribunals Bill to recognise selectively African trade unions
would, in fact, lead to a strengthening of state control over
them.[61] In such circumstances, the opposition of the A.D.P.
and its front organisations like the South African Democratic
Socialist Party (established by one of the A.D.P. organisers in
Johannesburg, Self Mampuru)[62] to the policy of boycott was
seen as increasingly coinciding with the more 'collaboration-
ist' followers inside congress, who both opposed the continuation of the boycott and supported the candidature of Douglas
Buchanan in the by-election in the Transkei in 1947. This also
encouraged *The Bantu World*, edited by Victor Selope Thema,
to become increasingly hostile to the congress policy in 1947
and 1948, leading it eventually to act as the vehicle for a
splinter group, organised inside Congress by Selope Thema,
called the National Minded Bloc.[63] It was, though, this paper
which began to give extensive coverage to the anti-boycott
speeches of Self Mampuru and Paul Mosaka in opposition to
the official policy of the A.N.C. and the C.Y.L.[64]

These political limitations on Basner's campaign to mobilise
African political support behind a radical liberal campaign
organised through the A.D.P., exemplified the problems of the
more democratic liberals in the late 1940s. Hemmed in by the
growing nationalism of the A.N.C., cut off by rivalries with his
former Communist colleagues and restricted in his appeal to

African support by only a selective regional following, Basner's position by 1948 was virtually untenable, and it was significant that he abandoned the campaign for re-election as senator for the Transvaal and Orange Free State to the more ineffectual William Ballinger. The success of the A.D.P. was confined only to its two main African organisers, Self Mampuru and Paul Mosaka, who were both elected to the N.R.C. that year, Paul Mosaka beating his Communist rival, Edwin Mofutsanyana, by some 52,524 votes to 12,812. The very fact that only three new members were elected to the council that year (including Mampuru) indicated the strength of the boycott campaign and that there were increasingly limited avenues in which the A.D.P. could develop. Furthermore, by virtue of the fact that Basner's appeal relied upon the channels of Native Representation, there was a tradition of legalism that pervaded his political appeal. In this sense, the A.D.P. was unable to develop such an opportunistic political platform as the Communist Party, which selectively advocated both boycotting and participating in elections to Advisory Boards, the N.R.C. and Natives Representation in Parliament.

While the A.D.P.'s strategy was based upon a long-term realignment in liberal forces within the structures of political representation in South Africa, the C.P.S.A. in some respects tried to exploit the prevailing local sympathies to representative structures by either engaging in elections or championing a boycott. In Johannesburg the local party committee advised a boycott of Advisory Board elections in support of the Pimville Sub Tenants Association[65]; in Orlando, Communist candidates were put up, unsuccessfully, against the Sofasonke Party of Mpanza[66]; and in Pretoria five candidates stood for ten seats in the Advisory Board elections.[67] Similarly in the Cape, C.P. candidates stood for Advisory Board elections where local figures like Johnson Ngwevela and W. Ndunyana continued to stand on the Advisory Board long after the party was banned in 1950, while in 1948 Sam Kahn defeated Douglas Buchanan in the election for Natives Representative for the Western Cape.[68] While Edwin Mofutsanyana defended this expediency on the grounds that 'a total boycott can only be achieved when sufficient organisational work has been achieved in this country',[69] clearly the C.P. did score against the A.D.P. in its ability to appease the radical support for the boycott, whilst at the same time using the election to the representative institutions to attack the 'collaborationism' of the more conservative liberals. In the Western Cape elections, for instance, Sam Kahn's supporters were able to muster extensive support in a 53 per cent poll when the slogan 'Votela Ngoluhlobo' was used to appeal against the somewhat ineffective campaign of Douglas Buchanan. Wining 3,780 votes against Buchanan's 754, Kahn declared that 'a vote for a communist is a vote for freedom. That is what the Africans think today.'[70]

In such circumstances, by 1948 Basner moved towards a more mainstream liberal position by coming out in favour of a liberal party led by Hofmeyr. Only such a party, he declared in the wake of the Nationalist election victory over the U.P., 'based on the needs of the industrialists of South Africa has a chance of finally defeating the feudal agrarian ideology and policy of the Nationalist Party'.[71] The statement was indicative of the state of the liberal position as a whole in the South African body politic, as independent political action to establish a power base amongst black political organisations, had so clearly failed. Though various further attempts were to be made by isolated liberal groups and individuals through the 1950s and early 1960s to repeat Basner's enterprise and seek some form of African following — most notably Patrick Duncan and the white student group in the somewhat inappropriately named African Resistance Movement[72] — it was clear by the time of the 1948 election that most liberal political initiative would be based upon party political action through the narrowly based white electoral franchise. The attempt at democratising liberalism in a social democratic direction had for the most part been unsuccessful, despite the period of wartime optimism, while in the period after the Nationalist election victory of 1948, a number of key liberals who had been hitherto involved in the governmental process itself via Natives Representation became released to become actively involved in leading political action in the direction of a political party. It was in circumstances such as these that the democratic challenge from left liberalism was met in the 1940s. As a consequence, the more conservative liberalism of the Institute of Race Relations became reconsolidated after 1948 on a stand-

point that continued to assert the primacy of the white electoral franchise.

FIVE

The failure of reform

1   *The erosion of 'trusteeship'*

The progressive isolation of the left liberals in the post-war period in South Africa was a reflection of growing political polarisation on both the internal and external political plane. Internally, as we have seen, the democratic liberalism of Basner became isolated as it was caught between a growing nationalism inside the African National Congress, favourable to the boycotting of Natives Representation, and the more conservative liberalism of the other Natives Representatives sheltering behind the Institute of Race Relations. Externally, it became caught up in the growing cold war political climate engendered by the Iron Curtain spreading down through Europe and struggles between East and West for political influence inside the United Nations. These latter influences began to play an increasing role in defining political ideologies in South African politics as the move towards national independence in both Asia and Africa began to shape increasingly the complexion of Union policy in international affairs.

In essence, the inter-war climate of 'trusteeship', underpinned by the League of Nations and the operation of mandates in such areas as Tanganyika and South West Africa, was now dead. National independence in countries like India in 1947 meant that it no longer became internationally acceptable for one country to be holding another country in 'trust', and this applied as much to South Africa's holding of South West Africa as anywhere else. Even if the western powers covertly sought continued South African control over a region that was beginning to emerge as a vital source of minerals, it was no longer possible to justify this internationally in terms of the old mandate concept. The growing attacks on South Africa in this respect, from both emergent states like India and from the South African A.N.C., left the country isolated politically and unable any longer to appeal to the old colonial allegiances of the pre-war years.[1] 'What has been evolving at Dumbarton Oaks, San Francisco and here in London,' wrote the Union High Commissioner in London, Heaton Nicholls, 'has been a new world system, which is very imperfectly understood in South Africa':

We have surrendered our old sovereignty. No longer will we be able to determine our own external policies without let or hindrance from outside. ... South African politics are quite out of date in the modern world. The political parties will have to realise that they are part of a greater whole and they cannot do what they like in Trade, Economics or in Politics, and that they are linked up with the rest of Africa in a unity of common interests. It is an interesting thought to realise that it is only the British Commonwealth and the support of the Western colonial powers which prevents the development of a movement initiated by Russia and its satellites to regard South Africa as a kind of Franco Spain, and thus turn the whole force of the United Nations against us.[2]

This realisation of South Africa's isolation in terms of her 'native policy' thus initiated a reappraisal within her administrative class of the working of segregationist legislation. While not necessarily concerned to move away from the basic assumptions of this policy, the administrators in charge of the old policy of 'trusteeship' increasingly recognised the need to reformulate this in more internationally respectable terms. At the same time, the widening of political opposition to the policy after 1946 by the A.N.C., in alliance with the Indian Congress and the Coloured Peoples Organisation and the growing radical influences from both the Congress Youth League and the Communists, emphasised the urgency of the situation.

2 Discussions on reform

Thus, soon after the adjournment of the Natives Representative Council in August 1946, a debate began within administrative and political circles on the methods that might be adopted to reconsolidate the original 1936 legislation on a new basis acceptable to the African political élite. The problem was, as the deputy Prime Minister, Jan Hofmeyr, pointed out to the Prime Minister, Smuts, that 'the hitherto moderate intellectuals of the Professor (Z. K.) Matthews type are now committed to an extreme line against colour discrimination, and have carried the chiefs with them. We can't afford to allow them to be swept into the extremist camp, but I don't see what we can do to satisfy them which would be tolerated by European public opinion.'³ Hofmeyr put with succinct brevity the dilemmas of political change in order to re-establish the structures of political co-optation over the African political élite. For how far would it be possible to engineer political change without risking the loss of further support from the white electorate to D. F. Malan's Nationalists?

In this respect, the question turned on using as far as possible the avenues of consultation, established under the 1936 legislation, as a means to win back the confidence of the 'moderate intellectuals' on the Natives Representatives Council and to use the liberals elected as Natives Representatives. As had been evidenced during the excursions of the Native Trust after 1936, the white parliamentary representatives often proved useful as channels to the African chiefs in the tribal reserves. Now the question turned on whether the Representatives could be employed in a similar fashion regarding the intelligentsia in both the Congress and the N.R.C. which had been swung behind the boycott motion.

The strategy proposed by the government was partly determined by the mutual consultation of both government representatives and white liberals, as both sought to exploit as far as possible a situation of relative flux in the immediate post-war period. For the government, the exact method of administrative reform remained unclear, given the somewhat shaky state of the Native Affairs Department that had been denuded of personnel for the duration of the war. The guiding influence of the Secretary of Native Affairs, Douglas Smit, ended in 1945 as he was appointed to the Trusteeship Committee of the United Nations — a post in which he remained until 1946 when he returned to a more advisory role as member of the Native Affairs Commission. However, during the time away in San Francisco and later in London, he had a chance to see, like Heaton Nicholls as High Commissioner in London, the development of newer ideas for native administration in the British African colonies and to meet with Lord Hailey, a key exponent of developing African councils as administrative units at the local level.[4]

Furthermore for the liberals, changes were occurring in the internal politics of the Institute of Race Relations by the end of the second world war, as the long-felt presence of Rheinnalt-Jones as director was clearly coming to an end. The election defeat by Basner in 1942 had led to some loss of political face, whilst some of the younger Institute members like Lynn Saffery were opposed to Jones's weak opposition to government segregation policy. The executive committee, therefore, decided in 1946 to begin relieving Rheinnalt-Jones of much administrative work and to place it in the hands of the more inexperienced Quintin Whyte. The latter's ideas revolved less around the interventionist approach carved out by Rheinnalt-Jones, as he sought a political power base, than as a research body with leanings towards the field of industrial relations and race relations.[5] In the period of transition before Whyte took over full control in 1947, after Rheinnalt-Jones accepted an offer to work as an adviser to Anglo-American in the opening up of its Orange Free State gold mines,[6] the Institute was in somewhat of a state of flux and was very much open to alternative influences. The way thus lay open for the one liberal whom Rheinnalt-Jones and Loram had cast aside in the early 1930s, Edgar Brookes. As a new member of the Native Affairs Commission as well as Native Representative in the Senate for Natal, Brookes by late 1945 was in a position of some authority to act as a mediator between the Institute, as it was being reshaped under the guiding hand of Quintin Whyte, and government discussions on the reform of native administration. For Brookes this was a golden opportunity, not to be missed, towards remodelling government native policy to involve the African intelligentsia and political élite at the local level, as well as carving out a new role for the liberals around the Institute in the field of local level adminstration and in industrial relations. In one sense, indeed, the opportunity that was presented took up some of his earlier suggestions made on the Pact government between 1924 and 1926.[7]

Brookes was especially convinced that, with the end of the second world war, the old 'welfare' approach of inter-war liberalism was no longer adequate and risked becoming increasingly irrelevant in the new political situation. Many of the Joint Councils were going into decline, either through apathy or open African hostility, and it was by no means certain that any active policy would be able to revive them. Brookes was in favour of avoiding the personality cult that had surrounded Rheinnalt-Jones and spreading out Institute representation on to various bodies and committees, as well as seeking, if possible, to reconcile the old differences with William Ballinger and the Friends of Africa so as to focus upon trade unions and industrial relations. At the same time, through avoiding direct research itself, except certain small-scale work, the Institute could act as the co-ordinator for many other types of research at the local level:

The work for racial co-operation is vital: We should not have an unintelligent policy of keeping Joint Councils as such alive artificially. Where they have lapsed, local branches of the Institute may be better. I know our difficulties in that these bodies tend either to get apathetic or to be run by the Leftists. We can combat that by encouraging constructive work, especially on actual local situations, and also study. Visits from Headquarters, with their stimulation and guidance, are very necessary. We shall miss R.J. in this, but it may also be a good thing if this work is more spread out. Marquard could be used, so could Maurice Webb. Regional Organisers could be exchanged from time to time. I also want to suggest that one of the ways in which the Carnegie Corporation could help us would be the setting aside of funds for travelling lecturers.[8]

Brookes' ideas for a more activist approach to race relations, backed up by increasing local-level research, coincided with his hopes for a more coherent stake by the white liberals in the working of the governments's native policy. The boycott resolution of the A.N.C. in 1946 indicated that in many respects the heartland of South African liberalism was for the first time under systematic attack. The consolidation of the Joint Councils and the Bantu Men's Social Centre in the 1920s had tended only to overlay the fundamental liberal structure at the local level, centred on the Cape, the African franchise, the Transkeian and Ciskeian General Councils and Fort Hare. These had been able to continue, even after the 1936 legislation ending the Cape common roll, for as a substitute there had been the direct representation of African representatives in Parliament and the election of such liberals as Donald Molteno and Margaret Ballinger. However, by the early 1940s, it was becoming clear that many of the traditional assumptions behind Cape liberalism at the local level were finally being eroded as the government's Betterment Areas Scheme took heavy tolls on the Easter Cape African peasantry. The South African Native Farmers Congress complained that many of the graduates in agriculture from Fort Cox and Fort Hare were frustrated in their ambitions to put their training into practice through the government's failure to employ them as agricultural instructors,[9] while in many parts of the Easter Cape, areas of African landholding that had been consolidated under the 1894 Glen Grey Act were being contracted in size. Despite attempts by Margaret Ballinger in the early 1940s to defend as far as possible the claims of individual landholders, the channels of communication through Native Commissioners to central decision-making became increasingly blocked, and the seeming effectiveness of Natives Representation in advancing the interests of African land claims progressively diminished.

'The effect and apparent intention of the present land policy of the Department of Native Affairs', Margaret Ballinger wrote despairingly to the Under Secretary of Native Affairs, Gordon Mears, in 1943, 'is that a Native peasantry shall not develop but that rather the African country man shall continue to be, and on an increasing scale, a town worker with a plot of land to subsidise his town earnings.' Even this trend, though, became checked by the actual forfeiture of many African claims to rural holdings after migrating to town locations, thus ensuring a complete proletarianisation of many former peasant landholders in the Eastern Cape.[10] This nullified the hopes of many of the Eastern Cape African political leaders, like D. D. T. Jabavu, who had originally considered that the instruments of Natives Representation established in 1936 could be used to extract large land settlements from the South African Native Trust.[11] As a consequence, by 1943, the position of Jabavu inside his own political body, the All African Convention, was becoming progressively weaker and he looked to his friend and mentor, Margaret Ballinger, for political assistance to defend himself from an increasingly vocal Trotskyite left wing.[12] A similar phenomenon occurred, too, with the Rev. James Calata in the Cape African Congress as attacks on the liberally inclined Secretary General mounted in the years after 1936 from an assorted collection of Communist and Africanist oriented political groupings. With Calata, however, the main source of political assistance came from DonaldMolteno who, until the middle 1940s, provided his client with considerable support in the form of attending African political meetings and acting as a covert lobbyer in Calata's favour against his more radical critics.[13]

With the end of the war, and particularly the boycott campaign initiated by the A.N.C. in September 1946, it became clear that this covert support by the Cape Representatives to the liberals inside both the A.N.C. and the All African Convention was ceasing to work. The structures of Natives Representation had failed to rectify the overall workings of government segregation policy, and it had not even been able to prevent the erosion of the remnants of the African franchise in the Cape which ensured the Representatives of their basic political support. The Cape African Voters Association, for example, indicated that the effect of the government's limitation on African landholding was the further narrowing of those eligible to the franchise: many applications for the vote under the old £50 property qualification, for instance, were refused because it was difficult for Africans to demonstrate that they were employed by a 'known' employer, while in the case of the £75 property qualification it became difficult for many Africans to prove that property they held in the rural areas amounted to this figure unless they had a house built on it 'in a European style'.[14]

This weakening of the economic basis of the old Cape liberalism at the local level by the mid-1940s, left the Cape liberal representatives in an increasingly marginal political position. Though a part of the caucus of Natives Representatives in Parliament, Margaret Ballinger had not necessarily agreed to all the political views of her more conservative colleagues like Rheinnalt-Jones and Brookes from the Transvaal and Natal. Considering Brookes a 'timid conservative', she had in the initial years after 1936 sought to develop her own specific channels of consultation on specific issues and had tended to avoid working in too close a harmony with the other Representatives, as Brookes in particular had at first hoped.[15] This strategy, however, left her politically weak after August 1946, when the boycott issue challenged the whole system of Natives Representation and, in particular, shattered the belief that the old structures of paternalist Cape liberalism could continue to be used to sustain the influence of the Cape representatives. In December of the same year, the Cape African Voters Association followed the A.N.C. in urging a boycott of Natives Representation, and the position of some of the white Cape liberals' closest African supporters, like R. H. Godlo, chairman of the Advisory Boards Congress, Professor Z. K. Matthews and D. D. T. Jabavu, became politically threatened. Jabavu declared that, despite opposing the boycott motion in both the A.A.C. and the Cape African Voters Association, he was 'overwhelmed by the youthful majority who were strong in their views and who forced me to refrain from exerting any influence on the discussion by reason of my being chairman'.[16] Similarly, Godlo pointed out that 'without the voice of the Council', the political efforts of the Natives Representatives would decline in their effectiveness, for they would lose a valuable means through which to disseminate their views to the African public.[17]

In comparison to the northern liberals, who were more closely associated with the Institute of Race Relations, there was little that such Cape Representatives as Donald Molteno and Margaret Ballinger could actively do in the critical period from the beginning of 1947 to the election in 1948. Having so closely based her political strategy on a parliamentary view of Natives Representation in the best Whig tradition, Margaret Ballinger was clearly taken very much unawares by events. 'We have a strong feeling that the African population are not yet ready for a complete repudiation of the Council', she wrote to Godlo in September 1946,[18] and it was only in December, on returning from a trip to India, that she sought a meeting of the Natives Representatives in Cape Town to seek some form of co-ordinated strategy *vis-à-vis* the boycott issue.[19]

Parliamentary lobbying, though, was increasingly seen as a far less effective means of seeking to influence government policy. Though the Cape Representatives did act as purveyors in the course of 1947 for resolutions by the Cape African Congress,[20] the more effective method lay in direct contact with government decision-makers on a personal basis and the formulation of clear-cut reformist proposals. In this respect, Edgar Brookes had the upper hand, for he not only had the advantage of being a member of the Native Affairs Commission and having close contact with his fellow member, Douglas Smit, but also the role of being mediator between the Institute of Race Relations and government policy. Furthermore, for the period immediately after the boycott resolution in 1946, Brookes was not hampered by any strongly radical African political influence in Natal, for the Youth League did not begin to expand into the province until 1947 and Congress politics were still dominated by the amenable presence of A. W. G. Champion, whom Brookes had secured as a supporter behind his senatorship in the late 1930s.[21] Thus, after securing the support of the four Natal members on the Natives Representative Council (including Champion) behind his policy of opposition to outright boycott in October 1946,[22] Brookes began a campaign of direct influence on Hofmeyr and central government decision-making. In comparison to the Cape Representatives, Brookes was far more concerned to create new and more direct platforms by which to co-opt the disaffected 'moderate' elements within African political leadership. Enclosing an article published in the *Manchester Guardian* in December 1946, Brookes suggested to Hofmeyr that a commission of enquiry on the N.R.C. be set up so as to 'hold the question in solution', while the N.R.C. at its next meeting could be asked to nominate a sub-committee to confer with the commission.[23] While Hofmeyr doubted the wisdom of a full-scale commission, which he felt would lead 'to crystallization of the issues and a deepening of the cleavage', undoubtedly Brookes's ideas for an administrative reform from the top downwards had some impact in the coming months, and indicated the changing nature of the political pressures from the white liberals.[24]

In essence, Brookes' differing approach to the 'solution' of the boycott issue to that of the Cape liberals, related not only to differences of temperament but also cultural and historical background. As a Natalian, Brookes was heir to a more systematised pattern of native administration, dating back to Shep-

stone, and he had a far greater faith in the virtues of administration than the Cape liberals. At the same time, in comparison with the more pragmatic approach of the Cape Representatives, Brookes' ideas were shaped in part by the previous
discussion in the Institute of Race Relations, and by Hoernle in
the early 1940s, on blueprints for the reform of race relations.
The problem was, for Brookes, to open up the avenues of native
administration and prevent it from hardening into a closed and
impermeable system. In a memorandum to the other members
of the N.A.C. in September 1946, for instance, he warned of the
dangers of allowing the boycott movement to extend itself:

If ... the Government stands on its dignity and gives the more moderate members of the Council no way of saving their faces, they will be
bound to repeat their resolutions and adjourn again indefinitely. If we
consider what that means, it means a declaration of civil war — a
bloodless war but war nevertheless — between Government and ac-
credited leaders of the Native people chosen by a system of election
which the Government itself has devised. It means that men who
have hitherto stood out as moderates will, by the logic of events, be
forced to take their place with the extremists. If we pause to think
what a nationally organised non co-operation movement among the
natives would mean, especially if among those leading it were such
men as Matthews, the Transkeian chiefs and Luthuli, who have won
the confidence of large numbers of Europeans and who are regarded as
moderates and responsible men, I do not see any end to such a
struggle.[25]

This meant, therefore, exerting pressure through such lob-
bies as the Native Affairs Commission and the Natives Representatives' caucus in Parliament for political reform that
would widen the political influence of the N.R.C., as well as go
some way toward meeting the hopes of African union leaders
for the legalisation of African trade unions. In the debate that
ensued on this, Brookes was partly supported by many of the
Native Affairs Department administrators who, though not
necessarily so directly beholden to liberal influences through
such bodies as the Institute of Race Relations, were nevertheless aware that the bureaucratic conception of Natives Representation created in 1936 was no longer operable. Douglas
Smit had long privately felt that the N.R.C. was an ill-devised
body that failed to meet the demands of the African intelligentsia,[26] while the new Secretary of Native Affairs, G.

Mears, who had the responsibility of chairing the council's meetings, confessed to difficulties in coping with its political nature. The council, he complained to the Native Affairs Commission, was 'a political body and does not fit into the administrative machine at all':

When it was born the analogy was taken of the Transkeian Council, that it had worked well and this would too, but actually it is a different body altogether. The Transkeian Council is an administrative machine but this is a political body which does not fit into the administration at all instead of being an advisory body as an adjunct to the departmental machine. For that reason I find it difficult to handle the situation and the whole thing is an embarrassment to me.[27]

Thus, in the course of 1947, following an initial instruction from Smuts, the Prime Minister, the administrative apparatus of native affairs began to discuss strategies for reform, based upon the idea of politicising in some way the existing body of the N.R.C. and widening its area of representation so that it could represent more fully the emergent interests of an African petty bourgeoisie in the urban areas. At the same time, though, the basic constraint on any such reformist programme was that it was still work within the basic structures of Stallardist urban segregation and merely to widen the linkages by which the urban intelligentsia maintained contact with its counterparts in the reserves. While much of the actual drafting of the proposals for the Native Affairs Department was done by the Secretary of Native Affairs, Mears, many of the strongest influences came from his former boss, Douglas Smit, and the N.A.C. who sought the recategorisation of Africans into 'Reserve Natives', 'Urban Natives' and 'Farm Natives', with the last in particular, having an increased stake in the composition of the N.R.C. via a Union Advisory Boards Congress.[28] Thus, in contrast to the somewhat more radical proposals of Mears for the establishment of an almost completely separate system of devolved local African-dominated administration, Smit urged only a partial reform that still ensured the continuation of white administrative officials from the N.A.D. 'You cannot eliminate the local officials from responsibility', he wrote to Mears in April 1947 when opposing the Secretary of Native Affair's ideas on local tribal councils conducting their own courts; for 'at present they do the bulk of the work and their withdrawal would deprive the Native Councils of the necessary driving power and the close association with our administration that is necessary to ensure success'.[29] Smit's desire to shield the existing area of responsibility held by the Native Affairs officials indicated the limitations on the debate on reform, conducted as it was within the confines of an administrative hierarchy anxious to preserve its own sphere of influence. Smit certainly recognised the need to bring in as far as possible the African intelligentsia into public administration, and the proposals that were drawn up by the N.A.D., entitled *A Progressive Programme for Native Administration*, went some way towards achieving this. They envisaged the establishment of a reconstituted 50 member Natives Representative Council that had powers to impose personal taxes on Africans, to consider the expenditure of the General Councils and to allocate funds to them, as well as having an executive committee to confer with the Secretary of Native Affairs. Furthermore, a separate 'Native Treasury' was proposed that would be responsible for revenue obtained by the N.R.C. and the system of local government that was envisaged to cover the whole of the Union, and which would be centred around a series of general and local councils modelled on the Eastern Cape and Transkeian precedents.[30] While being segregationist, the scheme was the most comprehensive plan for a delegation of powers to both a rural and urban African political élite yet evolved, and it recalled in some ways the promises made by General Hertzog to Sol Plaatje and African political representatives when he was Minister of Native Affairs in 1912. 'It should be our policy to associate the Natives with us in their own affairs,' Smit, the essential architect of the policy, wrote in some notes for Mears:

Unless we do this they will resent our presence more and more as the time goes on, as has been the case in India. The growing spirit of nationalism among them will be less bitter if we find more scope for members of the intelligentsia in the Public Service rather than in agitation... Lord Hailey has rightly drawn attention to the fact that throughout Africa there is a growing middle class among the Natives who are antagonistic to our Government and these people are gradually creating a position that may well prove insoluble in the future unless some effort is made to give them an outlet for their aspirations.[31]

The essentially bureaucratic context in which this policy for reform was conducted, however, indicated that the influences from the white liberals, led by Brookes and Institute of Race Relations, were ultimately blunted. The Native Affairs Commission by May 1947 was relegated to a more peripheral role, where it could do little more than urge greater political tact by the government leaders when it next met the African political leadership.[32] Furthermore, Brookes's pleas at one of the N.A.C.'s meetings for a complete overhaul of the Industrial Conciliation Act, so as to ensure a more wide-ranging measure than the proposed Native Industrial Bill fell on stony ground.[33] It became clear after 8 May when Smuts, in a meeting with a contingent from the N.R.C., promised to try to make the council into a 'real working institution, helpful to the good government of this country',[34] that the reformist programme was becoming increasingly bound up with the wider reconsideration of the Union's native policy, currently being undertaken by the Native Laws Commission under the chairmanship of H. A. Fagan. Though the N.A.D. proposals did not directly conflict with the ideas of the Fagan commission, the more detailed intricacies of the reform policy, such as the establishment of a Union Advisory Boards Congress, depended upon the final resolution of the commission's deliberations. In August 1947 Fagan urged that definition of the new scope and powers of the boards be shelved until after the commission's report and, in effect, until after the next general election.[35] It was essentially for this reason that, when the N.A.D. programme came up for renewed discussion on 1 September 1947, Smuts decided the final evolution of the policy should be delayed until after the election, which he confidently expected to win.[36] Administrative slowness thus delayed an early response to the N.R.C.'s boycott decision of September 1946 and, in the event, the United Party suffered election defeat by the Nationalists in May 1948 without any coherently evolved native policy.

3   The African response

The dilatoriness and uncertainty pervading the government's native policy in the months after September 1946 if anything helped to exacerbate the resolve amongst the African political leadership in the A.N.C. to step up the boycott campaign. Xuma found the initial blueprint of the N.A.D. reform policy in May 1947 'vague and disappointing', since the failure to remove the essentials of colour-bar legislation left even a revamped N.R.C. assisting the Africans 'to administer their own domination, discrimination and oppression under the cloak of giving Africans responsibility and participation in the administration of their own affairs'.[37] Meeting in the Johannesburg Trades Hall in June, 600 delegates of the Transvaal African Congress went on to condemn the proposals, especially the Industrial Disputes Bill which C. S. Ramohanoe argued would increase state surveillance over African unions by the N.A.D. which he described as an 'Intelligence Service Department surpassing even Marshall Square'.[38] Furthermore, even the most liberally inclined African leaders like Jordan Ngubane, who had written a pamphlet in 1946 arguing for an increase in the powers of the N.R.C.,[39] could not find much to support in the Smuts proposals since the executive powers that would be given the council would still be subject to a government veto, and would thus nullify any attempts to reverse some of the existing land provisions under the government's trusteeship policy:

As things now stand, the Native Affairs Department needs millions of pounds to rehabilitate African reserves alone. Parliament is now willing to vote the required amounts. The Africans see no reason why Parliament would suddenly change its attitude merely because the demand for the money came from an elected, wholly African body.[40]

These arguments reflected many of the pressures being exerted by Africans at the grass roots against collaborating with the government's attempts to reform the machinery of administering native affairs. In the Eastern Cape and Transkei, for example, widespread opposition began to be expressed against the seeming ineffectiveness of both local African representative bodies, such as the Ciskeian General Council and the Transkeian Bunga, and the representation in Parliament, to reverse the working of the government's rehabilitation policy. The promulgation of the scheme for the Ciskei in the form of Douglas Smit's *New Era of Reclamation* in 1945 had occurred at the same time as a devastating drought which

had led to considerable famine amongst the African peasantry,[41] and the complaint was expressed by villagers that the
South African Native Trust had effectively taken over most of
the administrative functions formerly conducted at the local
level via the Glen Grey Councils. This bureaucratisation
particularly removed many of the powers of local headmen
who had often been one of the basic pillars behind the
reconstituted Cape liberalism in the early years of the century. By 1947, however, in areas like the Healdtown Reserve,
groups of local headmen began to protest at the erosion of
their powers which, as one petition claimed, was drawing
local African dignatories 'into the policy of administration
implied in the Native Administration Act of 1927 which give
discretionary powers to officials to act without consulting the
people'.[42]

These protests against the workings of the rehabilitation
policy also became linked to the boycott campaign, and this
became manifest in the Transkei with the formation of an
'Anti Rehabilitation Government Scheme Committee, which
argued in a manifesto of October 1947 that 'the present
boycott in the Transkei is strengthened by the dissatisfaction
caused by the Government in the Transkeian Territories. We
fully endorse that if the scheme could be stopped at present
pending future consideration, the present state of mental
perturbation among Africans resulting in the anti white spirit
can be improved and bettered in the Native Reserves.'[43] The
manifesto warned that much of this depended upon how far
the Natives Representatives were prepared to fight the
scheme in Parliament, though the response indicated how
ineffective this was. William Ballinger, in a letter of reply to
the manifesto writers, personified the state of the more radical white liberals by simply repeating many of the ideas on
African peasant co-operatives in the reserves, linked to an
urban African working class in the town, that had been
debated in the 1930s; he expressed the additional hope that if
the African peasant farmers could 'get busy' and pass on their
ideas to the Natives Representatives, a 'plan of campaign
could be worked out', providing the conclusion were 'theore-
tically sound' for 'representatives cannot of themselves com-
pel the authorities to put them into operation'.[44]

Ballinger's hopes, however, depended upon the boycott campaign being in effect stifled and African consciousness at the grass roots being brought behind a more moderate leadership that was still prepared to work through the system of Native Representation.[45] Such hopes seemed increasingly implausible in the course of 1947 as, particularly in the Transkei, support began to be mobilised behind boycotting the by-election for the Native Representative to replace Advocate Hemming who died that year. The executive committee of the Transkeian African Voters Association declared the whole system of Natives Representation 'a farce and a mockery', since it meant that Africans were 'expected to elect a European to perpetuate the illusion that we are represented ... Let the people know that we are voiceless.'[46] At the same time a campaign began to be organised by Govan Mbeki and the Transkeian Organised Bodies that gathered considerable momentum despite the shortage of funds.[47] With the only known candidate being the Cape liberal Douglas Buchanan, who was still keen to trust to parliamentary tactics as far as possible,[48] the campaign was a considerable success. Despite the fact that Buchanan was able to claim that only a small number of African voters — allegedly some 94 out of 200 gathered at a meeting in Umtata in May — actually supported the boycott campaign,[49] the appeal of the boycotters to the large numbers of franchiseless African peasants and labour migrants undoubtedly acted as a considerable fillip to the general African feeling that Natives Representation lacked a basic political legitimacy. Alfred Xuma urged Mbeki to encourage African voters to press their own candidate or candidates forward in the election to succeed Hemming, since there was 'calamity awaiting the Transkei about its representation'[50] and Anton Lembede of the Congress Youth League urged Buchanan to stand down.[51] Indeed, the movement of congress organisation out into the reserves indicated the strength of the boycott appeal and Buchanan's eventual election in the Transkei in 1947 did nothing to nullify the growing African opposition to being represented by whites in an all-white Parliament.

By the time that General Smuts' proposals for reform of the Natives Representatives Council were finally revealed in September 1947, even some of the foremost congress moderates

like Selby Msimang were forced to concede that they would do
little to ease the political deadlock.[52] Pressure from the grass
roots had, in areas such as the Transkei, ensured that, by the
start of 1948, Natives Representation had become a political
symbol of the structures that were seen to be preventing the
development of mass African political consciousness. Only
those white radicals like the Communist Sam Kahn, who
stood outside the white liberal caucus of Native Representatives in Parliament, gained the support of the leading local
African political organisations. Justifying the support of Kahn
in the Western Cape election of 1948 after Donald Molteno's
decision to resign from Parliament, C. A. W. Sigila of the Cape
African Voters Association indicated the degree to which the
old paternal alliance with Cape liberalism had been eroded:
'We Africans since 1936,' he wrote to Margaret Ballinger,
'learnt to have no particular attachment to any political party,
except to individuals who promise to consistently and persis-
tently present our case with courage and honesty'.[53] It appeared
that now, even in the former heartland of the South African
liberal tradition, white liberals could no longer expect automatic support by organised African political opinion.

4   Moves towards a party base

In these political circumstances in 1947 and 1948, and the
general inadequacy of the Smuts reform proposals, liberals
began to look towards a more formal political organisation.
The election defeat of the U.P. turned many liberal hopes
towards a political party led by Hofmeyr, since this appeared
the obvious direction in which to go as the Nationalist policy
of ethnicisation through the apartheid conception; not only
cut the white liberals off from their African political base but
removed them from the institutions that could affect government policy at the centre. The attempts, however, by Brookes
and his fellow Institute liberals to influence government deci-
sions at the centre were dashed by the death of Hofmeyr at the
end of 1948, removing the one figure to whom liberals could
look to be included in a liberally inclined cabinet.[54] In addition,
in the course of 1949 both Brookes and Smit were put under
pressure by the Nationalist Minister of Native Affairs, E. G.

Jansen, to resign from the Native Affairs Commission.[55] Though government policy continued some aspects of the previous United Party government's reform programme by extending local and general native councils on a regional basis, hopes of extending urban African representation on to a revamped Natives Representative Council vanished as the Nationalists sought separate political outlets via the tribally dominated reserves.[56] For the new Secretary of Native Affairs, W. W. M. Eiselen, appointed over the head of Mears in September 1949, and his colleague M. D. C. de Wet Nel, chairman of the Native Affairs Commission, this became an extension of the neo-Fichtean or territorially based conception of Afrikaner nationalism to the African population in order to defuse African nationalism. It became clear, in the course of 1949 and 1950, that the Nationalist government could expect little or no support from the urban African intelligentsia beyond a small number of opportunists like S. N. Bennet Ncwana and the former treasurer of the A.N.C., the Alexandra business man, Richard Baloyi,[57] so the political pressure only increased for ethnic separatism. By 1950, the entire thrust of government policy had swung round towards by-passing the urban African petty bourgeoisie and the existing institutions of Natives Representation, via the N.R.C. and the white parliamentary representatives, and establishing instead new structures of control via Bantu Authorities in the reserves, under the control of a regenerated tribal political élite.[58] With the appointment of the apartheid ideologist, Dr. Verwoerd, in 1950 as Jansen's successor as Minister of Native Affairs, this policy received strong political support in the central echelons of the Nationalist-controlled state apparatus.

For the liberals, these new political trends necessitated a search for a new political strategy in order to cope with their weakened political base. Even before the U.P. election defeat in 1948, the government discussion on political reform had been seen in some quarters of the Institute of Race Relations as an opportunity to put into practice some of the previous ideological revision of liberalism propounded by Hoernle in the early 1940s. On the basis of a memorandum written by Brookes in January 1948 entitled 'Segregation and its Alternatives', the executive committee of the Institute had kept closely in mind the three political possiblities offered by Hoernle of total segregation, parallelism and assimilation.[59] The proposals of the Smuts government for a widening of the powers of the N.R.C., together with an extension of local government for Africans, received the committee's tentative support for, as it argued 'there is a certain incompatibility in the demands of the Natives Representative Council for increased powers for itself and for extension of the present system of African parliamentary representation'.[60] The Institute executive tended to place most faith in the proposals to extend representation to the urban African petty bourgeoisie via a Union Native Advisory Boards Congress, for it was in this direction that it saw its own influence in terms of an industrial relations and race relations research mediator. Echoing the previous trend towards a plural conception of democratic theory, the committee concluded that 'the application of democracy to a multi-racial society with peoples of different levels of development may involve forms not hitherto found necessary'.[61]

But what was to be the avenue by which these political ideas could now be put across, given the changed complexion of the South African state and the black political opposition to it? By the middle of 1949, Margaret Ballinger began to favour the idea of establishing a liberal political party, which was now being actively championed by diverse groups of liberals, including Leo and Hilda Kuper and Kenneth Kirkwood in Durban.[62] 'I am quite convinced,' she wrote to C. A. W. Sigila of the Cape African Voters Association, 'that it is a fruitless [?] waste of energy for those of us who have applied ourselves to the task of Native representation to continue longer as isolated units. It simply means that for much of the time we are beating the air.'[63] Similarly, Donald Molteno wrote that with the death of Hofmeyr there was an even greater need for the organisation of liberal leaders, since 'the need for inspiring leadership is perhaps greater in the case of liberalism than in that of any other political creed'.[64] The actual decision to organise such a party, though, was deferred until after the 1953 election, which many liberals hoped that the U.P. could still win from the Nationalists, despite the creation of six extra Nationalist seats through the incorporation of South West Africa into the Union.[65]

This idea of direct entry into party politics was not necessarily shared by all sections of the liberal establishment in South Africa, for in the Institute of Race Relations, particularly, there was still the view that liberals should keep to a bland and empirical programme.[66] However, the A.N.C. came under growing influence from the Communist/Youth League alliance in 1949, as Xuma and Calata were removed from the presidency and secretaryship and replaced by J. M. Moroka and Walter Sisulu; this made it essential that new avenues be found to appeal to the radicalised African political élite. Though some influence remained through Natives Representation, as Brookes held on to the senatorship for Natal in 1948 and William Ballinger easily won the Transvaal and Orange Free State the same year,[67] it was likely in some areas that continued liberal participation in the elections risked alignment with only the tiny faction of the African rural élite who continued to oppose the boycott. In the Transkei, for example the main support for the nomination of Alexander Kerr as parliamentary representative on his retirement as Principal of Fort Hare, came from the Bikitsha faction of Mfengu headmen who were linked in a political alliance with Kaiser Matanzima, chief of the emigrant Tembus. Though this group gained control of the old Transkeian African Voters Association in opposition to the pro-boycott Transkeian Organised Bodies, the partial nature of the support led even such a conservative chief as Victor Poto of the Pondo to advise Kerr to stand down.[68] In such circumstances, the avenues of political leaders via such channels as Natives Representation became increasingly unreliable and needed to be supplemented by a new political organisation based on a party apparatus.[69]

The formation of the Liberal Party after the defeat of the U.P. in the 1953 election should, therefore, be seen in a somewhat wider context than the pluralist party politics model suggested by Janet Robertson in her *Liberalism in South Africa, 1948–63*.[70] While clearly the timing of the white liberals' decision to form the party was dictated by the fortunes of the U.P. in oppositon to Malan's Nationalists, it is important to understand the structural context in which the party was formed. This was unlike western liberal democratic systems since, by 1950 at the latest, it was already beginning to be recognised that white liberals could not hope to reverse the general political direction that the South African political system was taking. As Edgar Brookes lamented in the Hoernle memorial lecture of the Institute of Race Relations that year,

a new golden image of nationalism had come to dominate South African politics and those of us who will not bow down to this golden image are threatened in our position and our fields of service. We may never, if the worshippers of the image have their way never, never, never hold public office in South Africa, never speak for our beloved country in the outside world, never be reckoned as one of the real family in our own country. As far as may be our freedom must be curtailed, our voices stilled, our pens struck from our hands.[71]

In a number of respects, therefore, the pressure towards creating a Liberal Party accrued from those interests frustrated by their exclusion from political influence since 1948, and at the same time alienated from the more diffuse efforts at mass protest by whites against government policy through a body like the Torch Commando. It was not so much a simple concern to maintain the values of the Cape liberal tradition,[72] though this could be appealed to politically, but a search to reinstate some of the channels of political influence with the government which had been enjoyed by liberal politicians as Natives Representatives and via informal contacts built up by the Institute of Race Relations. In the liberally inclined journal, *The Forum*, a political party to defend the liberal political standpoint was argued as essential. In June 1952 Anthony Delius wrote that 'at this desperate moment in our country's history ... there is no clearly expressed liberal policy before the people'.[73] When the Defiance Campaign organised by the A.N.C. in that year led to riots in some parts of the Eastern Cape, the pressure to some extent carried a momentum of its own[74] for the Liberal Association that was formed in March 1952 became transformed in May 1953 into a political party, 'before', it was claimed by one observer, 'all the implications of the step had been fully weighed'.[75]

The first issue of the Liberal Party magazine, *Contact*, in January 1954 indicated that the major premise behind the party was the search for political influence at the centre. 'We must try to win political power', it urged, 'and we must try to influence public opinion ... We must increase our knowledge of and strengthen our connections with Non European political organisations. It seems that these connections will be informal ones rather than political alliances.[76] The tone indicated the attempt to renew political influence over black organisations which had been lost with the breakdown in the political clientelism exerted via the Natives Representation in the 1940s. The political consequences of this, though were seen as profound. At the time of the Defiance Campaign, *The Forum* warned of the dangers of 'terrorism' if the 'moderate leaders' in the A.N.C. were not recognised as part of a 'basis for hopeful discussion'.[77] *Contact* took up the same theme, emphasising the importance of black members in Liberal Party organisation. 'The more white people see that non-white people support the Liberal Party, the more hope they will feel that a racial disaster is not our inevitable end. The more they will be inclined to join a Party that does not reason in terms of race or colour.'[78] There was a rather naïve optimism in this, but at the same time the mood indicated the more general state of political despair to which liberals had been driven by the middle 1950s, as the portent of a 'racial disaster' seemed to loom over the horizon. The novel *Episode* by Harry Bloom, set in a fictitious Transvaal town of 'Nylstroom', epitomised this pessimistic thinking in liberal circles at this time as both state repression and African response polarised society in a spiral of escalating hostility that led to massive bloodshed. Both sides were ultimately seen as barbaric and seemingly limitless in their capacity to inflict violence, and no positive alternative society could yet be seen to emerge out of this. It was also a type of race violence that was not yet seen to have any implicitly revolutionary implications.[79] Thus the Liberal Party, together with the allied organisations of the Institute, the Churches and intellectual circles, was seen as the only repository of political rationality which could prevent such a disaster. This was a rather benign political faith, though, which would not long survive the wave of political repression that followed Sharpeville in 1960 and the banning of the A.N.C. and P.A.C.

5   *Michael Scott and the beginnings of international isolation*

There was also an external dimension to this lurch towards party politics. Some liberals in South Africa became increasingly aware by the later 1940s and early 1950s that the changing international situation was beginning to isolate South Africa. Whilst there had been some international hostility to South African segregation policies in the inter-war years, the second world war popularised world-wide much of the hostility formerly felt in liberal intellectual circles towards philosophies based upon race. The foundation of Unesco in 1945 widened the critique made by such figures as Jacques Barzun and Julian Huxley of the political uses of racial ideology, and racialism now became both internationally disreputable and linked to fascism and philosophies underpinning right-wing and authoritarian societies.[80]

Charges that South African government policy was 'fascist' had been made for many years and stretched back to before the war. However, the development of articulate black criticism of South Africa after 1945, such as that by George Padmore in his book *Africa: Britain's Third Empire*[81], became linked to a radicalisation in non-Marxist political circles in the era of the post-war Labour government in Britain. For South African liberals, this latter trend was especially threatening, for hitherto these circles had usually been seen either as allies, or at best only half-hearted critics supporting comparatively minor groups such as *The Friends of Africa*. By the late 1940s, though, the Anglican priest Michael Scott began to drive a wedge between this political accord between English and South African liberals as he campaigned against the political injustices behind the South African farm labour sysem, which employed prison labour in near-slavery conditions in areas such as Bethal in the Eastern Transvaal, and the pleas for self-determination by the Herero in South West Africa before the United Nations General Assembly.[82]

Scott was a danger to the South African liberals precisely because his former missionary experience in Johannesburg had led him to become acquainted with their various political activites. In 1944 Scott had helped to form a left-liberal organisation called *The Campaign for Right and Justice* under the presidency of a liberal Afrikaner nationalist, Mr. Justice Krause. The campaign had sought to influence white party politics, but in as 'non-partisan' a manner as possible, through championing ideas for a welfare state, full political representation for all sections of South African society and the abolition of all racially discriminatory legislation.[83] The movement, though, soon foundered on a pamphlet that sought to publicise the political activites of the Afrikaner Broederbond, and Scott resigned in 1945, 'overcome', as he later recalled, 'by a sense of betrayal and frustration in face of what seemed the overwhelming forces of oppression both on the Government side and in the Opposition'.[84] Feeling especially let down by the Churches inside South Africa, Scott moved on to the international plane at a time when world-wide Christian opinion was starting to be mobilised through the formation of the World Council of Churches in 1948. By 1949 he warned such Christian groupings as the British Society of Friends against too close an identification with South African liberals after the South African Quaker, and president of the Institute of Race Relations, Maurice Webb, wrote an article attacking what he felt were the exaggerated criticisms of South African government made by Michael Scott, Yusuf Dadoo and Paul Robeson at a meeting in London.[85] Accusing the South African Churches of refusing to take a stand on racial segregation, Scott impressed on John Fletcher of the London Society of Friends that 'the evils of the South African situation have been too long concealed by the carefully moderate and scholarly sounding phrases of professedly "liberal-minded" statesmen. For these can be exaggerated by deliberate understatements and selection of truth as well as by overstatement.'[86]

Scott's activites outside South Africa increasingly embarrassed South African liberals at precisely the time when they were seeking to evolve a coherent political response the the government's apartheid policy. By 1950, Rheinnalt-Jones confessed to C. W. W. Greenidge, the successor to John Harris as president of the Anti Slavery Society, that Scott's methods, especially on South West Africa, made 'the position of liberals very difficult indeed', though the government majority in the Union Parliament 'increased our moral responsibility to insist that the non

European peoples shall be treated with justice and humanitarian care'. Rheinnalt-Jones, however, could only resort to the old tactic of seeking a commission to investigate the various issues that Scott had raised over the preceding years, such as the complaints of the Hereros, the situation on the land and the labour situation on the farms and in urban areas.[87] For the liberals overseas, this paternalism was no longer adequate to deal with a situation that was becoming increasingly politicised. In March 1952, Scott helped to found The Africa Bureau in London which had an objective 'to further the best traditions of Britain's policy in Africa'; in the aftermath of the Seretse Khama affair in 1950 which had done so much to focus British public attention on the racial issues in southern African politics,[88] a slow, gradualist approach appeared out of tune with the pace of events. With African nationalism being fanned all over the African continent, and especially in Central Africa with the creation of the Central African Federation in 1953,[89] the formation of a political party by South African liberals was dictated by an assessment of events external as well as internal to South Africa. In effect, it was a last, desperate attempt to keep the mantle of a liberal 'western civilisation' flying on a Continent that seemed to outsiders to be on the verge of being torn to ribbons.

CONCLUSION

Apartheid and the twilight of liberalism

South African liberalism has for the most part been the political expression of a small body of white educationalists, philanthropists, missionaries and social workers who have been concerned to alleviate the harsh economic and social consequences of industrialisation in a racially divided society. Although the South African liberal tradition from the time of Union in 1910 has taken over a fairly cohesive body of political values — freedom of expression, the parliamentary franchise and individual rights transcending racial or religious affiliation — from the nineteenth-century Cape,[1] it has been unsuccessful in translating these into a political programme that had real impact on the body politic. Instead, liberal political discourse from Union was increasingly defined by the alternative ideological concept of white settler segregationism, which became the chief political weapon by which the nascent white state sought to protect itself from the spectre of black proletarianisation and urbanisation. Thus the overall assessment of South African liberalism must not be guided by, as many liberal historians have imagined, the simple ability to keep certain political values intact, but by the way particular historical situations are confronted. As Eric Voegelin has warned, '[liberalism] is not a body of timelessly valid scientific propositions about political reality, but rather a series of political opinions and attitudes which have their optimal truth in the situation which motivates them, and are then overtaken by history and required to do justice to new situations.'[2]

Judged by these criteria, liberalism may be seen to have failed politically, whilst at the same time having a far wider

impact socially and ideologically. The important point about
segregationist ideology was that it did not incorporate in any
significant manner the tradition of European biological racism,
which was easily available to a settler regime seeking to defend
its ostensibly 'racial' identity. It could perhaps have done so,
for the phase of late nineteenth-century expansion of European
imperialism certainly acted as a powerful fillip to the tradition
of race-thinking which went back to the eighteenth century.
However, as Hannah Arendt has pointed out, 'race-thinking
was a source of convenient arguments for varying political
conflicts, but it never possessed any kind of monopoly over the
political life of the respective nations; *it sharpened and exploited existing conflicting interests of existing political problems, but it never created new conflicts or produced new
categories of political thinking*' (emphasis added).[3] There was
thus no necessary 'immanent logic' to race-thinking, and the
way racism came to penetrate and define the ideological con-
ceptions of a particular society depended very much on the
historical configurations at a particular time.

In South Africa, therefore, it may be argued that, as if in
compensation for its political defeat, liberalism was able to
exert considerable influence on the manner of race-thinking. If
white racism *per se* could produce no new categories of analysis, the compensating influence from the liberal tradition of
missionary interest in African societies, and the experience of
cultural and social mediation between African and white settler societies, ensured a fund of expertise which the nascent
settler state could not ignore. Thus the purely racist assertion
of white genetic superiority over non-white races became tem-
pered and deflected by the process of inter-racial mediation,
once the white territorial sphere in land from the 1913 Natives
Land Act onwards had been established and its sphere in the
towns and cities ensconced under the percept of Stallardism
(Africans should only be towns to minister to white labour
needs) after the 1923 Natives (Urban Areas) Act.

This tradition of inter-racial mediation became increasingly
sophisticated, as this study has pointed out. From the time of
the Joint Councils in the 1920s, the white liberals won over a
body of élite African opinion to the concept of racial harmony,
which Aggrey had likened to the black and white keys of a

piano. The political parameters of this approach became increasingly obfuscated as the discourse of positivist American race relations began to intrude from the late 1920s onwards. With the aid of American funding, the figure of C. T. Loram was crucial in establishing the Institute of Race Relations in 1929, and the concept of race relations became crucial in promulgating the idea of different races in South African society with inherently different interests which could best be resolved through a process of bargaining and mediation. Even the idea of some form of 'common society', as had underpinned the social settlement view of Frederick Bridgman in Johannesburg in the early 1920s and propagated by Ethelreda Lewis, became incompatible with this approach, and by the mid-1930s the main body of South African liberals looked, as did the government itself via the strategy of territorial segregation, to the rural reserves as the main repositories for African political and economic rejuvenation.

Given this basic ideological role of liberalism, in the unfolding of territorial segregation as political reality, the actual political role of liberalism by the 1930s narrowed considerably. Events both at home and abroad did a lot to shake liberal self-confidence, with the rise of fascism in Europe and the burgeoning of Afrikaner nationalism under the Broederbond and F.A.K.[4] World-wide individualist and metropolitan doctrines of liberalism were coming under challenge. The second world war acted as a further catalyst for forces that the liberals had hitherto been able to control. The growing pressure toward African unionisation in the late 1930s and the gradual reorganisation of the A.N.C. after A. B. Xuma became president in 1940, indicated the emergence of a democratic challenge to the élitism of the mainstream liberalism of the Joint Councils and Institute of Race Relations. The involvement of the liberal leadership with the system of African political representation established in 1936, was seen to compromise their ostensible opposition to segregation, or 'trusteeship' as it was increasingly becoming known. An indication of this trend was Rheinnalt-Jones' defeat for the senatorship representing the Africans in the Orange Free State and Transvaal in 1942 by the former Communist Hymie Basner on a democratic platform. The emergence, too, of the Congress Youth League and Africanist doctrines in the mid-1940s signalled a growing challenge to the liberal domination in African political thinking as the war came to an end.

Nevertheless, the democratic pressure from below in the 1940s did bring out some of the important political differences between the varying wings of South African liberalism. The more social-democratic wing had been led from the early 1930s by the Ballingers as they sought to maintain some of the old links with the liberal heartland in London. Aided by a small circle of English liberals concerned with African polics in the 1930s, the Ballingers' Friends of Africa organisation never looked like presenting any serious challenge to the Institute of Race Relations and its allies in the English-speaking universities and African colleges like Fort Hare, Lovedale and Adams. Its ties to the overseas metropolis were in many respects a colonial hangover, except that it coincided with a growing resurgance of political and moral criticism on the left in Britain towards British colonial policy in Africa. Furthermore it challenged the already insecure nature of the Johannesburg liberals' efforts to institutionalise a mainstream South African liberal tradition centred on the Witwatersrand.

The upsurge of political expectations engendered amongst the black population in South Africa during the second world war provided a fillip, therefore, to the political hopes of the left-liberals. The more limited horizons of the 1930s liberalism that had been so influenced by anthropology began to be overtaken by a more economically rooted analysis, exemplified by such works as Leo Marquard's *The Black Man's Burden* in 1943.[5] Through growing international influences, the South African liberal intelligentsia could be said to have become more cosmopolitan during the 1940s until, with the fissures of the Cold War and super-power rivalry putting paid to a more incisive economic analysis of South African class and racial divisions, the South African liberal intelligentsia could at last be said to have come of age. 'The rise of the intelligentsia,' Karl Mannheim wrote, 'marks the last phase of the growth of social consciousness.' Furthermore:

The intelligentsia was the last group to acquire the sociological point of view, for its position in the social division of labour does not provide direct access to any vital and functioning segment of society.

The secluded study and the dependence on printed matter afford only to derivative study view of the social process. No wonder that this stratum remained long unaware of the social character of change.[6]

Though directed at the European intelligentsia, Mannheim's remarks can be seen to apply to South Africa as well. The settler nature of South African society contributed to a mythical view of the past and the place of the white man in Africa. African societies were seen to lack history, and black people became pastoralised as part of a mythical African state of nature. In many respects this view spilled over into the first phase of serious social scientific study of South African society, through anthropology. While this discipline may be said to have contributed to the decline in the formal, governmental acceptance of biological racism, it reinforced the common perception of innate cultural African societies which were seen to be changing as they underwent a process of 'cultural contact' with the west. As William Macmillan remarked on this in the first edition of his book *Africa Emergent* in 1938, even the champions of African rights were reduced to a simple moral appeal as the 'culture contact' school avoided any incisive analysis of the political and economic conditions that both caused and explained this process.[7]

So the limitations and failures of South African liberalism cannot be completely explained in terms of the political limitation of the state system that was established in 1910. Such a view places liberals on a pedestal of righteous, but helpless, passivity which in real terms did not truly describe their behaviour.[8] As this study has argued, liberals from the time of their role in nineteenth-century Cape politics were very much involved in the politics of South Africa and, despite the failure to extend the Cape African franchise northwards with Union, still played an important part in the evolving policies of segregation in the years up to the Nationalists' triumph in 1948. Even the political defeat that that election entailed was not the end of the story, for in a number of respects the evolution of the apartheid ideology under Dr. Verwoerd and his Secretary of Native Affairs, Dr. W. W. M. Eiselen, in the 1950s grew out of some of the previous anthropological and economic analysis to which the liberals had contributed. 'Native Affairs has always impressed me as a Department of Development', wrote Dr.

Eiselen to Rheinnalt-Jones on becoming Secretary of Native Affairs in 1949, 'and I have on many occasions stressed the necessity of explaining its educational rather than its administrative functions.'[9]

The evolution of the apartheid doctrines indicated the double-edged nature of the new economic and sociological analysis that was increasingly influencing the behaviour of the South African State. Coming from backgrounds as professors of sociology and ethnology (Volkekunde) at the University of Stellenbosch, Verwoerd and Eiselen epitomised the receptiveness of the post-1948 Nationalist administration to a sociological analysis that had been in part developed by the liberals. While, in terms of political rhetoric, the ideological justification of apartheid to the white electorate was in terms of a Völkisch populism, the implementation of the doctrine owed far more to the previous administrative practice of adaptation and progressive modernisation of the control by chiefs of the reserves as the key instruments of social control.[10] Even on the ideological level, a continuity with the inter-war liberalism was maintained on the external plane as Dr. Strydom appointed the former chairman of the Native Economic Commission, John Holloway, as ambassador to Washington. Justifying apartheid as 'not a dogma but a policy', Holloway linked the doctrine to the developmentalist objectives of the 1930s and 1940s, for 'reforms ... have still to be introduced to make the Bantu survive at all in a civilised environment ... A totally improvident race will never become a civilised race.'[11]

The apartheid programme, therefore, owed far more to the previous development in administrative decentralisation and the build-up of chiefs on the British indirect rule model, than on a blind obeisance to a utopian cultural idealism which shaped the thinking of only the more fanatical of Afrikaner Nationalist supporters through such movements as the Ossewa Brandwag in the 1940s. The main features of the policy were the state nationalisation of many of the previous education and co-operative efforts which had been fostered under guidance from the liberal establishment. Government control of the chiefs was extended through the 1951 Bantu Authorities Act, and this was supplemented by a growing programme of ethnic education of chiefs and the creation of industrial loca-

tions in the reserves on the model of the Zwelitsha development
in the Ciskei, which had been begun under the Smuts government. Linking this to a wider strategy of 'rationalization of
labour' which could ensure 'its selective canalisation... into the
appropriate channels of occupation', Dr. Eiselen's scheme was
not substantially different from what many liberals had been
arguing for in the early 1940s.[12] On the basic premises of the
Betterment Areas Schemes in the reserves in the 1950s, many
liberals in the Institute of Race Relations such as Quintin
Whyte and Ellen Hellman, found themselves in substantial
agreement, criticising only the insufficient pace of the change.[13]
Margaret Ballinger, too, continued to argue right to the end of
her career as a Natives Representative in Parliament in 1960 the
case for both administrative decentralisation and the involvement of Africans in politics, first at the level of local councils,
before they could become 'full citizens' of the country.[14]

The political significance of the 1948 election, therefore,
detracts from a more fundamental consensus between both
Nationalists and liberals on the importance of development in
the African reserve and their guidance towards the essential
precepts of western civilisation. For this reason, the development of the Liberal Party after 1953 was only a somewhat tardy
and defensive reaction by liberals concerned with the political
consequences of the government's exclusive nationalism and
an attempt to try to revive as much as possible of the old Cape
liberal tradition's interest in the incorporation of at least the
educated African minorities into a single homogeneous State.
The parliamentary nature of the party indicated the continued
survival of a Whiggish belief in the political potential of Westminster-style constitutional systems, and this was reflected in
the protracted resistance put up by many liberals in the 1950s to
the removal of the Cape Coloured voters from the common
electoral roll. In an age, though, of the progressive devolution of
control by the big colonial powers to newly independent states
in Africa and Asia, constitutionalism was still an important
political creed which was not yet tarred by the failure of so many
of the Westminster-style constitutions in the 1960s.

The political break-point for South African liberalism, therefore, came at the end of the 1950s when the government's
Promotion of Bantu Self Government Act in 1959 indicated the

path of exclusive nationalism, and the Sharpeville shooting and the banning of the A.N.C. and P.A.C. the same year revealed the authoritarian political process that this nationalism would entail.[15] Consequently an essential moral pillar of South African liberalism began to crumble in the 1960s, as the stance of defending 'western civilisation' became untenable in a world being increasingly influenced by the non-western Afro-Asian bloc in the United Nations and other international organisations.

In one sense, this was the longer-term political fruition of an ideological hiatus in political thinking already visible in the early 1940s. In 1941, when Hoernle began pessimistically to apply a caste analysis to South Afican society in order to explain the failure of liberalism, thinking amongst liberals on the international plane was moving in the reverse direction. Whilst caste explanations for race relations had been much in vogue in the 1930s in the United States, the onset of war led to a liberal resurgence which received its most powerful affirmation in Gunnar Myrdal's survey, *An American Dilemma*, published in 1944. Here a different trajectory for race relations was pinpointed, as Myrdal argued that the dominant values within American society, which he termed 'the American creed', were likely to prevail over the minority values of Southern segregationism. The dominant values of the American creed were ultimately rooted in a 'humanistic liberalism' which, in a world where America was increasingly likely to exert global power, were strongly associated with American nationalism and the belief in manifest destiny.[16] More importantly, the values could be strongly reinforced through the legal system which Myrdal did not see as a passive instrument simply reflecting the conservative 'folkways', as some sociologists had argued since the time of William Graham Sumner, but as a powerful force to restructure American race relations in conformity with the dominant values of the American creed.[17]

The optimism of Myrdal's analysis could be said both to reflect, and in turn shape, a new mood in American race relations by the end of the second world war. It contributed to a faith in the legal process which ultimately led to the 1954 Supreme Court decision in Brown v. Board of Education outlawing segregation in education.[18] However, for South African liberals the reverse could be said to be taking place in the post-war era, especially with the entrenchment of apartheid in the 1950s. After the government's willingness to pack the Senate with its own supporters in order to alter the South African constitution and remove the Cape coloured voters from the Common Roll, a new situation occurred to which the American pattern could no longer apply. By 1959, Alan Paton reflected this new awareness amongst South African liberals after a period in the 1950s when a strong faith had been put in the ability of inexorable economic growth to liberalise the political system.[19] In a lecture organised by Christian Action in London, Paton appealed to the consciences of Christians to recognise that 'racial discrimination of dominance cannot be fought with the weapons that are readily available in a democratic country. Racial discrimination is practised in the United States, but in that country there are legal means of fighting it. In South Africa there are no such means.' This appeared to justify, Paton argued, the boycott which was a legitimate weapon when no other was available.[20]

Paton's appeal marked a new mood of militancy amongst Christian organisationsinternationally against racist political practice in southern Africa, that led, in the wake of the Second Vatican Council of 1962–65 and the papal encyclical *Populorum Progressio* in 1967, to the establishment in 1968 of the World Council of Churches' Programme to Combat Racism.[21] While the mainstream of South African liberalism appeared to be more and more out of touch with these developments, an important internal response was generated through the Christian Institute, which was established in 1960 after the World Council of Churches met in consultation with the South African Council of Churches at Cottesloe near Johannesburg.[22] A key figure from the Nederduitse Gereformeerde Kerk (N.G.K.), Dr. Beyers Naude, was appointed director of the Institute which began to eclipse in the late 1960s the empirical analysis of bodies like the Institute of Race Relations. The Study Project on Christianity in Apartheid Society (SPRO-CAS) led to six commissions being established to analyse the effects of apartheid in the different aspects of South African life. Politically, the C.I. began to move towards a more committed radical liberalism which involved a shift in both economic as well as political resources from the entrenched white ruling class to the black majority within a federal political structure.[23] While not overtly Marxist, the position of the commission recalled the stance of the more social-democratic liberals around the Friends of Africa in the 1930s and the platform of Hymie Basner and Stam Khan in the 1940s against the conservatism of the Institute of Race Relations.

Furthermore, with the winding up of SPRO-CAS in 1973, the C.I. moved in the direction of recognising that the central area of political initiative had to come from blacks and not whites. As 'Black Consciousness' began to surface in the 1970s to fill the political vacuum left by the banning of the A.N.C. and P.A.C. in 1960 a new generation of black political militants emerged through the ethnically segregated system of higher education instituted by the government in the 'bush universities' or tribal colleges in the homelands. This Black Consciousness scorned the efforts of white liberals to try to intervene in black politics; indeed, it was whites who were now seen as the 'problem', in contradistinction to the old 'race relations' philosophy of isolating African society and culture as the focal area for analysis of the 'native problem', as it had been so often called. It scorned, too, the homelands leaderships and the pretensions of Gatsha Buthelezi's Inkatha movement in Kwazulu to speak for the African majority; as a former student of Fort Hare, he was seen as a successor to the former client African politicians who had thrown in their lot with the white liberals in the pre-Sharpeville era.[24]

While Black Consciousness represented an important development in ideological form, it did not necessarily represent a complete break with the previous tradition of ideological liberalism in African nationalism. The degree to which South African liberalism was able to mould this nationalism into an effective ideological offshoot of itself, has been a question outside the main focus of this study and demands considerable further research. The relationship, though, appears never to have been automatic, reflecting to a considerable degree the political vagaries of the African petty bourgeois political leadership. There was undoubtedy an important traditon of attachment to liberal political ideas in the era before the banning of the A.N.C., reflected in the ideas of such figures as Z. K.

Matthews, Albert Luthuli and James Calata, and this tradition had sufficiently strong roots to survive throughout the 1950s during the growth of the A.N.C.'s popular base and the increasing attachment of liberation struggle strategies derived from such revolutionary precedents as Communist China. Even after the banning of the A.N.C., the move to armed struggle entailed some agonising debate: the original strategy of the underground movement Umkhonto we Size (Spear of the Nation) was one of sabotage that did not involve the unnecessary taking of lives. Thus, in many ways Black Consciousness represented the demonstration of black psychological reassertion in the early 1970s after a long period of political oppression, though its exact political demands did not necessarily imply the revolutionary overthrow of the State, which Black Consciousness activists continued to deny in several spectacular court trials. Indeed, even some of the old patron-client ties were in some respects reforged, with Steve Biko seeking the support of the editor of the *East London Daily Dispatch*, Donald Woods, who had a record of fairly benign liberalism on the issue of black economic and political demands.

Steve Biko, however, died in jail in Pretoria in 1977 and the Christian Institute was banned, and the further entrenchment of South African state power nullified what little credibility liberals still had in the political process. The Liberal Party itself had voluntarily gone into liquidation in 1968, following the passing of the Prohibition of Improper Interference Act which forbade political parties to have multi-racial memberships. Thus the more hard core of liberal activists became either politically silent or went into exile. With no coherent political base left, the rhetoric of liberalism increasingly took on the mantle of a charade, full of sound and fury but signifying very little. The classic example of this lay in one of the bastions of the old liberalism, that of the English universities. Since the Extension of University Education Act in 1959, these universities, especially the University of the Witwatersrand and the University of Cape Town, had been prevented from admitting black students, and as a consequence a triennial public lecture — The Chancellor's Lecture — was arranged as a form of protest, along with a plaque asserting the universities' commitment to academic freedom and the restoration of its right to admit students on a non-racial basis, though prior to 1959 only a small number of black students had gained such admittance. The protest was in many respects a good example of the ritualised nature of liberal political opposition to apartheid, and came to be seen increasingly by the more radical section of the students as a fossilised and ineffective way to combat the government strategy of racial compartmentalisation.

In the parliamentary sphere, however, liberal rhetoric continued to be mouthed by the sole representative of the Progressive Party in the House of Assembly during the 1960s, Helen Suzman. In many respects, Mrs Suzman took on some of the trappings of the African representative M.P.s, such as Margaret Ballinger, who were finally excluded from the House in 1960. Eventually the Progressive Party merged with elements of the old United Party to form the Progressive Federal Party, under the leadership of Professor Van Zyl Slabbert, which came to form the offical opposition to the National Party with some twenty-six M.P.s. The party sought a grand constitutional convention to thrash out a new political system based upon multi-ethnic political representation. On economic matters, however, the issue of common ownership of the resources of the country appears to have been fudged, and the party is hostile to the idea, for example, of some nationalisation of the mines and agricultural land; this was one of the objectives of the Freedom Charter signed by the A.N.C. and the more left-wing Congress of Democrats at Kliptown in 1955 at the Congress of the People.

The successors of the economic liberals in the 1940s looked increasingly less, however, to the parliamentary process, as the United Party declined as a credible political force, than to alternative mechanisms of political influence. The emergence of a *Verligte* or 'enlightened' wing of the National Party in the 1970s led to a new political alliance being formed between the élite of the English- speaking industrialists, led by Harry Oppenheimer of Anglo-American, and the new Afrikaner bourgeoisie represented by a figure like Anton Rupert of Rembrandt Tobacco. Though not leading to any extensive realignment of the National Party's parliamentary base, this movement represented a vaguely liberal pressure group for the amelioration of the apartheid in urban areas, the establishment of a black middle class and the relaxation of influx control for urban blacks. In the wake of the 1976 riots, it led to the establishment of the Urban Foundation and greater private initiative in the channelling of funds to help to create a black petty bourgeoisie.[26]

In contrast to such limited economic attempts that lacked any coherent political vision beyond the amelioration of separate development, the truer successors of the liberal tradition could be said to have either gone into exile or lapsed into silence. However, in the realm of literature (perhaps in some ways a substitute for political action in a society like South Africa), Nadine Gordimer has depicted the anxieties and helplessness of the white liberal intelligentsia in contemporary South Africa. In successive novels since *The Conservationist* in 1974, she has undermined one of the last bastions of the liberal world view in South African society. The assumptions of the conventional liberal novel of individual meliorism and character development are seen as false in a society like South Africa. Moving in the direction of post-modernism, she has turned the pastoral myth of white settlement back upon itself; now, in contradistinction to Haggard and Buchan, white settler society stands as rootless and divested of any real moral authority in a landscape that becomes identified with the folk traditions of the African majority. Returning out of the pastoral wilderness that the segregationist racism of the whites have put them in, the Africans are depicted as the true owners of the land of South Africa.[27] Liberal politics are seen as hopeless since, in the case of the most recent novel, *July's People*,[28] the future revolution within South Africa entails a transformation in the power relationships that underpin the relation between black and white. As the former white masters become increasingly beholden to their former servants in such a situation of radical structural change, the static and ahistorical view of the traditional liberal view of race relations becomes exposed. Liberalism, it can be concluded, remains a colonial importation and is unlikely, at least in the immediate future, to reproduce itself in a post-colonial situation of black majority rule. The best it can hope for is some form of compromise from a position of weakness with the forces of black nationalism.

The alternative task of seeking to use the ethnically defined black 'homelands' as political bases might produce some short-term benefits, but risks sacrificing everything should the policy come unstuck.

NOTES

Introduction

1 Stanley Trapido, '"The Friends of the natives": merchants, peasants and the political and ideological structure of Liberalism in the Cape, 1854–1910', in Shula Marks and Anthony Atmore (eds.), *Economy and Society in Pre-Industrial South Africa* (London, 1980), pp. 247–74.

2 *Ibid.*, p. 268; Colin Bundy, *The Rise and Fall of the South African Peasantry* (London, 1979), pp. 134–40.

3 'Vindex', *Cecil Rhodes: His Political Life and Speeches* (London, 1900), p. 371.

4 *Ibid.*, p. 372.

5 William Charles Scully, *The Native Question* (Lovedale, 1894), p. 2.

6 A further important component of this was the development of African Church separatism — commonly known in white settler society as 'Ethiopianism' — in the 1890s and early 1900s that fostered a growing sense of white racial solidarity. The phenomenon was to receive a popular treatment in novel form in John Buchan's *Prester John* in 1910.

7 George M. Fredrickson, *White Supremacy: A Comparative Study in American and South African History* (New York, Oxford, 1981), pp. 239–92.

8 *Ibid.*, p. 253; Jack Temple Kirby, *Darkness and the Dawning* (Philadelphia, 1972), pp. 119–54.

9 *Ibid.*, p. 117.

10 F. H. Matthews, 'The Revolt against Americanism: Cultural Pluralism and Cultural Relativism as an Ideology of Liberation', *The Canadian Review of American Studies*, 1 (1970), 4–31.

11 See pp. 66–69 ins. – Alfred Hoernle & Cultural Idealism).

12 R. W. Rose-Innes, *The Glen Grey Act and the Native Question* (Lovedale, 1903), p. 33. Copies of this paper were supplied to the South African Native Affairs Commission. Bundy has seen this paper as 'representative of the authentic voice of turn of the century liberalism in the Cape', op. cit., p. 139. See also Phyllis

Lewsen, 'Cape Liberalism in its Terminal Phase', African Studies Seminar Paper, University of the Witwatersrand, September 1980, which also sees turn-of-the-century Cape liberals moving towards segregation.

13 See in particular Shula Marks and Stanley Trapido, 'Lord Milner and the South African State', *History Workshop*, No. 8 (1979), 50–80.

14 Howard Pim, *Some Aspects of the Native Problem* (Johannesburg, 1905), p. 37.

15 For the origins of apartheid theory see W. A. de Klerk, *Puritans in Africa* (Harmondsworth, 1976), pp. 217–22.

16 William Empson, *Some Versions of Pastoral* (London, 1963), p. 22.

17 See for example, H. Alan C. Cairns, *Prelude to Imperialism: British Reactions to Central African Society, 1840–1890* (London, 1965), for the evolution of this colonial view of African societies and the rural African terrain in the nineteenth century.

18 F. W. Bell, *The Native as a Political Factor and the Native Franchise*, paper read to the Transvaal Native Affairs Society, 5 Dec. 1908, pp. 4–5.

19 F. W. Bell, *The South African Native Problem* (Johannesburg, 1909), p. 13.

20 For a study of the Act see Paul B. Rich, 'Ministering to the White Man's Needs: The Development of Urban Segregation in South Africa, 1913–1923', *African Studies*, XXXVII, 2 (1978), 177–91.

21 See pp. 114–19

22 Martin Legassick, 'Liberalism, Social Control and Liberation in South Africa', (unpublished paper, University of Warwick, 1977).

23 See for example, John Roach, 'Liberalism and the Victorian Intelligentsia', *The Cambridge Historical Journal*, XIII (1957), 58–81.

Chapter One

1 ABM F. B. Bridgman to H.Q., 24 Jan. 1913.

2 *Ibid.*, F. B. Bridgman to H.Q., 3 May 1912.

3 *Report of the Population Census 1921*, UG 37–'24, p. 244

4 Philip Bonner, 'The Transvaal Native Congress, 1917–1920' in Shula Marks and Richard Rathbone (eds.) *Industrialisation and Social Change in South Africa* (London, 1982), pp. 270–313.

5 ABM, F. B. Bridgman, *Annual Report*, June 1917; F. B. Bridgman to H.Q., 27 Sept. 1917.

6 Bonner *op. cit.*, pp. 305–6.

7 For a study of the relationship between this proletarianisation on the Witwatersrand and the emergence of the slumyard culture of Marabi, see David Coplan, 'African working class culture in Town and Country in South Africa, 1870–1930: Some Research Perspectives', paper presented to the conference, Class Formation, Culture and Consciousness; the Making of Modern South

Africa, University of London, Jan. 1980; Eddie Koch, 'Without Visible Means of Subsistence: Slumyard Culture in Johannesburg, 1918–1940', History Workshop Paper, University of the Witwatersrand, Feb. 1981. See also Ellen Hellman, *Rooiyard: A Sociological Survey of a Native Slum* (Manchester, 1948).

8   These social settlements appeared in Chicago and New York in the 1890s after the wave of immigration from eastern and southern Europe, and 'went beyond traditional humanitarianism in two respects: in wanting to work with the people of the slums as well as for them, and in wanting to learn from them as well as teach them', John Higham, *Strangers in the Land: Patterns of American Nativism, 1860–1925* (New York, 1978), p. 119.

9   ABM F. B. Bridgman, *Annual Report*, June 1917.

10 Ray Phillips, *The Bantu Are Coming* (London, 1930), p. 148; see also Martin Legassick, 'Frederick Bridgman, James Dexter Taylor and Ray Phillips, American Missionaries: The Urban Mission and Social Control' (unpublished paper, University of Warwick, n.d.).

11 ABM, F. B. Bridgman, *Annual Report*, June 1919; for a more detailed study of the club as part of a new-Victorian strategy of 'moral upliftment' of African female domestic servants, see Deborah Gaitskell, 'Christian Compounds for Girls: Church Hostels for African Women in Johannesburg, 1907–1970', *Journal of Southern African Studies*, V. 1 (1979), pp. 44–69.

12 Gaitskell *op. cit.*

13 For the development of this class see Charles Van Onselen, 'The Witches of Suburbia: Domestic Servants on the Witwatersrand, 1890–1914', History Workshop Paper, University of the Witwatersrand, Feb. 1978.

14 Phillips, *op. cit.*, p. 118; R. V. Selope Thema, *Autobiography*, unpublished ms. in School of Oriental and African Studies, p. 100

15 Phillips, *op. cit.*, p. 116

16 Selope Thema, *op. cit.*, p. 100

17 Selby Msimang, *Autobiography*, published ms. in School of Oriental and African Studies, p. 108

18 *Abantu Batho*, Feb. 1920, p. 3; Selope Thema, *op. cit.*, pp. 74, 78.

19 *Ibid.*

20 Address by Mr. Jas Henderson, Prinicipal of Lovedale College (Under the auspices of the Society of Friends) in the common room of the Johannesburg YMCA on Saturday 19 April 1919, in Howard Pim Papers.

21 ARTCM 1925/113 Misc. Extract from minutes of the Gold Producers Committee, 18 May 1925.

22 Interview with T. D. Mweli Skota, Pimville, Soweto, 17 June 1975.

23 ABM, F. B. Bridgman to H.Q., 28 June 1920.

24 *The Star* 26 November 1920; ABM, F. B. Bridgman to H.Q., 28 June 1920.

140   *White power and the liberal conscience*

25 *ABM*, Zulu Branch, Annual Letter, July 1919-July 1920; F. B. Bridgman to H.Q., 21 Sept. 1920.
26 The Bantu Men's Social Centre, *Report for 1927*, (Johannesburg, 1927) pp. 2–3.
27 C. T. Loram, 'The Separatist Church Movement', *International Review of Missions*, July 1926, p. 480.
28 Richard D. Heyman, 'C. T. Loram: A South African Liberal in Race Relations', *The International Journal of African Historical Studies*, V11 (1975), p. 41; Martin Legassick, 'C. T. Loram and South African "native policy", 1920–1929', (unpublished ms., University of Warwick, n.d.).
29 S. M. Molema, *The Bantu Past and Present* (Edinburgh, 1920), p. 366; the significance of Molema's book can be seen to lie in its raising doubts about Smuts' whole notion of a white *mission civilast rice* in Africa based on his essentially cultural idealism. At the same time, by questioning the values of British liberalism, it also doubted the assimilationist ideals of so many African political leaders up to that time, who sought a meliorist and modernisationist programme based on the British model. See John David Shingler, 'Education and Political Order in South Africa, 1902–1961' (Ph. D. Thesis, Yale University, 1973), pp. 22–9; see also D. D. T. Jabavu, *The Black Problem* (Lovedale, 1920), p. 1.
30 *Ibid.*, p. 351
31 Legassick, 'C. T. Loram', *op. cit*, p. 11.
32 For an analysis of this educational programme see Kenneth King, *Pan-Africanism and Education* (Oxford, 1971), p. 97; Shingler, *op. cit.*, pp. 200–2.
33 *Ibid.*, pp. 27–8; see also C. T. Loram, 'The Phelps-Stokes Education Commission in South Africa', *International Review of Missions*, (1921), pp. 496–508.
34 William M. Macartney, *Dr. Aggrey: Ambassador for Africa* (London, 1949), p. 74; Edwin W. Smith, *Aggrey of Africa* (London, 1929), p. 121; 1921 was the year that followed the great Convention of the Universal Negro Improvement Association in Madison Square Garden in New York and was the period when Garvey was making strenuous efforts to spread the movement overseas by touring Central America, Cuba and Jamaica. The second Convention in 1921 was not as successful as the first, though Garvey was not actually arrested until January 1922, on charges of defrauding the mails.
35 Francis Schimleck, *Against the Stream: Life of B. Huss, Principal of St. Francis College, Mariannhill* (Mariannhill, 1949), pp. 61–2.
36 *The Christian Express*, 1 June 1921; Aggrey described Lovedale as 'the Hampton of Africa', Smith, *op. cit.*, p. 168.
37 Quoted Smith, *op. cit.*, p. 175; see also Edgar Brookes, *A South African Pilgrimage* (Johannesburg, 1977), p. 29.
38 Selope Thema, op. cit., p. 101.

39 Michael Twaddle, 'The Politician as Agitator in Eastern Uganda' in W. H. Morris-Jones (ed.), *The Making of Politicians: Studies from Africa and Asia* (London, 1976), pp. 78–92.

40 W. H. Morris-Jones, ('Introduction' in *ibid.*, pp. 12–16; for a similar distinction between the 'agitator' in times of crisis and the 'conciliator' in intervening periods see Harold Lasswell, *Politics: Who Get What, When How* (New York, 1958), p. 177. A similar argument regarding African support for the Joint Councils is presented by Baruch Hirson, 'Tuskegee, the Joint Councils, and the All African Convention', London, I.C.S. mimeo, 1979, pp. 6–7.

41 Selby Msimang, *op. cit.*, p. 110.

42 *Ibid.*

43 *Ibid.*, pp. 113–4; *Umteteli wa Bantu*, 13 Sept. 1924.

44 Brian Willan, 'Sol Plaatje, De Beers and an Old Tram Shed: Class Relations and Social Control in a South African Town', *Journal of Southern African Studies*, IV (1978), pp. 195–215.

45 ARTCM 1920/54 'C.W.L.', Memorandum for members of board of management, 1 March 1920.

46 Howard Pim Papers, Box 2 Native Affairs 1905–1934, P. A. Gazana to The Gen. Manager, The N.R.C., 21 Oct. 1921, encl. in P.A. Gazana to H. Pim, 21 Oct. 1921.

47 C. van Onselen, 'The Role of Collaborators in the Rhodesian Mining Industry, 1900–1935', *African Affairs*, 72, (1973), pp. 401–18.

48 Selope Thema, *op. cit.*, p. 103.

49 Minutes of a Meeting of the Executive of the Johannesburg Joint Council of Europeans and Natives, 8 Aug. 1924.

50 *Umteteli wa Bantu*, 5 June 1926.

51 Alfred Xuma, *Charlotte Maxeke — 'What an Educated African Girl can do'* (Johannesburg, 1930), p. 16.

52 *Ibid.*, p. 17. The question of the wages of min clerks was a sensitive one politically, as Margaret Maxeke's husband had worked out a minimum expenditure for the 'ordinary native' in Nancefield of less than £7 a month. As a consequence, the Joint Council sought to approach the Native Recruiting Corporation to get it to enforce on individual mines a minimum wage level which the N.R.C. had advised mine managers to introduce from 1 November 1920. These levels raised the minimum pay from £7 10s to £9 for Chief Native Clerks and from £7 10s to £10 a month for indunas. Joint Council of Europeans and Natives, Report of Wages Committee, n.d.

53 J. B. M. Hertzog Papers, A32 Box 35, Ray Phillips to Hertzog 18 Jan. 1925. J. W. Horton has argued that Rheinnalt-Jones was the main figure behind the deputation to Hertzog, though he has presented no evidence to support this; in J. W. Horton, 'South Africa's Joint Councils: Black–White Co-operation between the two world wars', *South African Historical Journal*, No. 4 (1972),

p. 33. The government's introduction of women's night passes was short-lived, however, since the following year the courts threw them out. The measure was brought back again via the 1930 Amendment to the 1923 Natives (Urban Areas) Act.

54 Minutes of a Meeting of the Executive Committee of the Johannesburg Joint Council held in Mr. Pim's Office, 9 February 1925; Minutes of a Meeting of the Joint Council held in the Exploration Buildings on 16 March 1925 incl. report on two conferences of 14 Feb. and 7 March.

55 *Imvo* 17 Feb. 1925; in the event the goverment introduced night passes from 1 June 1925, *Hertzog Papers*, minute dated 2 June 1925.

56 For a study of this process in Bulawayo see Stephen Thornton, 'The Struggle for Profit and Participation by an emerging African Petty Bourgeoisie in Bulawayo: 1895–1933', Londo, I.C.S. mimeo, 1978.

57 Interview with Selby Msimang.

58 Selby Msimang, *op. cit.*, pp. 41–3.

59 *Umteteli wa Bantu*, 3 and 17 Nov. 1923.

60 Shingler, *op, cit.*, p. 17.

61 *The Star*, 1 Dec. 1924; A. B. Xuma, unpublished Autobiography, in *Xuma Papers*, p. 28. Xuma to H. Pim, 17 April 1930, asking for information on the S.A.I.R.R.

62 Legassick, 'C. T. Loram', *op. cit.*

63 C. T. Loram, 'Introduction' to *European and Bantu: Papers and Addresses given at the Conference on Native Affairs, held under the auspices of the Federal Council of the Dutch Reformed Church*, 27th and 29th Sept. 1923 (Johannesburg, 1923), p. 5

64 ArSAIRR, Pol. Educ. file No. 1, C. T. Loram to J. D. Rheinnal-Jones, 22 Sept. 1926; Rheinnalt-Jones drew up a draft constitution for a Federation of Joint Councils in 1923, MSS Brit. Emp. S22 G194, J. D. Rheinnalt-Jones to J. H. Harris, 25 Jan. 1923.

65 Edgar Brookes, *RJ*, Johannesburg, S.A.I.R.R., 1954, p. 6.

66 ARSAIRR B3 (e), J. D. Rheinnalt-Jones to Archbishop Owen, 20 Feb. 1928.

67 *Ibid.*, J. D. Rheinnalt-Jones to M. Alexander, 5 March 1928. The previous year Rheinnalt-Jones had suggested in Cape Town the formation of a federal body 'to gather together Native and European opinion in South Africa on native matters', MSS Brit. Emp. S22 G194, J. D. Rheinnalt-Jones to J. H. Harris, 25 June 1927.

68 Howard Pim Papers, H. Burton to H. Pim, 29 April 1928; J. W. Jagger to H. Pim, 27 Oct. 1927; ArSAIRR B72 (b), C. P. Crewe to H. Pim, 21 Feb. 1929. For the political development of the South African Party in this period see R. J. Bouch, 'The South African Party in Opposition, 1924–1929', (B.A. (Hons.) Disertation, University of the Witwatersrand, 1972).

69 *National European Bantu Conference*, Cape Town, 6–9 February 1929, Open Address by the Chairman, Howard Pim (Lovedale, 1929), p. 3.
70 ArSAIRR B79 (a), H. Pim to J. D. Rheinnalt-Jones 18 Feb. 1929.
71 *Imvo* 2 April 1929; ArSAIRR B79 (i), H. Burton to J. D. Rheinnalt-Jones 13 March 1929. The Non Racial Franchise Association was formally established early in April and some 55–60 names of prominent Cape liberals were associated with it. The committee included J. W. Jagger, Professor Freemantle and Sir James Rose-Innes who had left the bench in 1927 and was the dominant personality in the association. See B. K. Long Papers MS 6720, James Rose-Innes to H. Pim, 19 April 1929.
72 ArSAIRR B72 (f), H. Burton to H. Pim, 3 July 1929.
73 ArSAIRR B97 (3), Memorandum marked 'private and confidential' for special Committee on Carnegie and Phelps-Stokes Funds formed to meet in Howard Pim's Office, Exploration Buildings, Johannesburg, 9 May 1929; Brookes, *RJ*, p.7; Horton *op. cit.*, p. 36.
74 This approach also implied an increasing intervention into Joint Countil politics in order to bring them under the controlling influence of the Institute, Howard Pim Papers, 'Notes by R-J given by Stella Jones', 25 Sept. 1930; Horton *op. cit.*, p. 37.
75 Gilbert Murray Papers, MS 378, E. Lewis to G. Murray, 30 April 1928 encl. text of speech 'The Church and Race Relations: Address to the Church Synod in Johannesburg, 8 May 1926', p. 9.
76 *Ibid.*, C. T. Loram to E. Lewis, 8 Feb. 1928; William Ballinger Papers A410/CT, E. Lewis to the Lord Bishop of Zululand, 20 May 1927.
77 For an account of this see P. L. Wickens, *The Industrial and Commercial Workers Union* (Cape Town, 1977), esp. chap. 11.
78 G.M. Pap MS 378, Sir Willoughby Dickinson to E. Lewis, 9 April 1928.

Chapter Two

1 Edgar Brookes, *The History of Native Policy in South Africa*, Pretoria, 1927. Brookes's thesis was a firm apology for segregation dressed up in a historical garb derived from a reading of J. R. Seeley's *Introduction to Political Science*. This proved too much for English-speaking publishers in South Africa, so Brookes turned to General Hertzog for assistance with the publication. This came at an opportune time for Hertzog with the 1924 election pending, since an English-speaking apology for his own conception of segregation would be politically useful. 'If they had followed the draft bill of 1912,' Hertzog wrote to Brookes, 'with its suggestions for reserved areas — suggested by you as neutral areas — your indictment of the Act of 1913 would never have been necessary', Hertzog Papers, A32 Box 35, J. B. M. Hertzog to E. Brookes, 23 March 1924. As a consequence the book was first

published in 1924, and Hertzog was able to use it throughout 1925 while the debate on segregation ensued in the Pact government. Copies were despatched to party members in both the Labour and Nationalist parties and the reaction was probably typified by T. Boydell, the Minister of Labour, who considered it 'the standard work on the native question in South Africa', *ibid,* T. Boydell to J. Hertzog, 27 Feb. 1925. Throughout 1924 Brookes supported Hertzog in the election campaign; see *Rand Daily Mail,* 10 May 1924 and Edgar H. Brookes, 'Native Affairs — A Constructional National Policy', *The South African Quarterly,* 3 May 1924.

2 In November 1925 Hertzog outlined government segregation policy in a speech at Smithfield, which sought the removal of Cape African voters from the common roll and their replacement by seven representatives in the House of Assembly and a Union National Council. At the same time, he re-emphasised the government interest in fostering communal, as opposed to individual, tenure in the reserves so that 'within all Native areas the Native is trained and encouraged to be as much as possible self reliant, to make those areas as attractive as possible for himself, and also to govern himself as far as possible'; *The Star,* 15 Nov. 1925. However, the idea of parliamentary representatives for black voters met opposition: *The Star,* 11 Nov. 1925.

3 ArSAIRR B72 (2), E. Brookes to Steyn, 20 Oct. 1925, enclosing 'Memorandum Embodying Certain Suggestions on the Four Native Bills'. 'As the Act now stands', Brookes argued, 'the qualified Cape voter not only loses his parliamentary franchise, but does not exercise a direct vote for members of his own council', p. 1. 'Towards a Native Policy', *Cape Times,* 4 July 1925.

4 Edgar Brookes, *A South African Pilgrimage* (Johannesburg, 1977), p. 35. Brookes was especially influenced by a book that appeared in the United States by Alan Wolfe, *The New Negro, The Cape Times,* 11 Feb. 1929. Even before he left for America, though, it is clear that Brookes was increasingly aware of the political challenge posed by African radicalism. In 1925 he argued for increased political representation for Africans, since 'in conversation with a group of advanced and rather "agitator" natives the other day, I was spontaneously and unanimously assured that were the concesstion granted that they might be represented in the House by men of their own colour, all opposition would be dropped and nothing else asked for'; 'Memorandum embodying certain suggestions', p. 5. See, especially, Edgar Brookes, *Native Education in South Africa* (Pretoria, 1930) for the idea that 'industrially the only hope of "South Africa lies in the civilisation of the Native proletariate', p. 15.

5 After beginning his association with the Institute in 1930, Brookes moved to a position of defending 'the old Cape policy' and aligning with Smuts' S.A.P. In 1931 he sought the S.A.P.

candidacy for Woodstock in Cape Town, though without success; James Rose-Innes Papers 789, E. Brookes to J. Rose-Innes, 16 Aug. 1931. Brookes concentrated most of his political energies, therefore, into working for the Institute in 1932–33, especially organising a fund-raising campaign. His move towards an increasingly fervent Christian belief, though, alienated figures like C. T. Loram, and in 1934 he ceased work for the Institute to become principal of Adams College in Natal.

6 Margaret Ballinger Diary, BC 345, King Williamstown, 1929.

7 J. Rose-Innes Papers, 766, H. Pim to J. Rose-Innes, 1 Jan. 1930.

8 Eric Walker's pamphlet appeared in 1930, *The Frontier Tradition in South Africa: a lecture delivered at Rhodes House on 5th March 1930* (Oxford, 1930). The lecture seems to have made quite an impression upon William Ballinger at a time when he was beginning to formulate some of his ideas on South African industrialisation. 'I quite agree with you', Walker wrote to Ballinger, 'about the influences of the sudden rush of Big capital into South Africa in the nineties, but I… think… that it is still the principle [*sic*] factor (i.e. the frontier tradition). It has been longest in the field and it provided the atmosphere in which other and later factors have been able to flourish', William Ballinger Papers BC 347 F3 II 1.12, Eric Walker to W. Ballinger, 28 Nov. 1930.

9 William Ballinger Papers, BC 347 DI 1.1.2, W. Ballinger to W. Holtby, 10 April 1928.

10 *Ibid.*, F31.5.1., W. G. Ballinger to A. Creech Jones, 30 Jan. 1929.

11 William Ballinger Papers BC 347 A5 iV 3 I.C. 5., I.C.U. of Africa, *Administrative Report*, 20 June 1929.

12 *The South African Outlook* May 1929. In August 1929 Kadalie claimed that his organisation had spent £1,000 on land purchase. P. L. Wickens, *The Industrial and Commercial Workers Union* (Cape Town, 1978), p. 181.

13 I.C.U. *Administrative Report*, 20 June 1929. The originator of the scheme was apparently, according to Wickens, a Johannesburg lawyer, Peter Morris, who was the I.C.U.'s legal adviser in 1929 and was to put up £2,000 and to make his profit from the transfer fee which would be £22 on each sale, Wickens, *op. cit.*, pp. 180–1.

14 Peter Walshe, *The Rise of African Nationalism in South Africa* (London, 1970), pp. 213–15, 230–1.

15 See, for example, William Ballinger's report to the secretary, chairman and delegates, I.C.U. of Africa Conference, Heilbron, O.F.S., 14–16 June 1932, William Ballinger Papers, BC 346 A5 V 4. 23.

16 William Ballinger Papers, BC 347 F3 I.5.I., W. G. Ballinger to A. Creech Jones, 30 Jan. 1929.

17 William Ballinger Papers, BC 347 DI I 3.I.5., W. Holtby to W. G. Ballinger, 11 Aug. 1930. Part of the committee's concern was the organisation of hospitality for Africans visiting London. This was organised by Livy-Noble who had already gained such experience

from the Bantu Men's Social Centre; W. Holtby to W. B. Ballinger, 30 Aug. 1930.

18 It was as a result of a Conference on the Colour Bar in Great Britain, organised by the Society of Friends in 1929, that a Joint Council to Promote Understanding between White and Coloured People in Great Britain was established in 1931 with John Fletcher as the convenor. Winifred Holtby was one of the committee members. However, the Joint Council failed to gather the same degree of interest as its South African namesakes, and was superseded by 1934 by the League of Coloured Peoples, organised by Dr. Harold Moody. This was described as 'the first conscious and deliberate attempt to form a multi-racial organisation led by Blacks' in Britain. Roderick J. MacDonald, 'Dr Harold Arundel Moody and the League of Coloured Peoples, 1931–1947: A Retrospective View, *Race*, XIV (1973), pp. 291–310.

19 Winifred Holtby, *Mandoa Mandoa* (London, 1933). The radical character in the novel, Rollett, was based on Leys. See also Diana Wylie, 'Norman Leys and McGregor Ross: A Case Study in the Conscience of African Empire, 1900-39', *The Journal of Imperial and Commonwealth History*, V (1977), pp. 294–309. Vera Brittain, *Testament of Friendship* (London, 1980), describes Winifred Holtby's contacts with South Africa.

20 Stephen Constantine, 'The Formation of British Policy on Colonial Development, 1914–1929' (Ph. D. Thesis, University of Oxford), p. 2 and *passim*; David Meredith, 'The British Government and Colonial Economic Policy, 1919–39', *The Economic History Review*, XXVIII (1975), pp. 484–99.

21 Constantine, *op. cit.*, p. 6.

22 Martin Chanock, *Unconsummated Union: Britian, Rhodesia and South Africa, 1900–1945* (Manchester, 1977), pp. 251–3. This argues against the more orthodox historical view represented by Ronald Hyam, that British interests were defined mainly by a moral concern to promote the trusteeship conception. 'South Africa's expansion was self interested', he has argued, 'Imperial Britain was concerned about trusteeship'. Ronald Hyam, *The Failure of South African Expansion, 1908–1948* (London, 1972), p. 22.

23 Chanock, *op. cit.*, pp. 251–2.

24 'Trusteeship' was felt by reformers like Leys and Ross to be sufficiently vague both to justify the status quo and to rally the reformers around a platform of change; Wylie, *op. cit.*, p. 307.

25 Quoted in Chanock, *op. cit.*, p. 253.

26 Sidney Olivier, *The Anatomy of South African Misery* (London, 1927). Leonard Barnes, *Caliban in Africa* (London, 1930). Leonard Barnes, *The New Boer War* (London, 1932). Martin Chanock has argued that these books 'helped to build up the body of public opinion which acted as a brake on how far Britain could go in co-operation with the Union', Chanock, *op. cit.*, p. 201

27 Cmd. 4114 (H.M.S.O., 1932), *Financial and economic situation of Swaziland;* Cmd. 4368 (H.M.S.O., 1933) *Financial and economic position of the Bechuanaland Protectorate;* Cmd. 4907 (H.M.S.O., 1935) *Financial and economic postion of Basutoland.* Alan Pim went on to develop a more sophisticated conception of the mutualtiy of peasant production and foreign investment in colonial production by the post-world war two era of colonial planning. See Sir Alan Pim, *Colonial Agriculture Production* (London, 1946).

28 Howard Pim, *A Transkei Enquiry* (Lovedale, 1934). Pim spent £250 of funds provided by the Phelps-Stokes Fund to complete the report, H. Pim to Keppel, 29 May 1933 (mimeo), in H. Pim Papers.

29 All published at Lovedale.

30 *Report of the Native Economic Commission, UG 22–1932.* See Chapter three, pp. 00–00, for a discussion of the report.

31 Margaret L. Hodgson and W. G. Ballinger, *Indirect Rule in Southern Africa* (Lovedale, 1931), p. 13.

32 *Ibid.,* pp. 29–30.

33 MSS Brit. Emp. Afr. S1427 1/5, W. G. and M. L. Ballinger, 'The British Protectorates in South Africa: Should they be transferred to the Union?', n.d.

34 'Of course the fault really lies with the Colonial (or Dominion) office', wrote Margaret Hodgson to Winifred Holtby. 'They have not wanted Civil Servants with imagination and they have not themselves or demanded from others a knowledge either of economics or politics unless those of capitalist intrigue in the interests of capitalist enterprise. Where there is no little or no scope for these one gets, as in Basutoland, stagnation': Winifred Holtby Papers, M. Hodgson to W. Holtby, 14 Jan. 1931.

35 Hyam, *op. cit.,* p. 135. The threat failed, though, with the recession in 1929 and the flight of capital from the Union; Chanock, *op. cit.,* p. 204.

36 Chanock, *op. cit.,* pp. 195–7. Amery also tried to interest Oppenheimer in Swaziland, and the Dominions Office negotiated with the Mushroom Land Settlement Company to provide for thirty-five settlers on its land, but developments were slow; Hyam, *op. cit.,* p. 123.

37 MSS Brit. Emp. S1427 1/3, L. Barnes to F. S. Livy-Noble, 11 July 1933.

38 Hyam, *op. cit.,* pp. 140–3; M. Perham and L. Curtis, *The Protectorates and South Africa: The Question of their Transfer to the Union* (London, 1935).

39 MSS Brit. Emp. S1427 2/6, J. D. Rheinnalt-Jones to F. S. Livy-Noble, 2 Sept. 1933.

40 MSS Brit. Emp. S1427 1/3, J. D. Rheinnalt-Jones to F. S. Livy-Noble, 6 April 1935.

41 *Ibid.,* Lord Lugard to F. S. Livy-Noble, 19 July 1935.

42   MSS Brit. Emp. S1427 1/1, W. G. Ballinger to F. S. Livy-Noble, 3 June 1933.
43   *Ibid.*
44   William Ballinger Papers, BC 347 D.1.1.3.1.1., W. G. B. to W. Holtby, 15 and 31 Jan. 1930.
45   MSS Brit. Emp. S1427 1/1, W.G.B. to W. Holtby, 5 Feb. 1933 encl. report of I.C.U. of Africa, n.d.
46   MSS Brit. Emp. S1427 1/1, W.G.B. to F. S. Livy-Noble, 16 Aug. 1933.
47   Howard Pim Papers, W. Holtby to H. Pim, 14 Dec. 1933; William Ballinger Papers BC 347 D1.1.6.1.7., W. Holtby to M. Ballinger, 6 Dec. 1933.
48   William Ballinger Papers, BC 347 D1.1.6.3.1, W.G.B. to Lord Lothian, 27 Nov. 1933 encl. memorandum 'The Beginnings of Co-operative Retail Trading and Production in the Union of South Africa and the British Protectorates'; *Umteteli wa Bantu*, 20 Jan. 1934.
49   W. G. Ballinger, 'The Beginnings of Co-operative Retail Trading'; the impetus for Ballinger to work with the RM in Swaziland, C. F. Strickland, came from Livy-Noble who hoped that Ballinger could be Strickland's assistant in a survey of the Protectorates. Joint Council Archive, 1931–4 file, 'Afro-European 1933', F. S. Livy-Noble to J. D. Rheinnalt-Jones, 5 Aug. 1933.
50   Howard Pim Papers, Lord Lothian to H. Pim 8 Dec. 1933.
51   MSS Brit. Emp. S1427 1/3, E. Marsh to F. S. Livy-Noble, 22 Oct. 1933.
52   Howard Pim Papers, A. Pim to H. Pim, 8 Aug. 1933.
53   Chanock, *op. cit.*, pp. 204–10, 220–6.
54   *Ibid.*, pp. 224–5.
55   W. M. Macmillan, *Africa Emergent* (London, 1938); see also *My South African Years* (Cape Town, 1975). For an analysis of this change in the thinking of the colonial office see J. M. Lee, '"Forward thinking" and war: the Colonial Office during the 1940s', *Journal of Imperial and Commonwealth History*, V1 (1977), pp. 64–79.
56   This was formented in part by the African nationalism stimulated by the Italian invasion of Ethiopia in 1936. See Ras Maklonnen, *Pan Africanism from Within* (London, 1973), p. 113.
57   Though the I.A.S.B. sought public demonstrations on the Protectorates issue and to 'expose this crude form of Imperialist intrigue by the Anglo-Duch capitalism of South Africa'; MSS Afr. S.1429 1/3, T. R. Makonnen to F. S. Livy-Noble, 5 June 1938.
58   *The Bantu World*, 3 Dec. 1932.
59   Howard Pim Papers, H. Pim to A. Pim, 8 Aug. 1932.
60   *Ibid.*, H. Pim to A. Kerr, 1 Dec. 1933.
61   W. M. Macmillan Papers, W. Holtby to W. M. Macmillan, 20 Oct. 1933. W. Holtby went with Lionel Curtis to see Strickland to discuss wider applications of his ideas on co-operation. See also

the debate at the Royal African Society, in a joint meeting with the Africa Society on 24 April 1924, *Journal of the Royal African Society*, XXIV (1935), pp. 3–18.

62 MSS Brit. Emp. S22 G196, J. Lewin to T. Buxton, 24 Jan. 1935.
63 MSS Afr. S. 1427 Box 1/1, M. Ballinger to F. S. Livy-Noble, 15 Sept. 1934.
64 Western Native Township Coop, Balance for the year 1935–36, (n.p.n.d.), in William Ballinger Papers.
65 William Ballinger Papers, BC 347 A3 X 3, Report by Self Mampuru, 'The Organisation of Co-operative Societies and Development of Trade Unions Among the Africans in South Africa', August 1939.
66 *Ibid.*
67 J. D. Rheinnalt-Jones, 'Co-operative societies amongst Africans', *Race Relations*, VII (1936), p. 10–14.
68 Mark Stein, 'A History of African Trade Unions on the Witwatersrand, 1928–1940' (B.A. (Hons) thesis, University of the Witwatersrand, 1977), p. 36.
69 MSS Brit. Emp. S 1427 1/1, W. G. Ballinger to F. S. Livy-Noble, 15 Sept. 1934.
70 A. Lynn Saffery, 'African Trade Unions and the Institute', *Race Relations*, VIII (1941); Baruch Hirson, 'The Reorganization of African Trade Unions in South Africa, 1936–42', London, *The Societies of Southern Africa in the Nineteenth and Twentieth Centuries*, VII (1977), pp. 182–194.
71 Hirson, p. cit., p. 192
72 Lynn Saffery Papers, Minutes of a meeting held in the office of the Chief Native Commissioner, Witwatersrand, Johannesburg, on the 9 Aug. 1939 for the purpose of explaining conditions under which the Government is prepared to afford recognition to organisations of African workers in urban areas, p. 2.
73 For an analysis of the election see my 'The Kroonstad Connection: Rheinnalt-Jones, Urban African Trading and the Politics of Social Control', (unpublished paper, University of Warwick, 1978).
74 ArSAIRR B100 (e), J. D. Rheinnalt-Jones to E. J. Evans, 30 Sept. 1935.
75 *The Cape Argus*, 12 May 1936.
76 MSS Brit. Emp. S 1427 1/3, J. D. Rheinnalt-Jones to F. S. Livy-Noble, 6 April 1938.
77 Alfred Xuma Papers ABX 3905 15 b, W. G. Ballinger to A. B. Xuma, 15 May 1939.
78 Lynn Saffery Papers, W. G. Ballinger, 'African Industrial Organisations and their Recognition', paper prepared for delivery at monthly meeting of European and African Joint Councils, Johannesburg, 13 March 1939, p. 6.
79 John Benyon, *Proconsul and Paramountcy in South Africa* (Durban, 1980), p. 331.

80 The appeal failed and all African titles were called in in the Ciskei and new *limited* titles issed under the 1927 Native Administration Act.
81 ArSAIRR B100 (a), D. D. T. Jabavu to J. D. Rheinnalt-Jones, 2 May 1935.
82 Howard Pim Papers, W. G. Ballinger to H. Pim, 15 July 1933.
83 William Ballinger Papers, BC 347 C.5 III 6.1.4, Rev. R. G. Milburn, 'The Joint Councils and Politics', n.d; see also W. M. Macmillan, *My South African Years* (Cape Town, 1975), p. 218.
84 ArSAIRR B100 (a), James Rose-Innes to J. D. Rheinnalt-Jones, 15 July 1935.

Chapter Three

1 One of the key influences was Winifred Hoernle at the University of the Witwatersrand whose pupils included Ellen Hellman, Hilda Kuper (née Beemer) and Eileen Krige (née Jensen) as well as Max Gluckman. With the exception of Eileen Krige all went on to study under Malinowski at the L.S.E. See Adam Kuper, *Anthropologists and Anthropology: The British School, 1922–72* (Harmondsworth, 1975), pp. 91–2, 177–8. Monica Hunter (Wilson) studied by a different route at Cambridge, though her study of the Pondo was also influenced by advice and suggestions from Winifred Hoernle. See Monica Hunter, *Reaction to Conquest* (London, 1936), p. xvii. For Central Africa see Richard Brown, 'Anthropology and Colonial Rule: Godfrey Wilson and the Rhodes Livingstone Institute, Northern Rhodesia', in Talal Assad (ed.), *Anthropology and the Colonial Encounter* (London, 1973), pp. 173–97. Assad has pointed out that 'unlike nineteenth century anthropology the objectification of functional anthropologists occurred within the context of *routine colonialism*, of an imperial structure of power already established rather than one in process of vigorous expansion in which political force and contradiction are only too obvious', Talal Assad, 'Two European Images of Non European Rule', in Assad, *op. cit.*, p. 115. Questions of power relations therefore tended to be by-passed by default.
2 See, for instance, R. E. Park, 'The Nature of Race Relations', in R. E. Park (ed.), *Race and Culture: Essays in the Sociology of Contemporary Man* (New York, 1950).
3 C. T. Loram, *The Claims of the Native Question Upon Scientists*, Johannesburg, South African Association for the Advancement of Science, Presidential Address to Section E, delivered 13 July 1921, p. 99.
4 *Ibid.*, p. 100
5 Assad, 'Two European Images', *op. cit.*, p. 114.
6 A. R. Radcliffe-Brown'Some Problems in Bantu Sociology', *Bantu Studies*, I (1921–22).
7 Martin Legassick, 'The Frontier Traditism in South African his-

toriography' in Shula Marks and Anthony Atmore (eds.), *Economy and Society in Pre-Industrial South Africa* (London, 1980), pp. 44–79.

8 J. D. Rheinnalt-Jones, 'The Need of a scientific basis for South African Native Policy', *South African Journal of Science*, XXIII (1926), p. 80.

9 *Ibid.*, p. 87.

10 John David Shingler, 'Education and Political Order in South Africa, 1902–1961', (Ph.D. thesis, Yale University, 1973), p. 187

11 In 1929 he was prepared, during an illness, to give up his Joint Council activities rather than his teaching. ArSAIRR (c), J. D. Rheinnalt-Jones to Mabel Palmer, 1 April 1929.

12 W. M. Macmillan, *My South African Years* (Cape Town, 1975); J. D. Rheinnalt-Jones and A. L. Saffery, 'Social and Economic Conditions of Native Life in the Union of South Africa', *Bantu Studies*, VII, 3–4, VIII 1–2.

13 *Report of the Native Economic Commission*, UG 22 1932, p. 13.

14 *Ibid.*, pp. 12–13.

15 *Ibid.*, p.16; the commission significantly also encouraged the idea that 'steps should be taken to facilitate co-operation between officials dealing with Natives and scientific investigators, to enable the results of such work to be used to assist in dealing with administrative questions dependent on a knowledge of native customs', (p. 31).

16 *Ibid.*, p. 16.

17 *Ibid.*, p. 26.

18 *Ibid.*, p. 31: the distinctions were on the basis of evidence from Professor Lestrade. Both 'adaptation' and 'assimilation' seemed to be biological metaphors left over from the nineteenth-century Social Darwinism legacy and probably owed a great deal to the Chicago School as well.

19 See, for instance, David Hammond-Tooke, 'Chieftainship in Transkeian Political Development', *The Journal of Modern African Studies*, II (1964), pp. 513-9; 'Tribal Cohesion and the Incorporation Process in the Transkei, South Africa', in Ronald Cohen and John Middleton (eds.), *From Tribe to Nation in Africa* (Chicago, 1970), pp. 217–41.

20 Native Economic Commission, Report, p. 31, para. 291.

21 *The Star*, 15 July 1922, reporting a paper given by Roberts to a Science Association meeting in Lourenço Marques.

22 Howard Pim Papers, A. Roberts to H. Pim, 30 April 1923.

23 Native Economic Commission Report, pp. 149–52, est. paras. 1010, 1017,1022.

24 See pp. 65–66.

25 Alex Roberts, 'The problem of the urban native', *The Cape Argus*, 30 June 1922: '... the urban native is now a permanent dweller on the outskirts of European urban life, and in these new conditions he is rapidly evolving a new civilisation. However much we may

regret this, it is an inevitable outcome of the times in which we live. Inexorable economic laws have brought it to pass that the old floating condition of things could not continue. The great industrial activities and uncertainty in the labour supply is a fatal hindrance to progress. There must be permanence if the machine is to run smoothly.'

26   Diedrich Westermann, *The African Today* (London, 1934), p. 298, arguing that the efforts of the Joint Councils and European-Bantu Conferences proved the possibility that 'members of the two races, with approximately the same level of education and with serious goodwill, can discuss together on an equal footing their common weal and so open the way to co-operation'. See also Edgar Brookes, *The Colour Problems of South Africa* (Lovedale, 1934), p. 145: 'The "anthropological school" has taught us the importance of knowing the native, the dangers of attempting to interfere with his way of life if we are ignorant or scornful of his past... Assuredly it can only be a good thing for us to know more of native life and thought, to appreciate better the traditions which form the background to of Bantu life, to acknowledge frankly the differences between Bantu and European life no less than the points of contact.'

27   By the 1930s the anthropological conception of 'culture' in Europe had become reinforced by a widespread fear in non-Marxist circles of a threat posed by the rise of a 'mass society'. See Michael D. Biddiss, *The Age of the Masses* (Harmondsworth, 1977), p. 289.

28   ArSAIRR B43 (f), R. F. A. Hoernle, 'Notes on "Assimilation" with special reference to Dr. J. E. Holloway's "American Negroes and South African Bantu"', n.d. (c. 1936).

29   *Ibid.*

30   Jan H. Hofmeyr, 'The Approach to the Native Problem', *Race Relations*, 3rd Qtr (1936), p. 30.

31   *Ibid.*, p. 33.

32   Alfred Xuma Papers, ABX 361306, A. Xuma to Hofmeyr, 30 Nov. 1936; ABX 361202, Hofmeyr to Xuma, 2 Dec. 1936.

33   Shula Marks, 'Natal, The Zulu Royal Family and the Ideology of Segregation', *Journal of Southern African Studies*, VI, 2 (1978), pp. 179–83.

34   George Heaton Nicholls Papers, KCM 3350, J. Dube to G. Heaton Nicholls, 13 May 1931.

35   MSS Brit. Emp. s22 191, File on Ohlange Institute; Shula Marks, "The Ambiguities of Dependence: John L. Dube of Natal", *Journal of Southern African Studies*, I (1975), p. 174; letter William Campbell to *Ilanga*, 20 June 1953. For Dube's pessimism in the inability of African political leaders to inspire confidence in the African masses, see his article 'Native Political and Industrial Organisation in South Africa' in Rev. J. Dexter Taylor (ed.), *Christianity and the Natives of South Africa* (Lovedale, 1928).

36   George Heaton Nicholls Papers, KCM 3350, G. Heaton Nicholls to
     J. Dube, 9 July 1931.

37   For the development of the A.A.C., see my paper 'African Politics
     and the Cape African Franchise, 1926–1936', Institute of Com-
     monwealth Studies, 1977; see also Peter Walshe, *The Rise of
     African Nationalism in South Africa* (London, 1970), pp. 114–27.

38   ArSAIRR B100 (a), D. D. T. Jabavu to J. D. Rheinnalt-Jones, 2 May
     1935.

39   *Ibid.*, E. Brookes to J. D. Rheinnalt-Jones, 16 May 1935.

40   *Ibid.*, R. F. A. Hoernle to J. Smuts, 13 July 1935; Minutes of a
     meeting of the Executive Committee, SAIRR, in The Library,
     Natal Technical College, Durban, July 8–10 1935: Smit opposed
     the holding of one central conference which was liable to be
     'dominated by agitators'.

41   *Ibid.*, E. Brookes to J. D. Rheinnalt-Jones, 22 Oct. 1935, referring to
     correspondence with Dube.

42   *Ibid;.*, interview with H. C. Lugg, Durban, 1976. The decision to
     possibly use Matthews instead of Dube is of interest. Matthews
     was one of the products of the new positivist anthropology taught
     in Britain, where he had registered at the University of London for
     a Ph. D. under Malinowski after completing an M.A. at Yale. He
     was also less keen than D. D. T. Jabavu to emphasise the British
     connections in South African liberalism, following the failure of
     Jabavu's attempts to get the Rex v. Ndobe issue on African land
     tenure in the Cape referred to the Privy Council. Instead there
     should be, Matthews wrote, 'a marshalling of the forces on our side
     here in our own country' which would 'help us more than striving
     to maintain the British connection', *Ilanga*, 16 Jan. 1931. At Yale,
     Matthews came under C. T. Loram's influence.

43   *Ibid.*, E. Brookes to J. D. Rheinnalt-Jones, 25 Oct. 1935, enclosing
     letter from Z. K. Matthews to Brookes, 22 Oct. inst.

44   Interview with H. C. Lugg. Brookes wrote to Jones before the
     election. 'On the question of tactics, I feel that, if elected, we
     should not only hold up the right ultimate ideals in a wise and
     constructive way, but *make friends*, win confidence, and carry
     through smaller but definite constructive reforms. I do not feel
     that we should adopt an "all or nothing" attitude, and we should
     not stand for election on such lines', ArSAIRR BIII (b), E. Brookes
     to J. D. Rheinnalt-Jones, 4 Nov. 1936 (emphasis in original); see
     also Zulu Society Papers 11/9, E. Brookes to C. Mpanza, 24 Sept.
     1941.

45   George Heaton Nicholls Papers, KCM 3358, P. Grobler, Minister
     of Native Affairs, to Heaton Nicholls, 17 Dec. 1935.

46   ArSAIRR B100 (e), G. Heaton Nicholls to J. D. Rheinnalt-Jones, 11
     Nov. 1935.

47   ArSAIRR File Native Land Affairs, J. D. Rheinnalt-Jones to J Dube,
     26 Aug. 1937; J. B. M. Hertzog Papers, A32 Box 33, G. Heaton
     Nicholls to Hertzog, 14 Aug. 1936.

48   J. D. Rheinnalt-Jones, "circular letter to 'The Chiefs and Other Leaders of the African People of the Transvaal and Orange Free State,'" in Rheinnalt-Jones Papers, 8 September 1939.

49   ArSAIRR Native Land Affairs, J. D. Rheinnalt-Jones to A. J. M. Mtimkulu, 2 April 1938.

50   Heaton Nicholls Papers, KCM 3362 a, R. F. A. Hoernle to Heaton Nicholls, 25 April 1937.

51   Interview with Hymie Basner (tapes in SOAS library).

52   MSS Brit. Emp. S22 G196, R. F. A. Hoernle to John Harris, 1 July 1938.

53   R. F. A. Hoernle, *South African Native Policy and the Liberal Spirit* (Cape Town, 1939), pp. 149-150; see also my article 'Liberalism and Ethnicity in South African Politics, 1921-1948', *African Studies*, XXXV, 3-4, 1976.

54   *Ibid* p. 135. For the influence of Laski and Bosanquet on English pluralist thought, see David Nicholls, *Three Varieties of Pluralism*, London, Macmillan, pp. 5-15. See also Paul Rich, 'The South African Institute of Race Relations and the Debate on "Race Relations", 1925-1958,' *African Studies, XL (1981)*, p. 18.

55   R. F. A. Hoernle, *op. cit.*, p. 168

56   *Ibid.*, p. 178.

57   Fritz Stern, 'The Illiberal Society' in *The Failure of Illiberalism* (London, 1972), p. 5.

58   See for instance the selected essays published posthumously by R. F. A. Hoernle, *Race and Reason* (Johannesburg, 1945), esp. 'The Concept of the Soul of a People', where the concept of western civilisation stood counterposed to the Nazi conception of the interrelationship of race, people and culture. However, while it was easy to make an apparently liberal demonstration of political faith by setting up Naziism as the central target, Hoernle still effectively rested his case upon a group-defined view centred around a conception of culture that was not especially dynamic and bore close resemblances to its usage in the anthropology taught in Johannesburg in the 1930s.

59   Douglas Smit Papers, 24/41, Geoffrey Clayton to A. Hoernle, 25 Oct. 1941.

60   Gilbert Murray Papers, Audrey Richards to Gilbert Murray, 16 June 1940.

61   London (Oxford University Press, 1936, 1939 and 1943).

62   For Macmillan's battle at the University of the Witwatersrand after his return from leave in February 1931 to his departure at the end of the academic term of 1932, see W. M. Macmillan, *My South African Years* (Cape Town, 1975), pp. 214-30. Macmillan was especially critical of the conservatism of the anthropology taught by Rheinnalt-Jones and Winifred Hoernle, p. 214.

63   See for instance W. H. Hutt's position articulated in 'The Economic Position of the Bantu in South Africa' in I. Schapera *Western Civilisation and the Natives of South Africa*, pp. 195-237.

54 See my article, 'Administrative Ideology, Urban Social Control and the Origins of Apartheid Theory, 1930-1939', *Journal of African Studies*, VII (1980), pp. 70-82.

55 *Ibid.*; Rodney Davenport, 'The Triumph of Colonel Stallard: The Transformation of the Natives (Urban Areas) Act between 1923 and 1937', *South African Historical Journal*, II (1970), pp. 77-96.

56 R. F. A. Hoernle, 'The Africans in Urban Areas', in *The Union's Burden of Poverty*, Johannesburg, S.A.I.R.R. 1942, p. 35. See also the discussion in my article, 'The South African Institute of Race Relations and the Debate on "Race Relations", 1929-1958', *African Studies*, XL (1981), pp. 13-22.

57 South African Institute of Race Relations, Minutes of Executive Committee, 6-9 July 1942.

58 Alexandra Health Commitee, *The Future of Alexandra Township* (Johannesburg, 1941), p. 27.

59 Alfred Xuma Papers, Archie S. Mbelle to A. Xuma, 25 Oct. and 9 Dec. 1941 and 3 Feb. 1942. Mbelle attacked white liberal manipulation of African politics and the 'accommodationism', as he saw it, of James Calata in the Cape A.N.C. He was favourable though to Mrs. Ballinger being invited to open the Congress Conference in December 1941.

70 See Chapter Four pp.94-96.

71 Donald Molteno backed William Ballinger's efforts to get the whole issues of African trade unions and co-operation discussed in the Institute of Race Relations and campaigned for this on the executive. Donald Molteno Papers, BC 579 CI. 49, D. Molteno to W. G. Ballinger 28 Dec. 1939; W. G. Ballinger to D. Molteno, 14 Jan. 1940. William Ballinger Papers, BC 347 BS 111.3.3., A. Lynn Saffery to M. Ballinger, 21 Feb. 1940 refers to a decision by the council of the Institute not to organise a conference on African Co-operatives, despite a motion by Self Mampuru. Attacks on the 'broad and vague' articles on association by the Institute came from the Cape liberals, *ibid.*, D. Buchanan, D. Molteno, A. Davis and Helen Stohr to A. Lynn Saffery, 12 March 1940.

72 For the meaning of this see R. F. A. Hoernle *Race and Reason*, esp. the 'Memoir' by I. D. MacCrone, pp. XX-XXIII. The 'synoptic' method derived from a philosophical outlook of comprehensiveness and the ideal of establishing an all-embracing conception of race relations. See also Rich, 'The South African Institute', *op. cit.* pp. 17-18.

73 ArSAIRR Policy 1943, D. Buchanan to R. F. A. Hoernle, 2 and 6 Feb. 1943.

74 *Ibid.*, Memorandum by R. F. A. Hoernle, 25 Jan. 1943.

75 South African Institute of Race Relations, Minutes of the General Council Meeting, 13, 14 and 15 Jan. 1943.

76 See the critique of the caste thesis by Gunnar Myrdal, *An American Dilemma* (New York, 1944), esp. appendix 1 (2 vols), pp. 1027-34.

77 Douglas Smit Papers, 25/41, R. F. A. Hoernle to D. Smith, 27 Nov. 1941 encl. memorandum entitled 'Reflections on the Racial Caste Society of the Union'. Emphasis in original.
78 Heribert Adam, *Modernizing Racial Domination* (Berkeley, 1971).
79 R. F. A. Hoernle, 'Reflections on the Racial Caste Society of the Union.'.

Chapter Four

1 'Report of a Deputation from the A.N.C. and Congress of Urban Advisory Boards to the Minister of Native Affairs, May 15-17, 1939', in Thomas G. Karis and Gwendolen M. Carter (eds.), *From Protest to Challenge,* II (Stanford, 1973), pp. 138-45.
2 Alfred Xuma Papers, ABX 390407, A. B. Xuma to J. Calata, 9 May 1939.
3 *Ibid.,* ABX 390510, A. B. Xuma to R. F. A. Hoernle, 10 May 1939. For Xuma's career in America as student see Richard D. Ralston, 'American Episodes in the Making of an African Leader: The Case of Alfred B. Xuma (1893-1962)', *The International Journal of African Historical Studies,* VI (1973), pp. 72-93.
4 *Ibid.,* ABX 390620, R. F. A. Hoernle to A. B. Xuma, 2 June 1938; J. D. Rheinnalt-Jones to A. B. Xuma, 20 June 1939; J. D. Rheinnalt-Jones RR4/39, *Memorandum on Non Europeans Travelling Overseas,* 28 February 1939.
5 *Ibid.,* ABX 370204, M. Yergan to A. B. Xuma, 4 Feb. 1937.
6 Peter Walshe, *The Rise of African Nationalism in South Africa* (London, 1970), p. 339; 'Report of Max Yergan to the All African Convention', n.d., included in Minutes of the All African Convention, December 1937, pp. 34-46. Yergan advocated 'unity with the liberal forces in the trade union movements, unity with all liberals and progressive minded people' (p. 38). Later, in the 1960s, Yergan became a supporter of apartheid in South Africa.
7 When Xuma became president of the A.N.C. in 1940, there were only £13 in funds, *Unpublished Autobiography,* p. 48.
8 See pp. 44-5.
9 Alfred Xuma Papers, ABX 4106091, leaflet by Gau Radebe, 9 June 1941.
10 ArSAIRR f 77, Labour: African Trade Unions: Recognition, 1940.
11 Alfred Xuma Papers, ABX 410828, A. B. Xuma to R. F. A. Hoernle, 28 Aug. 1941; R. F. A. Hoernle to A. B. Xuma, 29 Aug. 1941.
12 ArSAIRR Policy 1943, A. B. Xuma to J. D. Rheinnalt-Jones 1 July 1942.
13 Alfred Xuma Papers, ABX 420912, A. B. Xuma to R. F. A. Hoernle, 12 Sept. 1942.
14 *Ibid.,* ABX 420831b, H. Basner to A. B. Xuma, 31 Aug. 1942. Basner pointed out that many Transvaal chiefs had changed their

allegiance from Rheinnalt-Jones to himself, including those in Sekukuniland.

15 *Ibid.*, ABX 420914, R. F. A. Hoernle to A. B. Xuma, 14 Sept. 1942.
16 Margaret Ballinger Papers, BC579 B.98.22, Meeting of Natives Representatives Parliamentary Group, Pretoria, 4-8 Dec. 1937.
17 *To the Electorate of the Transvaal and OFS* by H. M. Basner, n.p., 1942, p. 6.
18 Alfred Xuma Papers ABX 421228b, A. B. Xuma to R. F. A. Hoernle and J. D. Rheinnalt-Jones 28 Dec. 1942.
19 *Ibid.*, ABX 421230b, A. B. Xuma to R F. A. Hoernle, 30 Dec. 1942; ABX 411106c, Xuma to A. Mbelle 6 Nov. 1941, stating his refusal to join the Council of the S.A.I.R.R. Xuma always considered Howard Pim a friend, ABX 370218b, Xuma to J. C. Hardy, 18 Feb. 1937.
20 *Ibid.*, ABX 430113, A. B. Xuma to R. F. A. Hoernle, 13 Jan. 1943.
21 Evidence given by A. B. Xuma, president general of the African National Congress to the Native Mine Wages Commission, 13 July 1943, p. 6; based upon evidence given by the Friends of Africa to the Native Mine Wage Commission, Memorandum prepared by W. G. Ballinger, 31 May 1943.
22 For the development of the Congress Youth League see Walshe, *op. cit.*, pp. 349-61; Gail M. Gerhart, *Black Power in South Africa: The Evolution of An Ideology* (Berkeley, 1978), esp. Chapter three; Edward Roux, *Time Longer than Rope*, (Madison, 1964), p. 403.
23 Gerhart, *op. cit.*, though the influence of Lembede seems rather overstated. Jordan Ngubane in some unpublished memoirs wrote of this time that the Youth League had an underlying political pragmatism in its realisation that the Congress 'old guard' led by Xuma could not be removed straight away; Lembede's 'African-ism' was checked by A. P. Mda's more conventional 'African Nationalism', *I Shall Not Be Silenced*, n.d., p. 8.
24 Alfred Xuma papers, ABX 326329 (68), *Congress Youth League Manifesto*, dated 31 March 1944, p. 2.
25 *Ibid.*, p. 3; see also Janet Robertson, *Liberalism in South Africa, 1948-1963* (Oxford, 1971), pp. 36-7.
26 *Ilanga lase Natal*, 11 March 1944.
27 *Ilanga lase Natal*, 24 Feb. 1945, article by Lembede entitled 'Some Basic Principles of African Nationalism'.
28 *The Bantu World*, 27 December 1947.
29 See for example a description of an African meeting in Bloemfon-tein in 1942 by S. M. Molema, Alfred Xuma Papers, ABX 430128a, 'Some Thoughts and Reflections on the African National Con-gress', 28 Jan. 1943.
30 *Ilanga lase Natal* 31 July 1943.
31 O. Mannoni, *Prospero and Caliban*, trans. P. Powestand (New York, 1964); see also A. Memmi, *The Colonizer and the Colo-nized*, trans. H. Greenfield (New York, 1965), for a similar master-servant paradigm of colonialism.

32   African National Congress *African Claims* (Johannesburg, 1943), p. 15.

33   *Ibid.*, pp. 9-15.

34   Alfred Xuma Papers, ABX 431123c, E. T. Mah and Y. Dadoo to Sec. A.N.C., 23 Nov. 1943.

35   *Ibid.*, ABX 450804, A. B. Xuma, Opening Adress of the All in Conference of the Non-White Trade Unions, Bloemfontein, 4 Aug. 1945, p. 3; *A.N.C. Bulletin*, 1 Nov. 1945, p. 2.

36   *Ibid.*, ABX 460318a, J. Ngubane to A. N. Xuma, 16 March 1946.

37   *Ibid.*, ABX 361127c, A. B. Xuma to M. Yergan, 27 Nov. 1936.

38   *Ibid.*, ABX 480507b, A. B. Xuma to I. C. P. Molefe, 1 March 1948; see also Walshe, *op. cit.*, pp. 383–4. The Transvaal A.N.C. resolved at its annual conference in Germiston in 1946 to try to raise £20,000 for a printing company and float £1 shares 'for the rich class of the African Community' and 5sh shares 'for the masses', ABX 460329c, A. W. Bopape to A.B. Xuma, 29 March 1946. The matter does not appear to have been proceeded with.

39   James P. Barber, *South Africa's Foreign Policy, 1945–1970* (London, 1973), pp. 24–34.

40   *The Bantu World*, 21 Sept. 1946.

41   *Inkundla ya Bantu*, 2nd Fortnight, Sept. 1946; Alfred Xuma Papers, ABX 460921, A. B. Xuma, leaflet on Emergency Conference of All Africans, 21 Sept. 1946.

42   The conference decided in the end to adopt a strategy whereby the councillors on the N.R.C. resigned by degrees and was a middle position between one of complete boycott, demanded by Anton Lembede, and one of continuing to work through the council, championed by Selby Msimang. Of 510 delegates, Msimang's motion got hardly a dozen votes, and over 490 voted for the motion backed by Xuma which he arranged in close consultation with many of the N.R.C. councillors and Moses Kotane, *Inkundla ya Bantu*, First Fortnight, Oct. 1946.

43   Dan O'Meara, 'The 1946 African Mine Workers Strike and the Political Economy of South Africa', *The Journal of Commonwealth and Political Studies*, XIII (1975), pp. 146–73.

44   Interview with Adv. A. P. Mda and Godfrey Pitje; Baruch Hirson, *Year of Fire, Year of Ash* (London, 1979), p. 34.

45   *The Bantu World*, 17 July 1947.

46   *Imvo*, 10 Jan. 1948.

47   Interview with Julius Lewin.

48   John Burger (Leo Marquard), *The Black Man's Burden*, 2nd ed. (London, 1943), p. 244.

49   In the 1940s this belief was especially centred around the liberal journal *The Forum* which I have discussed more fully in my article, 'Liberalism and Ethnicity in South African Politics, 1921–1948', *African Studies*, XXXIV (1976), p. 229.

50 *Trek*, June 1947; Sachs had earlier abandoned the mainstream liberal argument on industrialisation by itself promoting political change. In 1942 he suggested at the national executive of the South African Trades and Labour Council the appointment of an advisory committee for the consultation on all matters affecting workers, but the idea was rejected by the government in March, 1943. 'We waited patiently for the realisation of some of the good things promised,' Sachs wrote to Smuts, 'but we soon became completely disillusioned and realised that the more lavish the promises the less intention was there to fulfil them,' *The Guardian*, 25 March 1943; see also E. S. Sachs, *The Choice Before South Africa* (New York, 1952).

51 *The Democrat*, 20 Oct. 1945.

52 Leo Marquard Papers, BC 587, L. Marqard to Jan Hofmeyr, 25 Sept. 1946; Jan Hofmeyr to Marquard, 12 June 1946.

53 *The Guardian*, 13 Feb. 1947.

54 Alfred Xuma Papers, ABX 470213b, A. B. Xuma to A. Champion, 13 Feb. 1947.

55 H. Basner, *A Nation of 10,000,000 — Challenge to S.A.'s Native Policy* (Johannesburg, 1947), p. 47.

56 Donald Molteno Papers, C5, 182, D. Molteno to .C H. Malcom ess, 21 Dec. 1946.

57 The Zoutpansberg Cultural Association was a peasant-based organisation in the Northern Transvaal that rose to resist the government's implementation of land consolidation under the 1936 Native Trust and Land Act. In the case of the Venda, four main areas of consolidation were proposed — Jelele, Sibasa, Mpafuri and Ramputa — which would lead to considerable overcrow ing, with taxpayers receiving 2 morgen of land and non-taxpayers 1½ morgen. Maliba led protests against the scheme and was arrested in 1941 under the Riotous Assemblies Act, and by the time of the 1942 senatorial election, even Chief Sibasa gave Maliba's backer, Hymie Basner, his support against Rheinnalt-Jones. *The Guardian*, 30 Oct., 6 Nov. and 18 Dec, 1941, 30 July 1942; Donald Molteno Papers, B8. 58., Zoutpansberg Cultural Association, leaflet by J. M. Muthibe, Secretary, 7 Nov. 1941; Baruch Hirson, 'Rural Revolt in South Africa, 1937–41', London ECS, CSP, Vol 8, 1978, pp. 115–32.

58 Hirson, *op. cit.*; Alfred Xuma Papers, ABX 480402b, N. K. Peele to A. B. Xuma, 2 April 1947.

59 Godfrey Pitje Collection, Institute of Race Relations Library, Johannesburg, A. P. Mda to G. Pitje, 15 Sept. 1948.

60 Minutes of a Special Meeting of the National Executive held at Community Hall, Batho Location, Bloemfontein, 1 and 2 Feb. 1947. Msimang's motion, which resolved that the boycott weapon was 'dependent for its success entirely on a powerful and nation-wide campaign, or as a weapon to be resorted to after all constitutional means have been exhaused in the struggle for the

full attainment of political rights', was supported by both Champion and James Calata, the secretary general of congress.

61 *The Bantu World*, 17 May 1947.

62 *The Bantu World*, 14 June, 5 and 12 July 1947.

63 Walshe, *op. cit.*, pp. 357, 359. The National Bloc emerged in 1951 when J. B. Marks was elected president of the Transvaal African Congress. The executive of the congress had equivocated on the boycott resolution as far back as 1947, *Imvo*, 21 June 1947.

64 *The Bantu World*, 5 and 12 July 1947, 24 Jan. and 3 April 1948.

65 Johannesburg Dist. Committee of the Communist Party, *Boycott of Advisory Board Elections*, n.d.; *Guardian*, 20 Feb 1947; *Inkululeko*, May 1946.

66 *The Bantu World*, 4 Jan 1947.

67 The *Guardian*, 18 Sept 1947.

68 Rosalie Kingwill, 'The African National Congress in the Western Cape' (B.A. (Hons) Dissertation, University of Cape Town, 1977), pp. 61–4.

69 The *Guardian*, 15 Jan 1948; see also *Freedom* No. 11 (1947).

70 The *Guardian*, 11 Nov 1948.

71 The *Guardian*, 4 Nov 1948.

72 For a discussion of Patrick Duncan see Tom Lodge, 'Patrick Duncan and Radical Liberalism' (unpublished seminar paper, University of York, 1977); for the A.R.M. see Janet Robertson, *op. cit.*, pp. 223–5.

Chapter Five

1 See, for instance, Dr. A. B. Xuma, *South West Africa : Annexation or United Nation's Trusteeship?* (New York, 1946), for A.N.C. opposition to the incorporation of South West Africa into the Union.

2 Douglas Smit Papers, 4/46, G. Heaton Nicholls to D. L. Smit, 18 Feb. 1946.

3 Keith Hancock and Jean Van der Poel (ed.), *Selections from the Smuts Papers*, VII (Cambridge, 1973), Hofmeyr to Smuts, 8 Sept. 1946.

4 Douglas Smit Papers, 165/45, D. L. Smit to G. Mears, 9 Aug. 1945 encl. Notes of Discussion with Colonial Office Officials, 31 July and 1 Aug. 1945; 169/45, Notes of Interview with Dr. Margaret Read, head of the Colonial Dept. of the Institute of London University, 8 Aug. 1945; 175/45, D. L. Smit to Piet Van der Byl, noting British expenditure of £120,000,000 over next ten years under Colonial Development and Welfare Act of 1940. 'What we want,' Smit argued, 'is an overall plan so that we may look ahead without fear of interruption half way'; Note Book No. 3, dined with Lord Hailey, 24 Sept. 1945.

5 ArSAIRR BIV Q., Whyte to B. Pim, 4 July 1945. See also RR72/46 J.D. Rheinnalt-Jones, circular (marked 'strictly confidential') to

Members of the Executive Committee, 17 June 1946. A fund-raising campaign by Oscar Wollheim, full-time organiser of the Institute, brought in £4,782 between April 1945 and March 1946, and Quentin Whyte inherited from Jones an Institute interested in moving towards research to be funded by the Scientific and Industrial Research Council and the Council for Educational, Social and Humanistic Research.

6 Rheinnalt-Jones only took up this job after being advised by both Smuts and Hofmeyr to do so. Shepherd Papers, MS 14/713 (w), J. D. Rheinnalt-Jones to D. Shepherd, 8 March 1947.

7 See p. 38.

8 ArSAIRR BIV E. Brookes to Q. Whyte, 17 April 1947.

9 Margaret Ballinger Papers, A410/B2, D. D. T. Jabavu to M. Ballinger, 4 March 1942, encl. Memo of S.A. Native Farmers Congress.

10 *Ibid.*, M. Ballinger to G. Mears, 13 Dec. 1943; to D. L. Smith, 11 Dec. 1943; Notes entitled 'Complaints from the Glen Grey District Re Allocation of Lands', November 1943; D. L. Smit to B. B. Mdlele, 16 Dec. 1943.

11 *Select Report of the Natives Representative Council, UG10–'38*, motion by D. D. T. Jabavu, Nov. 1938.

12 Margaret Ballinger Papers D70/80 5 (n), D. D. T. Jabavu to M. Ballinger and D. Molteno, 26 Nov. 1943, asking M. Ballinger to appear at the triennial conference of the A.A.C. at Bloemfontein on 16 Dec.; M. Ballinger to D. D. T. Jabavu, 4 Dec., stating that she did not feel well enough qualified to advise Jabavu on his position: 'I am always a little bit nervous of interfering in purely African matters, unless I have some grasp of all the issues involved.' As an M.P. Margaret Ballinger appears to have been consistently 'hazy' of the nature of African political cleavages.

13 Donald Molteno Papers, BC 579 A 10 B, J. Calata to Cape Parliamentary Representatives, 2 July 1941; J. Calata to D. Molteno, 4 Oct. and 16 Dec. 1941, 7 Jan. 1942, 19 June 1946, 14 June 1947.

14 Margaret Ballinger Papers A410/C2, C. A. W. Sigila to M. Ballinger, 26 June 1943.

15 *Ibid.*, E. Brookes to D. Buchanan, 10 Feb. 1943.

16 *Ibid.*, D. D. T. Jabavu to M. Ballinger, 23 Sept. 1947.

17 *Ibid.*, R. H. Godlo to M. Ballinger, 16 April 1947.

18 *Ibid.*, M. Ballinger to R. H. Godlo, 3 Sept. 1946; Memorandum on the Adjournment of the Natives Representative Council, 11 Aug. 1946, advocating a do nothing policy by the Natives Representatives in the wake of the N.R.C. resolution condemning the government's native policy.

19 *Ibid.*, M. Ballinger to C. H. Malcommess, 31 Dec. 1946.

20 *Ibid.*, D. Molteno to J. Calata, 29 April 1947, describing interview with the P.M.

21 A.W.E. Champion Papers, A922, Caroline Frost to A. Champion, 20 April 1936, indicating the first overtures from Brookes even before his election; Champion to Brookes, 10 Aug. 1937, indicat-

ing messages passed from Brookes to Champion via the Durban
Bantu Men's Social Centre for a meeting; BC 581 A1 128, E.
Brookes to Champion, 16 Aug. 1937, promising to keep in touch
with Champion on the wage question; Champion to The Editor,
Natal Mercury, 11 March 1940, indicating his support for Brookes;
Champion to Brookes, 5 Sept. 1941; Brookes to Champion, 2 and
15 Oct. 1941; Champion to Brookes, 18 Nov. 1941, thanking
Brookes for making it possible to attend a conference of Chiefs and
leaders of Pietermaritzburg.

22 Jan Hofmeyr Papers, E. Brookes to J. Hofmeyr, 22 October 1946,
describing meeting with the Natal members of the N.R.C.
23 *Ibid.*, E. Brookes to J. Hofmeyr, 3 Dec. 1946, encl. article 'Racial
Tension in South Africa'.
24 *Ibid.*, J. Hofmeyr to E. Brookes, 5 Dec. 1946.
25 Douglas Smit Papers, 29/46, E. Brookes to D. L. Smit, 2 Sept. 1946,
encl. Memo dated 2 Sept. 1946.
26 *Ibid.*, GM 69/35/D 13.1/43, D. L. Smit to wife, 13 May 1943,
lamenting that the N.R.C. was so dominated by 'the urban element'; 16 May 1943; Note Book No. 4, entry dated 7 Sept. 1946,
noting that Hofmeyr felt that the events in the N.R.C. had occurred as he had foreseen at its inception in 1936.
27 *Ibid.*, 31/46, Notes of Discussion by Native Affairs Commission,
27 Sept. 1946, p. 6.
28 *Ibid.*, 5/47, G. Mears to the Prime Minister, 15 Feb. 1947, encl.
draft memo, A Progressive Programme for Native Administration;
D. L. Smit to G. Mears, 8 March 1947; Memo on Native Councils.
29 *Ibid.*, 13/47, D. L. Smit, Further Notes re Native Representation, 2
April 1947.
30 *Ibid.*, 55/47, A Progressive Programme for Native Administration,
revised after correspondence between G. Mears and H. A. Fagan,
20–22 Aug. 1947.
31 *Ibid.*, 10/37, D. L. Smit to G. Mears, 24 March 1947, encl. Notes on
Further Development of Native Councils.
32 *Ibid.*, 22. 1/47, Native Affairs Commission to G. Mears, 2 April
1947.
33 *Ibid.*, 21/47, Notes of Discussion of N.A.C. re Native Industry Bill,
3 May 1947.
34 *Ibid.*, 23/47, Notes of Interview between the Prime Minister and
members of the N.R.C., 8 May 1947, p. 4; Smit indicated the
political constraints on the whole reform programme when he
privately minuted on 25 March that he did not think that the
general and local councils would accept the scheme, 'and the
intelligentsia will object that they want much more than is
visualised. But within the orbit of the present political outlook I
cannot suggest a suitable alternative.' 11.1/47, Notes re Representation.
35 *Ibid.*, 45/47, H. A. Fagan to G. Mears, 23 Aug. 1947; G. Mears to H.
A. Fagan, 20 Aug. 1947 re to conversation re same.

36 *Ibid.*, 57/47, Notes of Discussion with the Prime Minister, Union Buildings, Pretoria, 1 Sept. 1947; see also my article, 'Liberalism and Ethnicity in South African Politics, 1921–1948', *African Studies*, XXXV (1976), p. 250.

37 *The Bantu World*, 17 May 1947; *The Democrat*, July 1947.

38 *The Bantu World*, 14 June 1947; The *Guardian*, 15 and 29 May 1947.

39 Jordan Ngubane, *Should the N.R.C. be Abolished?* (Cape Town, 1946). The N.R.C. was envisaged as becoming merely an administrative institution, responsible for the administration of reserves and locations and the appointment of Native Commissioners, while Ngubane sought a drastic overhauling of the 1936 legislation to ensure the extension of the Cape franchise to the other provinces and the increase in the number of senators representing Africans. 'So far,' he concluded, 'the Council has been a fairly good school of political training; now it must be turned into a training centre for Africans in the art of administration' (pp. 27–8). An idea exactly opposite, in many respects, to the scheme of Mears and Smit who sought to politicise the N.R.C. as an outlet for the urban African petty bourgeoisie and to confine administrative matters in detail to local and general councils under the guiding influence of the N.A.D.

40 *The Forum*, 21 June 1947. Selby Msimang, too, considered that Smuts's 'tentative proposals' did not 'in any way' disturb the political deadlock in the N.R.C. Furthermore 'any comment on the proposals I regard to be innocuous until the issue reaches the realm of practical politics', Alfred Xuma Papers ABX 470917c, H. Selby Msimang to A. B. Xuma, 17 Sept. 1947.

41 *A New Era of Reclamation, Statement of Policy made by Mr. D. L. Smit, Secretary for Native Affairs, at a Special Session of the Ciskeian General Council at Kingwilliamstown, the 8th January 1945*, Pretoria, 1945. The Ciskeian famine the same year was to some extent a propaganda coup for the *Guardian* newspaper which organised a relief fund which was assisted by Dr. Bokwe. Donald Molteno Papers, BC 579 C4 148, M. Ballinger to D. Molteno, 25 Oct. 1945.

42 Margaret Ballinger Papers, Memorandum drawn up by C. A. W. Sigila from Healdtown Farmers, 24 May 1947; *Imvo*, 18 June 1947.

43 *Ibid.*, A410/B2; Hamilton G. Kraai *etal.*, 'The Anti Rehabilitation Government Scheme Committee for the Transkeian Territories Manifesto', East London, 14 Oct. 1947.

44 *Ibid.*, W. G. Ballinger to Messrs. Hamilton G. Kraai, M. P. Ngloshe and W. Jingo, 22 Nov. 1947.

45 *Ibid.*, W. G. Ballinger to C. H. Malcommess, 2 Dec. 1947; Malcommess to W. G. Ballinger, 13 November 1947.

46 *The Guardian*, 3 July 1947.

47 Alfred Xuma Papers, Govan Mbeki to A. Xuma, 27 June 1947; Mbeki started the anti-boycott campaign initially through the Transkeian African Voters Association in the period following the adjournment of the N.R.C. in 1946, before establishing the rival T.O.B. ABX 400411, G. Mbeki to A. Xuma, 11 Sept. 1946. There were charges, though, that the A.N.C. leadership did nothing to help the campaign in the Transkei during 1947. *Inkululeko*, December 1947. See also Brian Bunting, *Moses Kotane* (London, 1975), p. 145.

48 Margaret Ballinger Papers, A410/B2, M. Ballinger to D. Buchanan, 1 Sept. and 13 Nov. 1947.

49 Donald Molteno Papers, BC 579 C6 96, D. Buchanan, leaflet *New Transkei By Election*, 15 July 1947.

50 Alfred Xuma Papers, ABX 570604, A. B. Xuma to G. Mbeki, 4 June 1947.

51 Brian Bunting, *op. cit.*, p. 146.

52 Alfred Xuma Papers, ABX 470917c, Selby Msimang to A. B. Xuma, 17 Sept. 1947.

53 Margaret Ballinger Papers, A410/B2, C. A. W. Sigila to M. Ballinger, 31 Jan. 1949.

54 Edgar Brookes, *A South African Pilgrimage* (Johannesburg, 1977), pp. 89–99. 'Gone with him were most of our facile political hopes. Parliament was now an altogether different place. We could no longer go to Ministers' offices and hope for a friendly reception', p. 98.

55 Douglas Smit Papers, 18–25/49, corr. re removal of Brookes and Smit from N.A.C.; Edgar Brookes, *op. cit.*, p. 95.

56 E. G. Jansen, *Native policy of the Union of South Africa* (Pretoria, 1950), pp. 7–9.

57 No Sizwe writes that only 'half-hearted and tentative overtures' were made to the Africanists in the A.N.C. 'to probe the stability of the links between African nationalism and communism', and 'the Nationalists soon abandoned the idea of co-opting petty bourgeois African leadership,' *One Azania, One Nation* (London, 1979), pp. 64–5. For the general ideological climate in which Nationalist apartheid policy began to be implemented see David Welsh, 'The Cultural Dimensions of Apartheid', *African Affairs*, LXXI (1972), pp. 35–53.

58 Welsh, *op. cit.*, pp. 46–9. See also Jeffrey Butler, Robert I. Rotberg and John Adams, *The Black Homelands of South Africa* (Berkeley, 1977); Patrick Laurence, *The Transkei: South Africa's Politics of Partition* (Johannesburg, 1976). For African resistance to Bantu Authorities see Goven Mbiki, *South Africa: The Peasants Revolt* (Harmondsworth, 1964).

59 ArSAIRR Memo R.R. 3/48 CT. 8.1.48, Memo entitled 'Segregation and its Alternatives'.

60 ArSAIRR R.R. 2/48 CT. 8.1.49, mimeo marked 'Private and Con-

fidential', *Considerations of Proposals Regarding Natives' Representative Council*, p. 2.

61 *Ibid.*, p. 4.
62 William Ballinger Papers, BC 347 G2 11 19, K. Kirkwood to M. Ballinger, 21 Aug. 1948.
63 Margaret Ballinger Papers, A410/B2, M. Ballinger to C. A. W. Sigila, 21 June 1949.
64 Donald Molteno, 'The Situation after Hofmeyr', *Trek*, January 1949, p. 1.
65 Margaret Ballinger Papers, A410/B2, A. Paton to M. Ballinger, 22 Sept. 1952, stating that he felt a Liberal Party would be established after the 1953 election.
66 This was especially the view in the Institute of Race Relations under Quintin Whyte's influence. See Q. Whyte, *Apartheid and Other Policies* (Johannesburg, 1950). Whyte made a visit to the United States in 1950 and came under the influence of various techniques of race relations involving inter-group contact via holiday camps and social welfare via the National Urban League. Drawing on the American parallel, he concluded that given the limited funds of the Institute and its difficulties in specialisation, the main approach should be an eclectic one: 'American experience would appear to point to this line of approach — to seek lines of least resistance in whatever field, probing each to the limit where opposition might be severely provoked', Quintin Whyte, *Report of Trip to Europe, Britain and the U.S.A., 1950*, p. 6.
67 *The Guardian*, 23 Sept. 1948.
68 Alexander Kerr Papers, B. B. B. Bikitsha to A. Kerr, 18 April 1948; Victor Poto to A. Kerr, 27 April 1948; A. Kerr to V. Poto, 11 May 1948, declining nomination.
69 Margaret Ballinger also confessed to confusion in knowing the exact policies of African leadership, Margaret Ballinger Papers, A410/B2, M. Ballinger to J. Hlehani, 10 Feb. 1953.
70 Oxford, 1971.
71 Edgar H. Brookes, *We Come of Age* (Johannesburg, 1950), p. 20.
72 Janet Robertson, *Liberalism in South Africa, 1948–1963* (Oxford, 1971), pp. 106, 111–12. The Liberal Party's emergence after 1953 can be partly explained, Robertson has argued, by the fact that the Torch Commando was dominant in anti-government white protest in the previous era since it still seemed possible between 1948 and 1953 to defeat the government (p. 61).
73 A. R. Delius, 'The Missing Liberal Policy', *The Forum*, June 1952, p. 40.
74 For an account of the Defiance Campaign and the riots see Leo Kuper, *Passive Resistance in South Africa* (New Haven, 1957).
75 C. W. M. Gell in *The Forum*, Sept. 1953, p. 13; see also Robertson *op. cit.*, pp. 108–11.
76 *Contact*, January 1954.

77 *The Forum*, December 1952, p. 1.

78 *Contact*, February 1954.

79 Harry Bloom, Transvaal *Episode* (London, 1956); Michael Wade, 'Black Heroes, White Writers... some notes on South African novels, 1945–60', paper presented at the Centre for West African Studies, University of Birmingham, November 1981, discusses Bloom's novel in terms of the traditional pastoral concept of Africans in South African fiction, and the failure to depict them as full human beings capable of initiating radical political change. In some ways this is a legacy of Victorian evolutionary thought in modern Marxist philosophy and its belief in applying scientific principles to the study of society. In these terms Africans 'fail' in the context of scientific evolutionism.

80 Jacques Barzun, *Race; A Study in Modern Superstition* (New York, 1937); Julian S. Huxley and A. C. Haddon, *We Europeans: A Survey of 'Racial' Problems* (London, 1935). See also M.F. Ashley Montagu, *Man's Most Dangerous Myth: The Fallacy of Race* (New York, 1942).

81 George Padmore, *Africa: Britian's Third Empire* (London, 1949). Padmore's book was written at the request of the fifth Pan-African Congress, held in Manchester in 1945 (p. 9).

82 Michael Scott, *A Time to Speak* (London, 1958), pp. 169–90, 219–35, 242–68, and *Civilisation Indivisible*, London, African Bureau, 1953; Freda Troup, *In Face of Fear: Michael Scott's Challenge to South Africa* (London, 1950).

83 Scott, *op. cit.*, pp. 113–32. Scott's vision contained a powerful intellectual challenge to conventional liberal thinking in South Africa in that it sought to break down the distinction between cities and countryside and, in a programme stimulated by Lewis Mumford's *The Culture of Cities*, integrate both into 'unit areas' of regional development. Scott also sought not to poach on the territory of the A.N.C. though he campaigned for the recognition of African trade unions. Alfred Xuma Papers, ABX 430903C, M. Scott to A. B. Xuma, 3 Sept. 1943.

84 *Ibid.*, p. 121.

85 Maurice Webb, leading article in *Race Relations News*, June 1949, pp. 51–3. 'We need', Webb concluded, 'to help people in other countries know and understand the truth about South Africa and to get their help is a difficult task' (p. 53).

86 John Fletcher Papers, M. Scott to J. Fletcher, 27 Sept. 1949.

87 MSS Brit. Emp. S19 D10/8 file 3, J. D. Rheinnalt-Jones to C. W. W. Greenidge, 3 March 1950.

88 For the Seretse Khama affair and the role of the Africa Bureau, see Scott, *op. cit.*, pp. 272–6.

89 See, for example, Robert Rotberg, *The Rise of Nationalism in Central Africa: The Making of Malawi and Zambia, 1873–1964* (Cambridge, 1965), esp. chs. 9 and 10.

Conclusion

1   'Cape liberalism served to unify at least an articulate minority of the white races in South Africa. Conversely, it was a set of values antipathetic to uncompromising Afrikaner nationalists, particularly in the Boer Republics.' Janet Robertson, *Liberalism in South Africa, 1948–1963* (Oxford, 1971), p. 3.

2   Michael D. Biddiss, 'Myths of the Blood: European Racist Ideology, 1850–1945', *Patterns of Prejudice*, VII, 5 (1975), pp. 11–19.

3   Eric Voegelin, 'Liberalism and its History', *Review of Politics*, XXXVI, 4 (1974), p. 506.

4   T. Dunbar Moodie, *The Rise of Afrikanerdom: Power, Apartheid and the Afrikaner Civil Religion* (Berkeley, 1975), *passim*.

5   John Burger (Leo Marquard), *The Black Man's Burden* (2nd edn., London, 1943). A similar example of this radicalisation of political thought is provided by W. M. Macmillan in an Intelligence memorandum, 'African Background — III and IV, Part III: The Central and East African Colonies', 20 November 1942, written for the B.B.C. and found in the W. M. Macmillan papers. Here the South African segregation model is especially stressed on wider white settlement in East and Central Africa.

6   Karl Mannheim, 'The Problem of the Intelligentsia', in *Essays on the Sociology of Culture* (London, 1956), p. 101.

7   W. M. Macmillan, *Africa Emergent* (London, 1937), p. 31 and pp. 374–379.

8   For a view that classically restates this liberal moralism see Pierre L. Van den Berghe, 'The Impossibility of a Liberal Solution in South Africa', in Pierre L. Van den Berghe, *The Liberal Dilemma in South Africa* (London, 1979), pp. 56–67.

9   Rheinnalt-Jones Papers, C8/3, W. W. M. Eiselen to J. D. Rheinnalt-Jones, 24 Ocotber 1949.

10   A. J. Gregor, 'Apartheid', in *Radical Political Ideologies* (New York, 1968), pp. 221–276, states the view of apartheid as Volkisch populism.

11   John E. Holloway, 'Apartheid', *Annals of the American Academy of Political and Social Science*, CVI (1956), p. 33.

12   W. W. M. Eiselen, 'Plan to Rationalise South Africa's Native Labour', *Native Affairs Fact Paper No. XIII* (September 1950), p. 10.

13   See, for example, ArSAIRR BX(k), Q. Whyte, 'Report of a visit to Transkei-Ciskei', 16 May 1955.

14   Mrs. Margaret Ballinger, 'A Programme towards a Democratic South Africa', in Hildegarde Spottiswoode (ed.), *South Africa: The Road Ahead* (Cape Town, 1960), pp. 13–27.

15   For an account of these events see dal, *An American Dilemma*, Vol. 1 (New York 1972), esp. chap. 1.

17   *Ibid.*, Vol. 2, Appendix, 'A Methodoligical Note on Valuations and Beliefs', pp. 1027–34. For Sumner's conception of conserva-

tive 'folkways', which he saw as underlying the legal process, see William Graham Sumner, *Folkways* (New York, 1959; first edition, 1906). For a critique of Myrdal's conception of the 'American creed', see Nahum Z. Medalia, 'Myrdal's Assumptions on Race Relations: A Conceptual Commentary', *Social Forces*, XL (1962), pp. 223–7.

18 C. Van Woodward, *The Strange Career of Jim Crow* (New York, 1974; third edition) p. 147.

19 See, for instance, Paton's article, 'An Economic Policy', *Contact*, January 1955.

20 Alan Paton, *The Christian Approach to Race Relations in the Modern World* (London, 1959), p. 5. For the move towards a boycott in 1958, see Robertson, *op. cit.*, pp. 196–7.

21 Peter Walshe, 'Church versus State in South Africa: The Christian Institute and the Resurgance of African Nationalism', *Journal of Church and State*, XIX (1977), pp. 357–79; 'Mission in a Repressive Society: The Christian Institute of Southern Africa', London, I.C.S. (mimeo), October 1980. For the international context see Adrian Hastings, 'The Christian churches and Liberation Movements in Southern Africa', *African Affairs*, LXXX (1981), pp. 345–54.

22 For a discussion of the Cottesloe Consultation, see John W. de Gruchy, *The Church Struggle in South Africa* (London, 1979), pp. 62–9.

23 Report of the SPRO-CAS Political Commission, *South Africa's Political Alternatives* (Johannesburg, 1973); Alf Stadler has pointed out, though, the limitations in much of the Study Project's analysis, which still tended to see the economy as being hampered by racism and ignored the links between business and the existing South African power structure: 'Anxious Radicals and the Apartheid Society', *Journal of Southern African Studies*, II (1975), pp. 102–8. See also de Gruchy *op. cit.*, pp. 104–15.

24 The Inkatha yeNkululeko yeSizwe or 'The national cultural liberation movement' claims some 300,000 members and some 700 registered branches, many of which are in non-Zulu areas. This makes it even larger than the old African National Congress before its banning in 1960. Significantly, it has attracted some support from former liberals like Jordan Ngubane who, after returning to South Africa after nineteen years in exile, sees the movement as having transformed KwaZulu from a segregated homeland into a weapon against racism. See *The Observer*, 29 Nov. 1981. See also Roger Southall, 'Buthelezi, Inkatha and the Politics of Compromise', *African Affairs*, LXXX (1981), pp. 543–81.

25 Joanna Strangewayes-Booth, *A Cricket in the Thorn Tree: Helen Suzman and the Progressive Party* (Johannesburg, 1976).

26 For a critical analysis of the continuing liberal hopes for a 'new deal for urban blacks', see John Kane-Berman, *South Africa: The Method in the Madness* (London, 1979). Heribert Adam has writ-

ten: 'What continues as the liberal spirit in South Africa today represents either a diluted version of traditional liberalism or is sufficiently adjusted and patriotic to be tolerated by an even more powerful Afrikaner nationalism'; 'The Failure of Political Liberalism' in Heribert Adam and Hermann Giliomee, *Ethnic Power Mobilized : Can South Africa Change?* (New Haven and London, 1979), p. 260.

27 Paul B. Rich, 'Tradition and Revolt in South African Fiction: The novels of André Brink, Nadine Gordimer and J. M. Coetzee', *Journal of Southern African Studies*, IX, 1 (1982), pp. 54–73.

28 London, 1981. Stephen Clingman, 'Writing in a Fractured Society: the case of Nadine Gordimer', paper presented to the Conference on Literature and Society in Southern Africa, University of York, September 1981.

BIBLIOGRAPHY

1   Interviews

Edgar Brookes, Pietermaritzburg, Natal, 13 September 1975
Julius Lewin, London, 12 June 1979
H. C. Lugg, Durban, 15 December 1976
Advocate A. P. Mda, Mafeteng, Lesotho, 2 July 1977
Gordon Mears, Cape Town, 15 July 1977
Dr. James Moroka, Thaba 'Nchu, O.F.S., 7 December 1976
  and 29th June 1977
H. Selby Msimang, Pietermaritzburg, 14 September 1975
Joe Nkatlo, Mt. Moorosi, Lesotho, 27 June 1977
O. D. Schreiner, Johannesburg, 2 September 1975
T. D. Mweli Skota, Pimville, Soweto, 17 June 1975
O.D. Wollheim, Cape Town, 12 August 1977

2   Newspapers and periodicals

Abantu Batho (the only files that exist for this are between 1929–31
  in the Cape Town Public Library)
The Bantu World
Cape Argus
Cape Times
Contact
The Christian Express, renamed after 1922 the *South African Outlook*
The Democrat
The Forum
Freedom
The Guardian
Ilanga lase Natal
Inkululeko
Inkundla ya Bantu
International Review of Missions
Rand Daily Mail
The Star
Trek
Um Afrika

Umsebenzi
Umteteli wa Bantu

3   Manuscript sources

(i) Unofficial

Margaret Ballinger Papers. These are divided between the Jagger Library, University of Cape Town and the Church of the Province Archives, University of the Witwatersrand.

William Ballinger Papers. Jagger Library, University of Cape Town.

A. W. G. Champion Papers. These are divided between the Church of the Province Archives, University of the Witwatersrand and the Lionel Forman Collection in the Jagger Library, University of Cape Town.

Patrick Duncan Papers. Jagger Library, University of Cape Town.

John Fletcher Papers. Library of Society of Friends, London.

James Henderson Papers. Cory Library, Rhodes University, Grahamstown.

Herbst Papers. Jagger Library, University of Cape Town. This collection contains the minutes of evidence to the 1930–32 Native Economic Commission.

J. B. M. Hertzog Papers. Union Archives, Pretoria. Permission was required from Mr. Albert Hertzog to consult these papers.

Jan Hofmeyr Papers. Church of the Province Archives, University of the Witwatersrand.

Winifred Holtby Papers. Hull Public Library.

Alexander Kerr Papers. Cory Library, Rhodes University, Grahamstown. I would like to thank Mr. A.J. Kerr, Alexander Kerr's son, for granting me permission to consult his father's papers.

B. K. Long Papers. Cory Library, Rhodes University, Grahamstown.

W. M. Macmillan Papers. In the private possession of Mrs Mona Macmillan.

Leo Marquard Papers. Jagger Library, University of Cape Town.

Donald Molteno Papers. Jagger Library, University of Cape Town.

Gilbert Murray Papers. Bodleian Library, Oxford.

George Heaton Nicholls Papers. Killie Campbell Library, Durban.

Howard Pim Papers. Church of the Province Archives, University of the Witwatersrand.

J. D. Rheinnalt-Jones Papers. Church of the Province Archives, University of the Witwatersrand.

James Rose-Innes Papers. Cape Town Public Library.

Lynn Saffery Papers. Library of the South African Institute of Race Relations, Johannesburg.

Robert Shepherd Papers. Cory Library, Rhodes University, Grahamstown.

Douglas Smit Papers. Albany Museum, Grahamstown.

Alfred Xuma Papers. Church of the Province Archives, University of the Witwatersrand.

(ii) *Official*

Files of the Union Native Affairs Department, Union Archives, Pretoria. Code letter NA.

(iii)*Organisations: documents, mimeographs and typescripts*

Files, reports and correspondence of the Aborigines Protection Society, Rhodes House, Oxford. Code MSS Brit. Emp. S22 G203.

Correspondence of the American Board Mission, Harvard University Library. Code letter ABM.

Files, mimeographed minuted and printed reports of the Johannesburg Joint Council, Church of the Province Archives, University of the Witwatersrand.

Files, reports and correspondence of the London Group on African Affairs, Rhodes House, Oxford. Code MSS Brit. Emp. S1427.

Files, reports and minutes of the South African Institute of Race Relations, Church of the Province Archives, University of the Witwatersrand. Code letter ArSAIRR.

4   Government publications

(i) *Annual reports*

South Africa Native Affairs Department, Report 1919–1921, UG 34–'22.

South Africa Native Affairs Department, Report 1922–1926, UG 14–'27.

South Africa Native Affairs Department, Report 1944–1945, UG 44–'46.

South Africa Native Representatives Council, Select Reports.

(ii) *Commisssions and related material*

South Africa Native Affairs Commission, Memorandum on the Native Administration Bill 1927 (AN404–1927) (Library of Parliament, Cape Town).

South Africa Native Churches Commission, Report 1915, UG 39–'25.

South Africa Native Economic Commission, Report 1932, UG 22–732. The minutes of evidence for this may be found in part in the Herbst Papers, Jagger Library, University of Cape Town, together with a further collection in the Library of the South African Institute of Race Relations, Johannesburg.

South Africa Native Laws Commission, Report 1946–1948, UG 28–'48.

Transvaal, Local Government Commission, Report 1922, TP1–'22.

(iii) *Miscellaneous*

South Africa, House of Assembly, Debates.

South Africa, Inter-Departmental Committee on the Social, Health and Economic Conditions of Urban Natives, Pretoria, Report 1942.

South Africa, Report of the African Population Census, 1921, UG 37–'24.

South Africa Select Committee on Native Affairs, Report 1923, SC2–'23.
South Africa, Social and Economic Planning Council, The Native Reserves and Their Place in the Economy of South Africa, 1946, UG 32–'46.

5   *Books and excerpts*

Adam, Heribert. *Modernizing Racial Domination.* Berkeley, 1971.
Adam, Heribert. *South Africa: Sociological Perspectives.* London, 1971.
Adam, Heribert, and Giliomee, Hermann. *Ethnic Power Mobilized: Can South Africa Change?* New Haven and London, 1979.
Arendt, Hannah. *The Origins of Totalitarianism* (2nd edn.), London, 1958.
Assad, Talal (ed.). *Anthropology and the Colonial Encounter.* London, 1973.
Ballinger, Margaret. *From Union to Apartheid.* Cape Town, 1969.
Ballinger, W. G. *Race and Economics in South Africa.* London, 1934.
Barber, James P. *South Africa's Foreign Policy, 1945–70.* London, 1973.
Barnes, Leonard. *Caliban in Africa: An Impression of Colour Madness.* London, 1930.
Barzun, Jacques. *Race: a Study in Modern Superstition.* New York, 1937.
Benyon, John. *Proconsul and Paramountcy in South Africa.* Durban, 1980.
Bloom, Harry. *Transvaal Episode.* London, 1958.
Bolton, Geoffrey. *Britain's Legacy Overseas.* London, 1973.
Bonner, Philip. 'The Transvaal Native Congress, 1917–20', in Shula Marks and Richard Rathbone (eds.), *Industrialization and Social Change in South Africa.* London, 1982, pp. 270–313.
Briggs, Asa. 'The Language of "Class" in Early Nineteenth Century England' in M.W. Flinn and T.C. Smout (eds.) *Essays in Social History.* Oxford, 1974.
Brittain, Vera. *Testament of Friendship.* London, 1980. (1st ed. 1940.)
Brookes, Edgar. *The Colour Problems of South Africa.* Lovedale, 1934.
Brookes, Edgar. *The History of Native Policy in South Africa,* (From 1830 to the Present Day, 2nd ed.). Pretoria, 1927.
Brookes, Edgar. *Native Education in South Africa.* Pretoria, 1930.
Brookes, Edgar. *The Political Future of South Africa.* Pretoria, 1927.
Brookes, Edgar. *South Africa in a Changing World.* Cape Town, 1953.
Brookes, Edgar. *A South African Pilgrimage.* Johannesburg, 1977.
Bundy, Colin. *The Rise and Fall of the South African Peasantry.* London, 1979.
Burger, John (Leo Marquard). *The Black Man's Burden.* London, 1943, 2nd ed.
Butler, Jeffrey, Rotberg, Robert I., and Adams, John. *The Black Homelands of South Africa.* Berkeley, 1977.

Cairns, H. Alan C., *Prelude to Imperialism: British Reactions to Central Africa, 1840–1890*, London, 1965.

Carter, Gwendolen. *African Concepts of Nationalism in South Africa.* Edinburgh, 1965.

Carter, Gwendolen. *Politics of Inequality: South Africa Since 1948.* New York, 1962

Carter, Gwendolen, and Karis, Thomas. *South Africa's Transkei: The Politics of Domestic Colonialism.* Evanston, 1967.

Chanock, Martin. *Unconsummated Union: Britain, Rhodesia and South Africa, 1900–45.* Manchester, 1977.

Cox, Oliver Cromwell. *Caste, Class and Race.* New York, 1970.

Crossick, Geoffrey. *The Lower Middle Class in Britain.* London, 1977.

Danziger, Kurt. 'Modernisation and the Legitimation of Social Power' in H. Adam (ed.), *South Africa: Sociological Perspectives.* London, 1971.

Davenport, T. R. H. *South Africa: A Modern History.* Johannesburg, 1977.

de Gruchy, John Wesley. *The Church Struggle in South Africa.* London, 1979.

De Kiewiet, Cornelis Willem. *The Anatomy of South African Misery.* London, 1956.

De Kiewiet, Cornelis Willem. *A History of South Africa: Social and Economic.* London, 1941.

de Klerk, W. A. *Puritans in Africa.* Harmondsworth, 1976.

Dexter-Taylor, Rev. J. (ed.) *Christianity and the Natives of South Africa.* Lovedale, 1928.

Dollard, John. *Caste and Class in a Southern Town.* New Haven, 1937.

Empson, William. *Some Versions of Pastoral.* London, 1963.

Erwin, Alec, and Webster, Eddie. *Change, Reform and Economic Growth in South Africa.* Johannesburg, 1978.

Evans, Ifor L. *Native Policy in Southern Africa: An Outline.* Cambridge, 1934.

Feit, Edward. *African Opposition in South Africa: The Failure of Passive Resistance.* Stanford, 1967.

Feit, Edward. *South Africa: The Dynamics of the African National Congress.* London, 1962.

Fredrickson, George M. *White Supremacy: A Comparative Study in American and South African History.* New York, 1981.

Freeden, Michael. *The New Liberalism: An Ideology of Reform.* Oxford, 1978.

Gerhart, Gail M. *Black Power in South Africa: The Evolution of an Ideology.* Berkeley, 1978.

Habermas, Jurgen. *Legitimation Crisis.* London, 1976.

Hancock, Sir William Keith, and Van der Poel Jean. *Selections from the Smuts Papers, Vols I-IV.* Cambridge, 1966.

Harris, David. 'European Liberalism and the State' in Heinz Lunacz (ed.), *The Development of the Modern State.* New York, 1964.

Hellman, Ellen (ed.). *Handbook on Race Relations in South Africa*. Cape Town, 1949.

Hellman, Ellen. *Rooiyard: A Sociological Survey of a Native Slum*. Manchester, 1948 (repr. 1969).

Hetherington, Penelope. *British Paternalism and Africa, 1920–1940*. London, 1978.

Higham, John. *Strangers in the Land: Patterns of American Nativism, 1860–1925*. New York, 1978.

Hirson, Baruch. 'The Reorganisation of African Trade Unions in South Africa, 1936–42', London, I.C.S., *The Societies of Southern Africa in the Nineteenth and Twentieth Centuries*. VII (1977), pp. 182–94.

Hirson, Baruch. 'Tuskegee, the Joint Councils, and the All African Convention', in *ibid.*, X (1981), pp. 65–76.

Hirson, Baruch. *Year of Fire, Year of Ash*. London, 1979.

Hoernle, R. F. A. *Race and Reason*. Johannesburg, 1945.

Hoernle, R. F. A. *South African Native Policy and the Liberal Spirit*. Cape Town, 1939.

Horrell, Muriel. *Action, Reaction and Counteraction*. Johannesburg, 1971.

Hyam, Ronald. *The Failure of South African Expansion, 1908–1948*. London, 1972.

Jabavu, D. D. T. *The Black Problem: Papers and Addresses on Various Native Problems*. Lovedale, 1920.

Jabavu, D. D. T. *The Findings of the All Africa Convention*. Lovedale, 1935.

Jabavu, D. D. T. *Native Disabilities in South Africa*. Lovedale, 1932.

Jabavu, D. D. T. *The Segregation Fallacy and Other Papers: A Native View of Some South African Inter-racial Problems*. Lovedale, 1928.

Johnstone, Frederick. *Class, Race and Gold*. London, 1976.

Kane-Berman, John. *South Africa: the Method in th Madness*. London, 1979.

Karis, Thomas D., and Carter, Gwendolen M. (eds.). *From Protest to Challenge: A Documentary History of African Politics in South Africa, 1882–1964*. Stanford, 1972–1977 (4 vols.).

King, Kenneth. *Panafricanism and Education*. London, 1971.

Kirby, Jack Temple. *Darkness and the Dawning*. Philadelphia, 1972.

Kuper, Adam. *Anthropologists and Anthropology: The British School, 1922–1972*. London, 1973.

Kuper, Leo. *Passive Resistance in South Africa*. New Haven, 1960.

Kuper, Leo, and Smith, M. G. (eds.). *Pluralism in Africa*. Berkeley, 1969.

Laurence, Patrick. *The Transkei: The Politics of Partition*. Johannesburg, 1977.

Leftwich, Adrian. *South Africa: Economic Growth and Political Change*. London, 1974.

Legassick, Martin. 'South Africa: Forced Labour, Industrialisation and Racial Discrimination' in R. Harris (ed.), *The Political Economy of Africa*. Boston, 1974.

Loram, Charles Templeman. *The Education of the South African Native.* London, 1917.
Macartney, William M. *Dr. Aggrey: Ambassador for Africa.* London, 1949.
Macmillan, W. M. *Complex South Africa.* London, 1930.
Macmillan, W. M. *Africa Emergent.* Harmondsworth, 1949; 2nd ed.
Macmillan, W. M. *Bantu, Boer and Briton: The Making of the South African Native Problem.* Oxford, 1973.
Macmillan, W. M. *My South African Years.* Cape Town, 1975.
Magubane, Bernard. *The Political Economy of Race and Class in South Africa.* New York, 1979.
Mannheim, Karl. *Essays on the Sociology of Culture.* London, 1956.
Marks, Shula. *Reluctant Rebellion.* Oxford, 1970.
Marks, Shula and Atmore, Anthony. *Economy and Society in Pre-Industial South Africa.* London, 1980.
Mbeki, Govan. *South Africa: The Peasants' Revolt.* Harmondsworth, 1964.
Molema, S. M. *The Bantu Past and Present.* Edinburgh, 1920.
Morris-Jones, W. H. (ed.). *The Making of Politicians: Studies from Africa and Asia.* London, 1976.
Moody, T. Dunbar. *The Rise of Afrikanerdom.* Berkeley, 1974.
Myrdal, Gunnar. *An American Dilema.* New York, 1972; 1st ed. 1944 (2 vols.).
Nicholls, George Heaton. *Bayete.* London, 1923.
Nicholls, George Heaton. *South Africa in My Time.* London, 1961.
No Sizwe, *One Azania, One Nation.* London, 1979.
Oliver, Sidney. *The Anatomy of African Misery.* London, 1927.
Palmer, Robin and Parsons, Q. N. (eds.). *The Roots of Rural Poverty.* London, 1977.
Park, Robert E. 'Social Control' in Ralph E. Turner (ed.), *On Social Control and Collective Behaviour.* Chicago, 1967.
Paton, Alan Stewart. *Apartheid and the Archbishop: The Life of Geoffrey Clayton, Archbishop of Cape Town.* Cape Town, 1973.
Paton, Alan Stewart. *Cry the Beloved Country: A story of Comfort in Desolation.* London, 1948.
Paton, Alan Stewart. *Hofmeyr.* Cape Town, 1964.
Paton, Alan Stewart. *Hope for South Africa.* London, 1958.
Perham, Margery and Curtis, L. *The Protectorates and South Africa: The Question of their Transfer to the Union.* London, 1935.
Philip, John. *Researches in South Africa.* New York, 1969, 1st ed., London, 1828 (2 vols.).
Phillips, Ray Edmund. *The Bantu are Coming: Phases of South Africa's Race Problem.* London, 1930.
Phillips, Ray Edmund. *The Bantu in the City: A study of Cultural Adjustment in the Witwatersrand.* Lovedale, 1938.
Pim, Sir Alan. *Colonial Agricultural Production.* London, 1946.
Pim, Howard. *A Transkei Enquiry.* Lovedale, 1934.
Robertson, Janet. *Liberalism in South Africa, 1948-1963.* Oxford, 1971.

Roux, Edward. *Time Longer Than Rope: A History of the Black Man's Struggle for Freedom in South Africa.* Madison, 1964; 2nd ed.

Sachs, E. S. *The Choice Before South Africa.* New York, 1952.

Schimlek, Francis. *Against the Stream: Life of B. Huss, Principal of Mariannhill.* Mariannhill, 1949.

Schapera, I. (ed.). *Western Civilisation and the Natives of South Africa.* London, 1967; 1st ed. 1934.

Scott, Michael. *A Time to Speak.* London, 1958.

Simons, H. J. and Simons, R. E. *Class and Colour in South Africa, 1850-1950.* Harmondsworth, 1969.

Sizwe, No. *One Azania, One Nation.* London, 1979.

Smith, Edwin William. *Aggrey of Africa: A Study in Black and White.* London, 1929.

Spottiswoode, Hildegarde. *South Africa: The Road Ahead.* Cape Town, 1960.

SPRO-CAS Political Commission. *South Africa's Political Alternatives.* Johannesburg, 1973.

Stern, Fritz. *The Failure of Illiberalism.* London, 1972.

Strangewayes-Booth, Joanna. *A cricket in the Thorn Tree: Helen Suzman and the Progressive Party.* Johannesburg, 1976.

Tatz, C. M. *Shadow and Substance in South Africa.* Pietermaritzburg, 1962.

Thompson, L. M. and Wilson, M. (eds.). *The Oxford History of South Africa.* Oxford, 1966-70, (2 vols).

Trapido, Stanley. 'The Friends of the Natives: merchants, peasants and the political and ideological structure of liberalism in the Cape, 1854-1910' in Shula Marks and Anthony Atmore (eds.), *Economy and Society in Pre-Industrial South Africa.* London, 1980.

Troup, Freda. *In Face of Fear: Michael Scott's Challenge to South Africa.* London, 1950.

Van den Berghe, Pierre L. (ed.). *The Liberal Dilemma in South Africa.* London, 1979.

Van den Berghe, Pierre L. *Race and Racism: A Comparative Perspective.* New York, 1978, 2nd ed.

Van den Berghe, Pierre L. *South Africa: A Study in Conflict.* Middletown, Conn., 1965.

'Vindex' pseud. *Cecil Rhodes: His Political Life and Speeches.* London, 1900.

Walker, Oliver. *Kaffirs are Lively: Being Some Backstage Impressions of the South African Democracy.* London, 1948.

Walshe, Peter. *The Rise of African Nationalism in South Africa.* London, 1970.

Welsh, David. *The Roots of Segregation.* Cape Town, 1970.

Westermann, Diedrich. *The African Today.* London, 1934.

Wickens, P. L. *The Industrial and Commercial Workers Union.* Cape Town, 1973.

Williams, Raymond. *The Country and the City.* London, 1975.

Wilson, Francis, and Perrot, Dominique, (eds.) *Outlook on a Century: South Africa, 1870–1970*. Lovedale, 1973.

Wilson, William J. *Power, Racism and Privilege: Race Relations in Theoretical and Sociohistorical Perspectives*. New York, 1973.

Woodward, C. Van. *The Strange Career of Jim Crow* (3rd edn.). New York, 1974.

Wolpe, Harold. 'Industrialisation and Race in South Africa', in S. Zubaida (ed.), *Race and Racialism*. London, 1970.

Wright, Harrison M. *The Burden of the Present*. Cape Town, 1977.

6   Pamphlets

Basner, H. *A Nation of 10,000,000 — Challenge to S.A.'s Native Policy*. Johannesburg, 1947.

Bell, F. W. *The Black Vote*. Johannesburg, 1909.

Bell, F. W. *The Native as a Political Factor and the Native Franchise*. Johannesburg, 1908.

Bell, F. W. *The South African Native Problem*. Johannesburg, 1909.

Bokwe, John Knox. *The Native Land Question*. Lovedale, 1904.

Brookes, Edgar. *RJ*. Johannesburg, 1954.

Brookes, Edgar. *We Come of Age*. Johannesburg, 1956.

Crocker, H. J. *The South African Race Problem: The Solution of Segregation*. Johannesburg, 1908.

Duncan, Patrick. *Suggestions for a Native Policy*. Johannesburg, 1912.

Dutch Reformed Church, Federal Commission of the. *European and Bantu: Papers and Addresses given at the Conference on Native Affairs, held under the auspices of the Federal Commision of the Dutch Reformed Church, 27th and 29th September 1923*. Johannesburg 1923.

Eiselen, W. W. M. *Die Naturelle Vraagstuk*. Pretoria, 1929.

Garthorne, E. R. *The Application of Native Law in the Transvaal*. Pretoria, 1924.

Hodgson, Margaret L. and Ballinger, W. G. *Indirect Rule in Southern Africa*. Lovedale, 1931.

Holloway, J. E. *Apartheid — A Challenge*. Johannesburg, 1964.

Horwitz, Ralph. *Expand or Explode*. Johannesburg, 1954.

Houghton, Desmond Hobart. *Enlightened Self Interest and the Liberal Spirit*. Johannesburg, 1970.

Huss, B. *Social History of the Rochdale Co-Operative Store for African Students*. Mariannhill, 1925.

Jansen, E. G. *Native Policy of the Union of South Africa*. Pretoria, 1950.

Kerr, A. *The Need for Higher Education: An Address to the Alice TOCH*. Lovedale, 1931.

Lewis, Stakesby. *Kaffir Beer Halls*. Johannesburg, 1941.

Loram, C. T. *The Claims of the Native Question upon Scientists*. Johannesburg, 1921.

Majeke, Nosipho (Dora Taylor). *The Role of Missionaries in Conquest.* Johannesburg, 1953.
Marquard, Leo. *Liberalism in South Africa.* Johannesburg, 1965.
Marquard, Leo. *South Africa's Internal Boundaries.* Johannesburg, 1958.
Mbeki, Govan. *Let's do it Together: What Co-operative Societies Are and Do.* Cape Town, 1944.
Ngubane, Jordan. *Should the N.R.C. be Abolished?* Cape Town, 1946.
Nicholls, George Heaton. *The Native Bills.* Petoria, 1936.
Pim, Howard. *The Native Question in South Africa.* Johannesburg, 1903.
Pim, Howard. *A plea for the Scientific Study of the Races Inhabiting South Africa.* Johannesburg, 1910.
Pim, Howard. *The Question of Race.* Johannesburg, 1906.
Pim, Howard. *Some Aspects of the Native Problem.* Johannesburg, 1905.
Rheinnalt-Jones, J. D. *At the Cross Roads.* Johannesburg, 1954.
Rose-Innes, R. W. *The Glen Grey Act And the Native Question.* Lovedale, 1903.
Scott, Michael. *Civilisation Indivisible.* London, 1953.
Scully, William Charles. *The Native Question.* Lovedale, 1894.
Smuts, J. C. *The Basis of Trusteeship.* Johannesburg, 1942.
SPRO-CAS *South Africa's Political Alternatives.* Johannesburg, 1973.
Walker, Eric Anderson. *The Frontier Tradition in South Africa: a Lecture delivered at Rhodes House on 5th March 1930.* Oxford, 1930.
Walker, Eric Anderson. *The Cape Native Franchise.* Cape Town, 1936.
Whyte, Q. *Apartheid and other Policies.* Johannesburg, 1950.
Xuma, Alfred. *Bridging the Gap Between White and Black in South Africa.* Lovedale, 1930.
Xuma, Alfred. *Charlotte Manye.* Johannesburg, 1930.
Xuma, Dr. A. B. *South West Africa: Annexation or United Nations Trusteeship?* New York, 1946.

7 Journal articles

Atmore, Anthony, and Westlake, Nancy. 'A liberal dilemma: a critique of the Oxford History of South Africa.' *Race* XIV (1972), 107-36.
Biddiss, Michael D. 'Myths of the Blood: European Racist Ideology, 1850-1945.' *Pattern of Prejudice,* VII (1975), 11-19.
Bundy, Colin. 'The Emergence and Decline of a South African Peasantry.' *African Affairs,* LXX1 (1972), 360-88.
Davenport, Rodney. 'The Triumph of Colonel Stallard: The Transformation of the Natives (Urban Areas) Act between 1923 and 1937,' *South African Historical Journal,* II (1970), 77-96.
Du Toit, Brian. 'Colour, Class and Caste in South Africa.' *Journal of Asian and African Studies,* I (1966), 197-212.

Gaitskell, Deborah. 'Christian Compounds for Girls: Church Hostels for African Women in Johannesburg, 1907-1970.' *Journal of Southern African Studies*, VI (1979), 44-69.

Good, Kenneth. 'Settler Colonialism: Economic Development and Class Formation.' *The Journal of Modern African Studies*, XIV (1976), 597-620.

Hammond-Tooke, David 'Chieftainship in Transkeian Political Development', *Journal of Modern African Studies*, II (1964), 513-519.

Heyman, Richard D. 'C. T. Loram: A South African Liberal in Race Relations.' *The International Journal of African Historical Studies*, V (1975), 41-50.

Horton, J. W. 'South Africa's Joint Councils: Black–White Co-operation between the two world wars.' *South African Historical Journal*, No. 4, (1972), 29-44.

Hughes, K. R. 'Challenges from the Past: Reflections on Liberalism and Radicalism in the Writing of South African History.' *Social Dynamics*, III, No. 1 (1977), 45-62.

Hunter, Monica 'Methods of Study of Culture Contact', *Africa*, VII, No. 3 (1934), 335-50.

Kuper, Leo. 'Class and Colour in South Africa: Some Problems in Marxism and Pluralism. *Race*, XII (1971), 495-500.

Kuper, Leo. 'Race, Class and Power: Some Comments on revolutionary Change.' *Comparative Studies in Society and History*, XIV (1972), 400-21.

Legassick, Martin. 'Legislation, Ideology and Economy in Post-1948 South Africa.' *Journal of Southern African Studies*, I (1974), 5-35.

Legassick, Martin. 'Race, Industrialisation and Social Change in South Africa: The Case of R. F. A. Hoernle.' *African Affairs*, LXXV (1976), 224-39.

Legassick, Martin. 'South Africa: Capital Accumulation and Violence.' *Economy and Society*, III (1974), 253–91.

Lewsen, Phyllis. 'The Cape Liberal Tradition: Myth or Reality? *Race*, XIII (1971), 65–80.

Mair, L. P. 'The Study of Culture Contact as a Practical Problem.' *Africa*, VII, No. 4 (1934), 415-22.

Marks, Shula. 'The Ambiguities of Dependence: John L. Dube of Natal. *Journal of Southern African Studies*, I (1975), 162-80.

Marks, Shula. 'Natal, the Zulu Royal Family and the Ideology of Segregation.' *Journal of Sout African Affairs*, LXXV (1976), 224-39.

Matthews, F. H. 'The Revolt against Americanism: Cultural Pluralism and Cultural Relativism as an Ideology of Libereration', *Canadian Review of American Studies*, I (1970), 4-31.

Medalia, Nahum Z. 'Myrdal's Assumptions on Race Relations: A Conceptual Commentary.' *Social Forces*, XL (1962), 223-7.

Morris, Michael L. 'The Development of Capitalism in South African Agriculture: Class and Struggle in the Countryside.' *Economy and Society*, V (1979), 292-343.

Nairn, Tom. 'The Modern Janus.' *New Left Review*, 94,)1975), 3-29.

O'Meara, Dan. 'The 1946 African Mine Workers Strike and the Political Economy of South Africa.' *The Journal of Commonwealth Political Studies*, XIII, No. 2 (1975), 146-73.

Perham, Margery. 'A Re-statement of Indirect Rule.' *Africa*, VII, No. 3 (1934), 321-34.

Pim, Sir Alan. 'The Question of The South African Protectorates.' *International Affairs*, XIII (1934), 668-88.

Ralston, Richard D. 'American Episodes in the making of an African leader: the case of Alfred B. Xuma (1893-1962), *International Journal of African Historical Studies*, VI (1973), 72-93.

Rex, John. 'The Plural Society: The South African Case.' Race, XII (1971) 401-13.

Rich, Paul B. 'Administrative Ideology, Urban Social Control and the Origins of Apartheid Theory, 1930-1939.' *Journal of African Studies*, VII (1980) 70-82.

Rich, Paul B. 'Liberalism and Ethnicity in South African Politics, 1921-1948.', *African Studies*, XXXV, No. 3/4 (1976), 229-51.

Rich, Paul B. 'Ministering to the White Man's Needs: The Development of Urban Segregation in South Africa, 1913-1923.' *African Studies*, XXXVII (1978), 177-91.

Rich, Paul B. 'The Origins of Apartheid Ideology: The Case of Ernest Stubbs and the Transvaal Native Administration, 1902-1932.' *African Affairs*, LXXIX (1980), 171-94.

Rich, Paul B. 'The South African Institute of Race Relations and the Debate on "Race Relations", 1925-58.' *African Studies*, XL, No. 1 (1981), 13-22.

Rich, Paul B. 'Tradition and Revolt in South African Fiction: the novels of Andre Brinkz, Nadine Gordime and J. M. Coetzee,' *The Journal of Southern African Studies*, IX, No. 1 (1982), 54-73.

Roach, John. "Liberalism and the Victorian Intelligentsia", *The Cambridge Historical Journal*, XIII (1957), 58-81.

Shannon, H. A. 'Urbanization, 1904-1936.' *South African Journal of Economics*, V (1937), 164-90.

Shepperson, George. 'Notes on Negro American Influences on the emergence of African Nationalism.' *Journal of African History*, No 2 (1960), 299-312.

Stadler, A. W. 'Birds in a Cornfield: Squatter Movements in Johannesburg, 1944-47'. *Journal of Southern African Studies*, VI, No. 1 (1979), 93-123.

Stedman Jones, Gareth. 'From Historical Sociology to Theoretical History.' *British Journal of Sociology*, XXVII (1976), 295-305.

Strickland, C. F. 'The Co-operative Movement in South Africa.' *Journal of the Africa Society*, XXVI (1937), 461-8.

Swanson, Maynard W. 'Urban Origins of Separate Development.' *Race*, X (1968), 31-40.

Trapido, Stanley. 'African Divisional Politics in the Cape Colony, 1884 to 1910.' *Journal of African History*, IX, No. 1 (1968), 79-98.

Trapido, Stanley. 'South Africa in a Comparative Study of Industrialisation.' *Journal of Development Studies*, VII (1971), 309-20.

Van Onselen, Charles. 'The Role of Collaborators in the Rhodesian Mining Industry.' *African Affairs*, LXXII (1973), 401-18.

Van den Burghe, Pierre L. 'Apartheid, Fascism and the Golden Age.' *Cahiers d'Etudes Africaines*, VIII (1962), 598-608.

Voegelin, Eric. 'Liberalism and its History. *The Review of Politics*, XXXVI, No. 4 (1974), 504-20.

Walshe, A. P. 'Black American Thought and African Political Attitudes in Southern Africa.' *Review of Politics*, (1970), 51-77.

Walshe, A. P. 'The Changing Content of Apartheid.' *Review of Politics*, (1963), 343-61.

Walshe, A. P. 'The Origins of African Political Consciousness in South Africa.' *Journal of Modern African Studies*, VII, (1969), 583-610.

Walshe, A. P. 'Church versus State in South Africa: The Christian Institute and the Resurgence of African Nationalism'. *Journal of Church and State*, XIX, 23 (1977), 357-79.

Welsh, David. 'The Cultural Dimensions of Apartheid.' *African Affairs*, LXXI (1972), 35-53.

Welsh, David. 'The Nature of Racial Conflict in South Africa.' *Social Dynamics*, IV, No. 1)1978), 29-39.

Welsh, David. 'Urbanization and the Solidarity of Afrikaner Nationalism.' *Journal of Modern African Studies*, VII (1969), 265-76.

Willan, Brian P. 'The Anti-Slavery and Aborigines' Protection Society and the South African Natives' Land Act of 1913.' *Journal of African History*, XX (1979), 83-102

Willan, Brian P. 'Sot Plaatyje, De Beers and an Old Tram Shed: Class Relations and Social Contrast in a South African Town,' *Journal of Southern African Studies*, IV (1978), 195–215

Wolpe, Harold. 'Capitalism and Cheap Labour Power in South Africa: From Segregation to Apartheid.' *Economy and Society*, XIV (1972), 425-56.

Wylie, Diana. 'Norman Leys and McGregor Ross: A Case Study in the Conscience of African Empire, 1900-39.' *Journal of Imperial and Commonwealth History*, V (1977), 294-309.

Yudelman, David. 'Industrialisation, Race Relations and Change in South Africa.' *African Affairs*, LXXXIV (1975) 82-96.

8   Theses

Bouch, R. J. 'The South African Party in Opposition, 1924-1929.' B.A. (Hons) Dissertation, University of the Witwatersrand, 1972.

Constantine, Stephen. 'The Formation of British Policy on Colonial Development, 1914-1929.' Ph.D. Thesis, University of Oxford, 1974.

Kingwill, Rosalie. 'The African National Congress in the Western Cape.' B.A. (Hons) Dissertation, University of Cape Town, 1977.

Shingler, John David. 'Education and Political Order in South Africa, 1902-1961.' Ph.D. Thesis, Yale University, 1973.

Stein, Mark. 'A History of African Trade Unions on the Witwatersrand, 1928-1941.' B.A. (Hons) Dissertation, University of the Witwatersrand, 1977.

Yudelman, David. 'From Laissez Faire to Interventionist State: Subjugation and Co-optation of Organised Labour on the South African Gold Mines, 1902-1939.' Ph.D. Thesis, Yale University, 1977.

9 Unpublished papers

Koch, Eddie. '"Without visible means of Subsistance": Slumland Culture in Johannesburg, 1918-1940', History Workshop Paper, University at the Witwatersrand,' Feb. 1981.

Legassick, Martin. 'The Making of South African "Native Policy", 1903-1923: The Origins of Segregation.' London, Institute of Commonwealth Studies, 1972.

Legassick, Martin. 'British Hegemony and the Origins of Segregation, 1900-1914.' London, Institute of Commonwealth Studies, 1974.

Legassick, Martin. 'Liberalism, Social Control and Liberation in South African' (published paper, University of Warwick, 1977).

Lewsen, P. 'Cape Liberalism in its Terminal Phase.' African Studies Seminar Paper, University of the Witwatersrand, 1980.

Lodge, Tom. 'Patrick Duncan And Radical Liberalism, University of York, 1977.

Van Onselen, Charles. 'The Witches of Suburbia: Domestic Service on the Witwatersrand, 1890-1914.' History Workshop Paper, University of the Witwatersrand, 1978.

Wolpe, Harold. 'Pluralism, Forced Labour and Internal Colonialism in South Africa.' Paper presented at Conference at University of York, 1973.

10 Unpublished documents

Basner, Hymie. Taped interviews with Brian Willan deposited in the Library of the School of Oriental and African Studies.

Fox, E. William and Douglas Black *A Preliminary Survey of the Agricultural and Nutritional Problems of the Ciskei and Transkeian Territories* (marked 'private and confidential'), microfilm version in the Library of the University of the Witwatersrand.

Jokl, E. A *Labour and Manpower Survey of the Transkeian Territories*, no place, n.d., (1943?), Library, S.A.I.R.R.

Msimang, H. Selby. *Autobiography*, copy deposited in the Library of the School of Oriental and African Studies. This is based on tape interviews.

Ngubane, Jordan. *I shall not be silenced*, unpublished autobiography, no place, n.d., photocopy in the Library of the School of Oriental and African Studies.

Selope Theme, R. V. *Autobiography*, n.d., photocopy in the Library of the School of Oriental and African Studies.

Xuma, A. B. *Autobiography*, n.d., in A. B. Xuma Papers, Church of the Province Archives, University at the Witwatersrand.

Index

People (N.A.A.C.P.), 83

N.R.C., *see:* Natives
    Representative Council

National European Bantu
    Conference, 1929, 29

National Minded Bloc, 94

Nationalist Party, 96, 100, 116–7,
    134; Election victory of 1948,
    110, 127

Native Administration Act,
    1927, 40, 59, 112; Bill, 1926, 58

Native Advisory Boards, *see:*
    Advisory Boards

Native Affairs Act, 1920, 33, 71

Native Affairs Commission, 17,
    21–2, 26, 28, 60, 66, 100–1,
    106–7, 110, 115

Native Affairs Department, *see:*
    Department of Native Affairs

Native Affairs Reform
    Association, Durban, *see:*
    Native Welfare Associations

Native Agricultural Bank, 59

Native Building Workers Union,
    49

Native Churches Commission,
    1925, 16–17

Native Development and Trust
    Company Ltd., 36

Native Economic Commission,
    1932, 40, 51, 58, 60, 62, 68

Native Franchise Act, *see:*
    Representation of Natives Act

Natives Land Act, 1913, 6, 59,
    124

Native Laws Commission, 1948,
    110

Native Mine Clerks Association,
    22–25

Native Mines Commission,
    1943, 83

Native Ministers Association, 25

Native Recruiting Corporation,
    15, 23 and *Umteteli wa Bantu,*
    23

Native Teachers Association, 25

Native Trust, 100, 103, 112

Native Trust and Land Act, 1936,

50–51, 66, 78

Native Welfare Association, 21;
    Durban Native Affairs Reform
    Association, 13

Natives representation, 8, 81, 87,
    93–95, 103–5, 107, 113–8;
    Boycott of, 87, 92, 98

Natives Representative
    Council(N.R.C.), 65, 86–7, 95,
    100, 106–7, 109, 111;
    Adjournment of, 91, 99, 110;
    Boycott of, 106; Reform of,
    113, 115–6

Natives Representatives, 89, 98,
    100, 104, 112, 114, 118; in
    Cape, 104

Natives (Urban Area) Act, 1923,
    6, 25, 60, 71, 124;
    Amendments of 1930 and
    1937, 71; Bill, 22

Naude, Dr. Beyers, 131

Ncwana, S.N. Bennet, 115

Ndunyana, W., 95

Ngabane, Jordan, 86, 90, 111

Ngwevela, Johnson, 95

Nicholls, George Heaton, 63–7,
    99–100

Noble, F.S. Livy–, *see:*
    Livy–Noble F.S.

Non–European Conference,
    1930, 43

Non Racial Franchise
    Association, 29; Franchise
    Defence Organisation, 29

North East District Protection
    League, 73

Ohlange Institute, *see:* Dube,
    John

Olivier, Sidney, 45; *The
    Anatomy of South African
    Misery,* 1927, 39

Oppenheimer, Sir Ernest, 39, 42

Oppenheimer, Harry, 134

Ossewa Brandwag, 128

Pact Government, 24, 26–7, 29,
    33, 38–9, 101

190 *Index*

DATE DUE